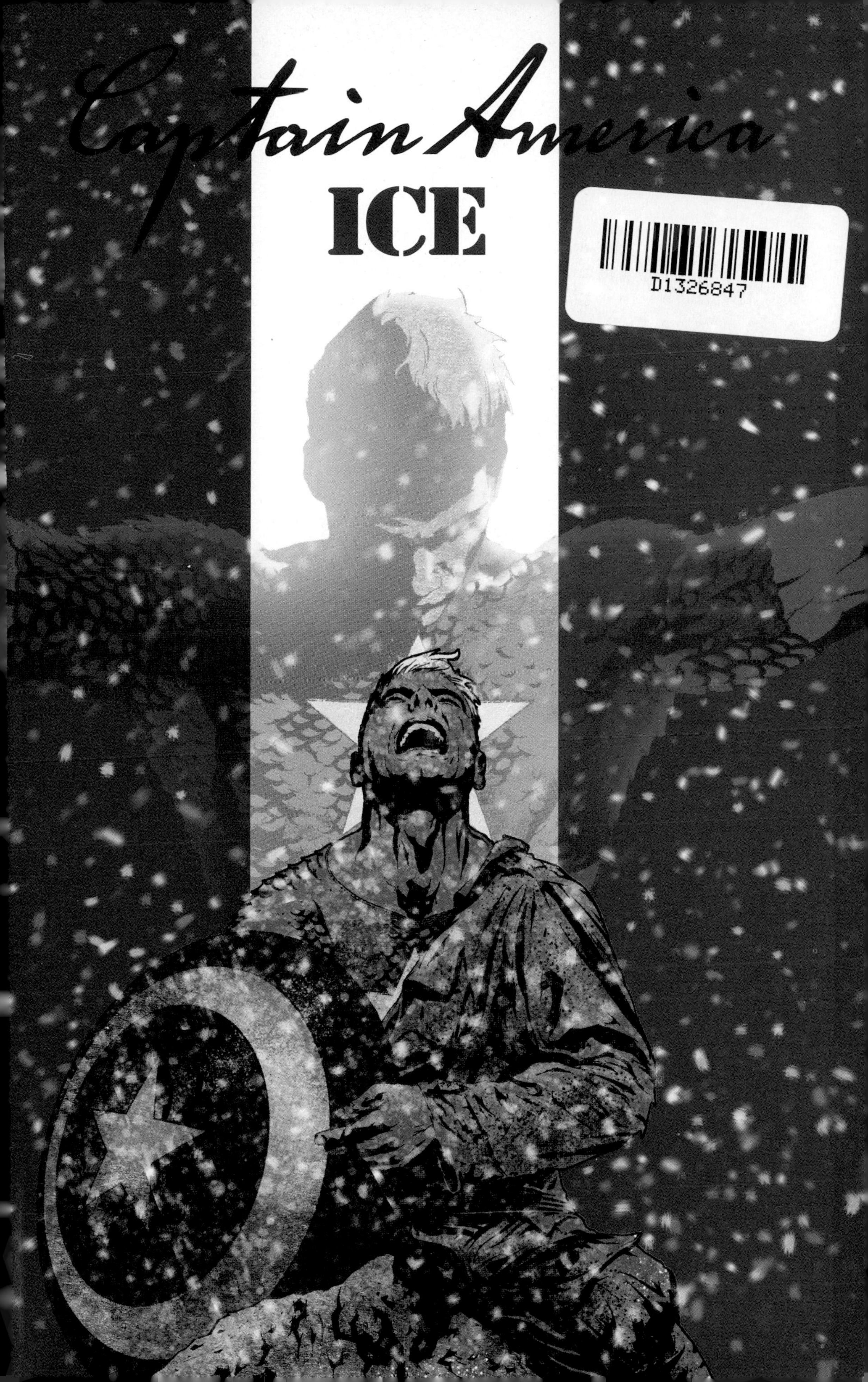
Captain America
ICE

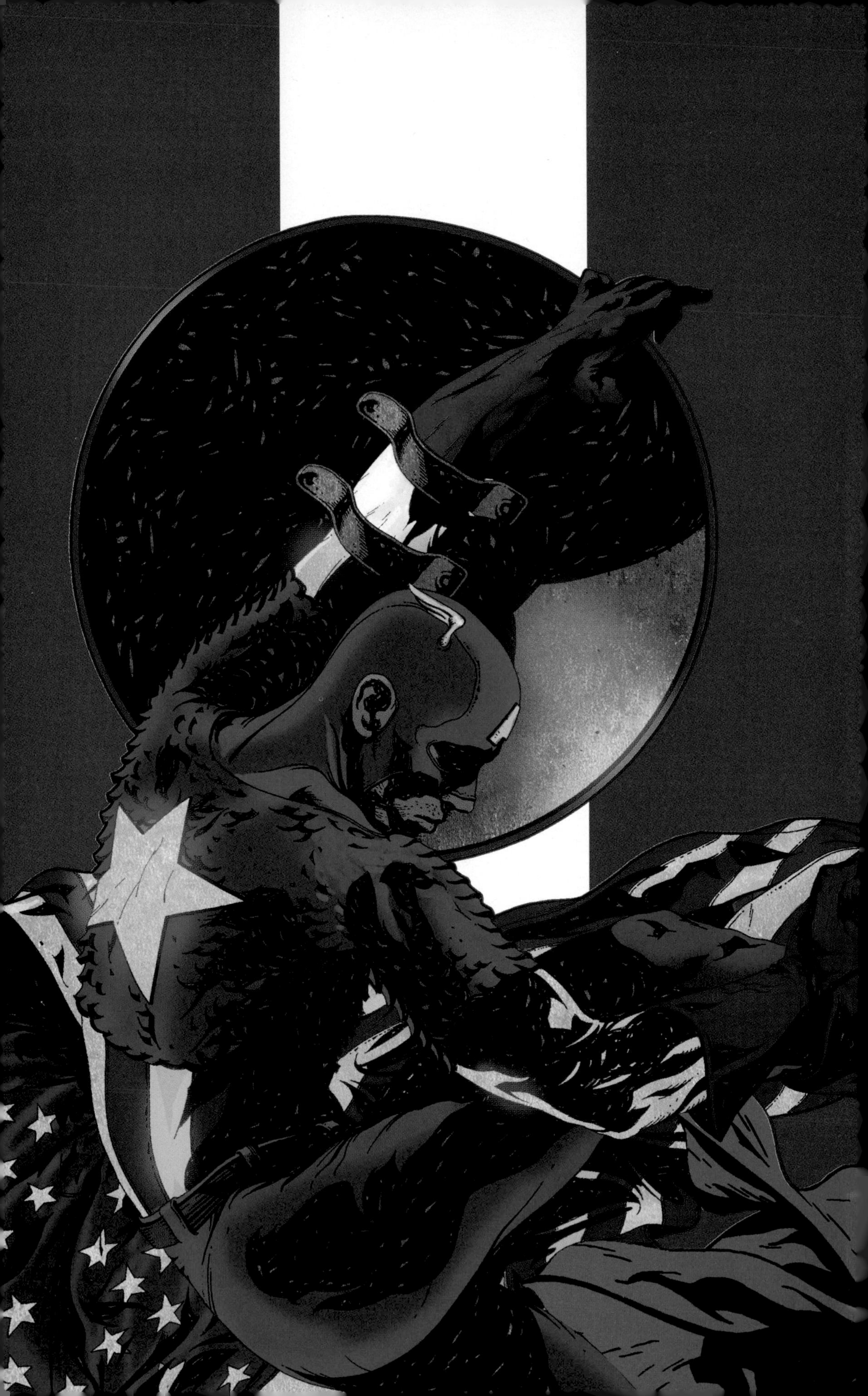

Captain America

ICE

Writers
Chuck Austen
with John Ney Rieber

Artist
Jae Lee

Colors
Jose Villarrubia

Letters
Dave Sharpe and
Virtual Calligraphy's
Russ Wooton

Cover Art
John Cassaday

Assistant Editor
Nick Lowe

Editor
Joe Quesada

Associate Managing Editor
Kelly Lamy

Managing Editor
Nanci Dakesian

Collections Editor
Jeff Youngquist

Assistant Editor
Jennifer Grünwald

Book Designer
Julio Herrera

Editor in Chief
Joe Quesada

President
Bill Jemas

PREVIOUSLY

During a battle, Inali Redpath, a revolutionary who was merged with a Sioux storm god, drugged Captain America with some Native American bitters that gave him hallucinogenic visions of his past. Having defeated Inali, Captain America was left with some burning questions. How many of the mental images were true, and how many were simple delirium?

Is it true that during World War II the American military had determined that Captain America's moral code of ethics and amazing powers might lead him to attempt to stop the bombing of Hiroshima and Nagasaki , whichthey felt was necessary to end the war in the Pacific? Were they right in assuming that a man known for putting his moral code before his military duty might actually turn against his own country, thus making him a liability instead of an asset? Would Captain America actually have put his moral belief in the sanctity of human life ahead of his dedication to his country, even if those lives were the lives of his country's enemy?

And most important, had the American military knowingly left Captain frozen in a block of ice to prevent just such an act?

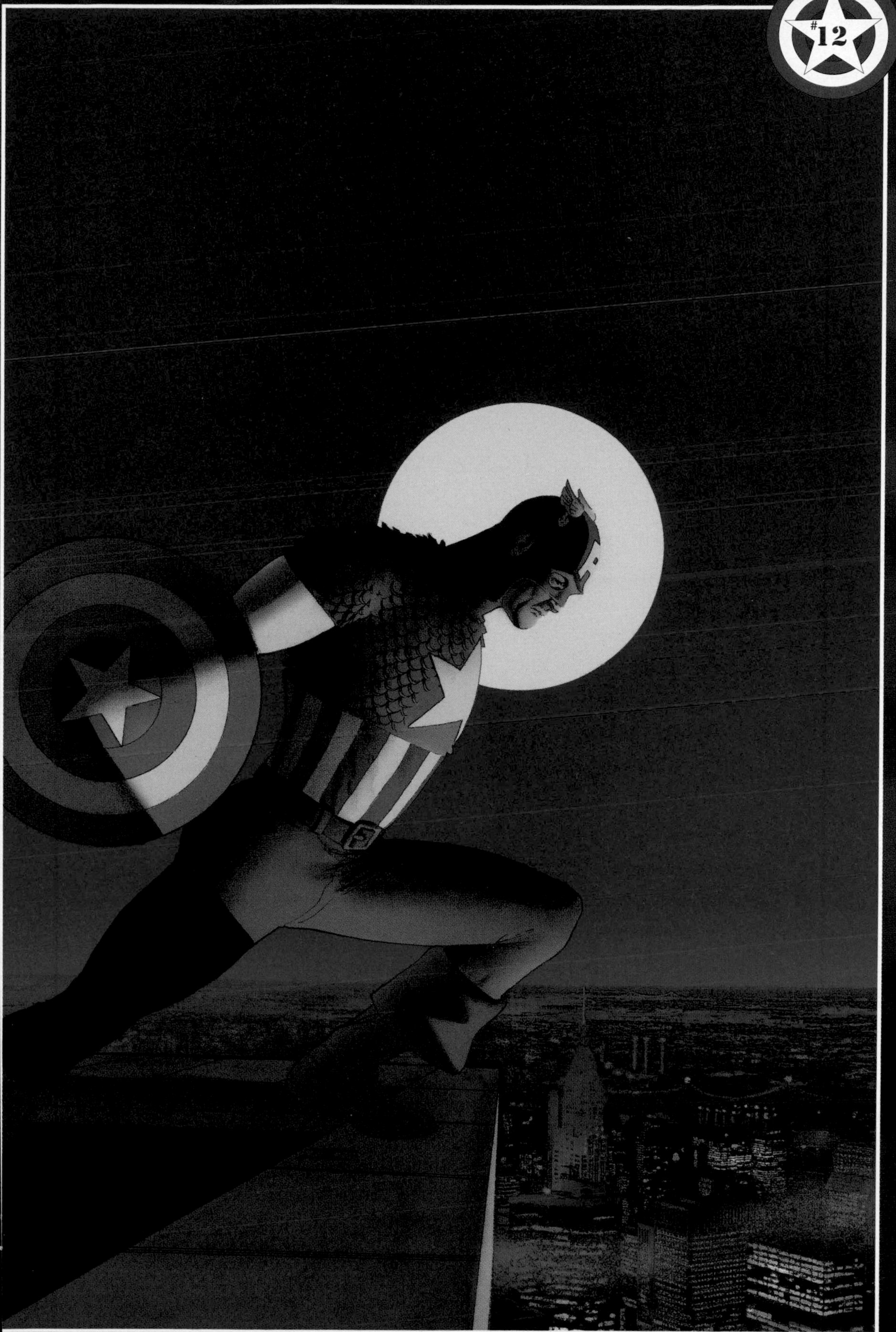
#12

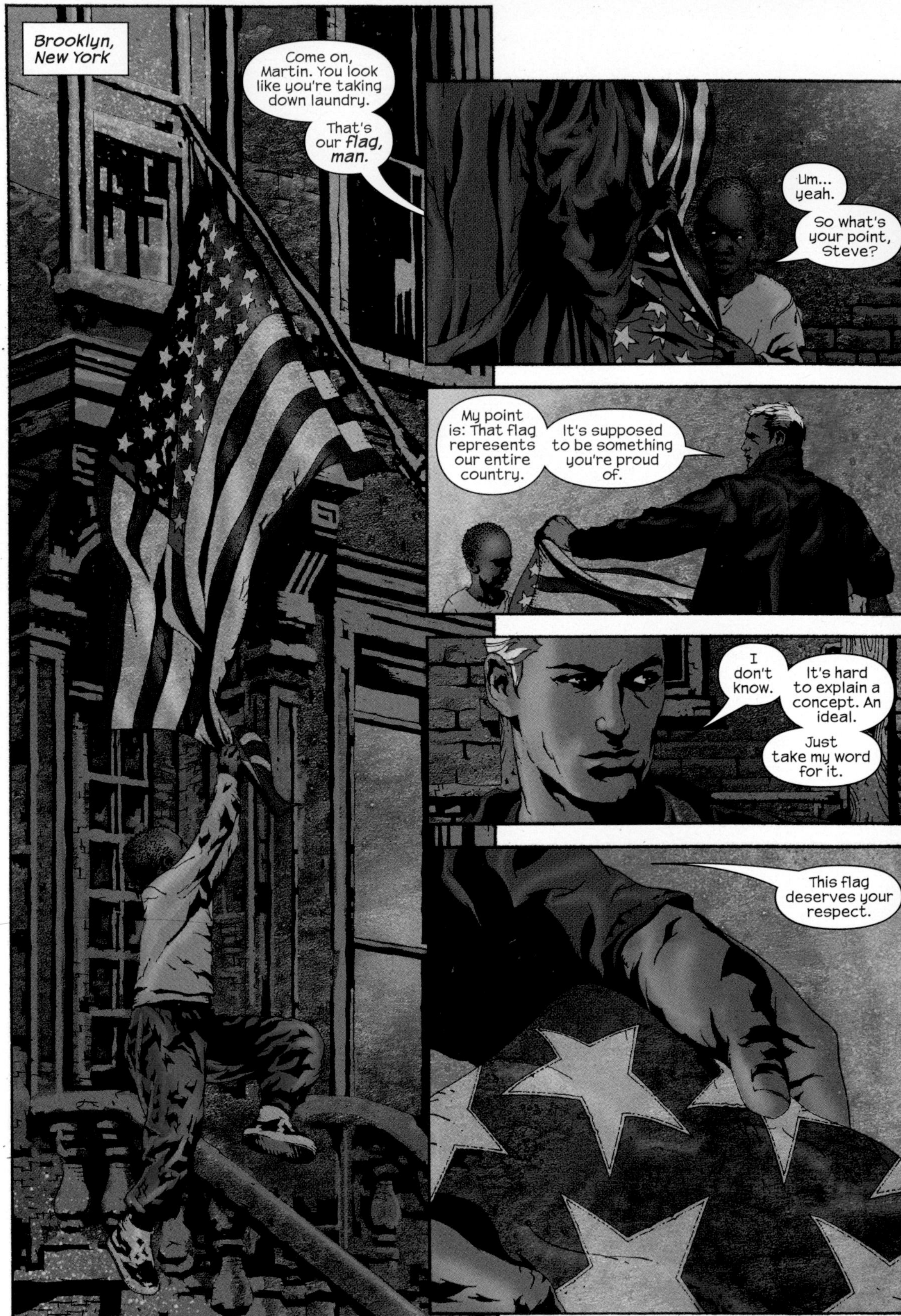
Brooklyn, New York
Come on, Martin. You look like you're taking down laundry.
That's our *flag, man.*
Um... yeah.
So what's your point, Steve?
My point is: That flag represents our entire country.
It's supposed to be something you're proud of.
I don't know.
It's hard to explain a concept. An ideal.
Just take my word for it.
This flag deserves your respect.

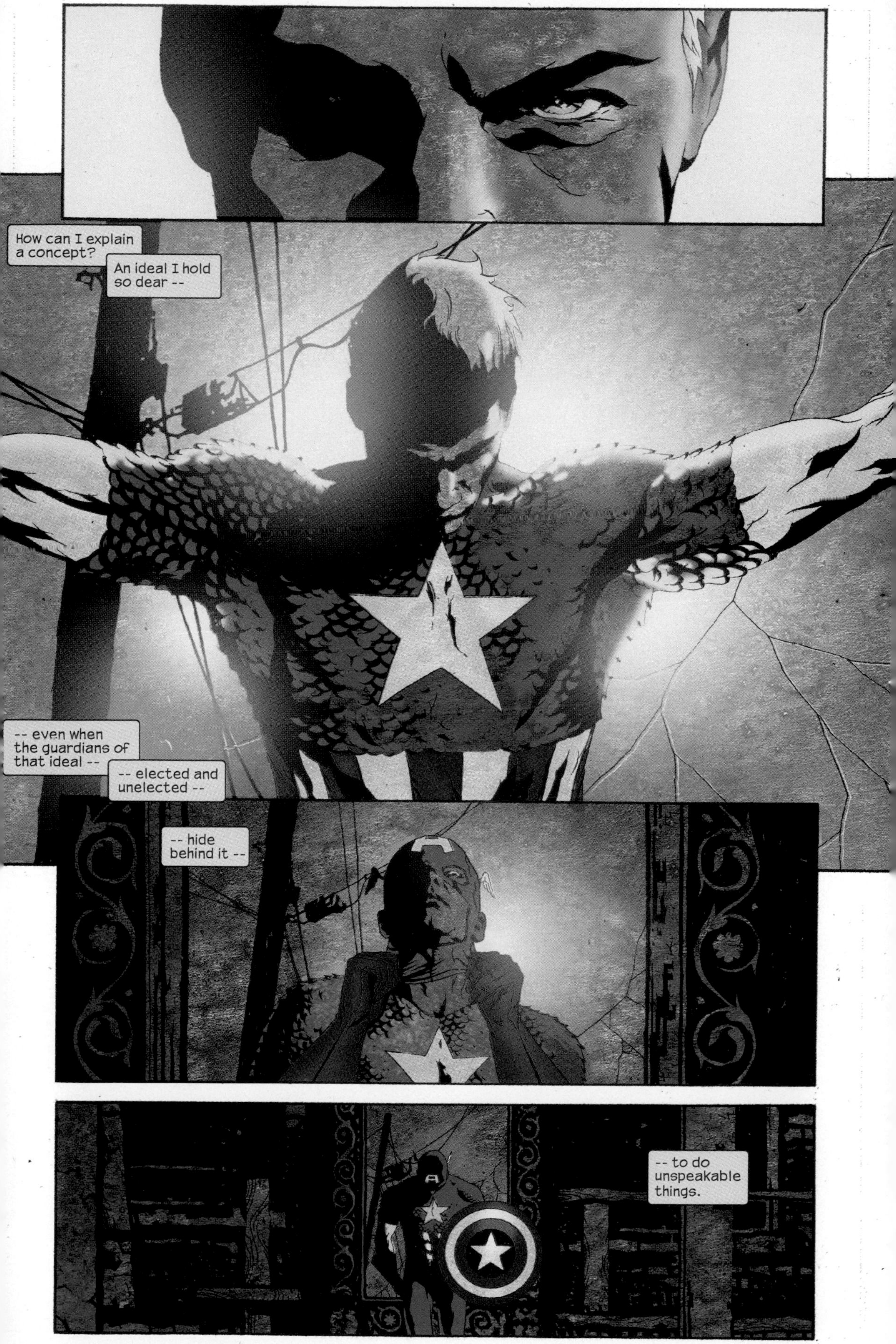
How can I explain a concept?
An ideal I hold so dear --
-- even when the guardians of that ideal --
-- elected and unelected --
-- hide behind it --
-- to do unspeakable things.

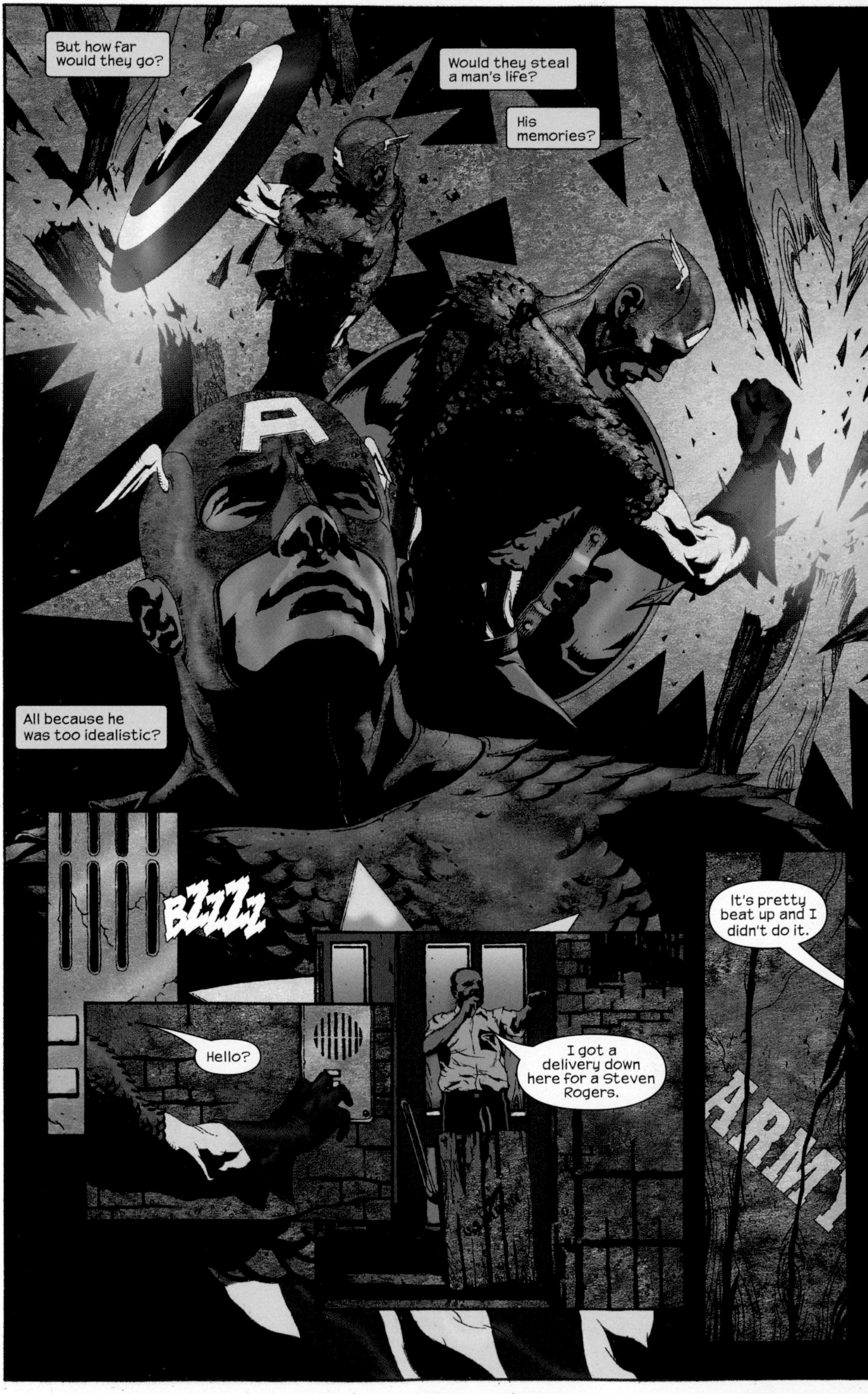
But how far would they go?
Would they steal a man's life?
His memories?
All because he was too idealistic?
BZZZZ
Hello?
I got a delivery down here for a Steven Rogers.
It's pretty beat up and I didn't do it.
ARMY

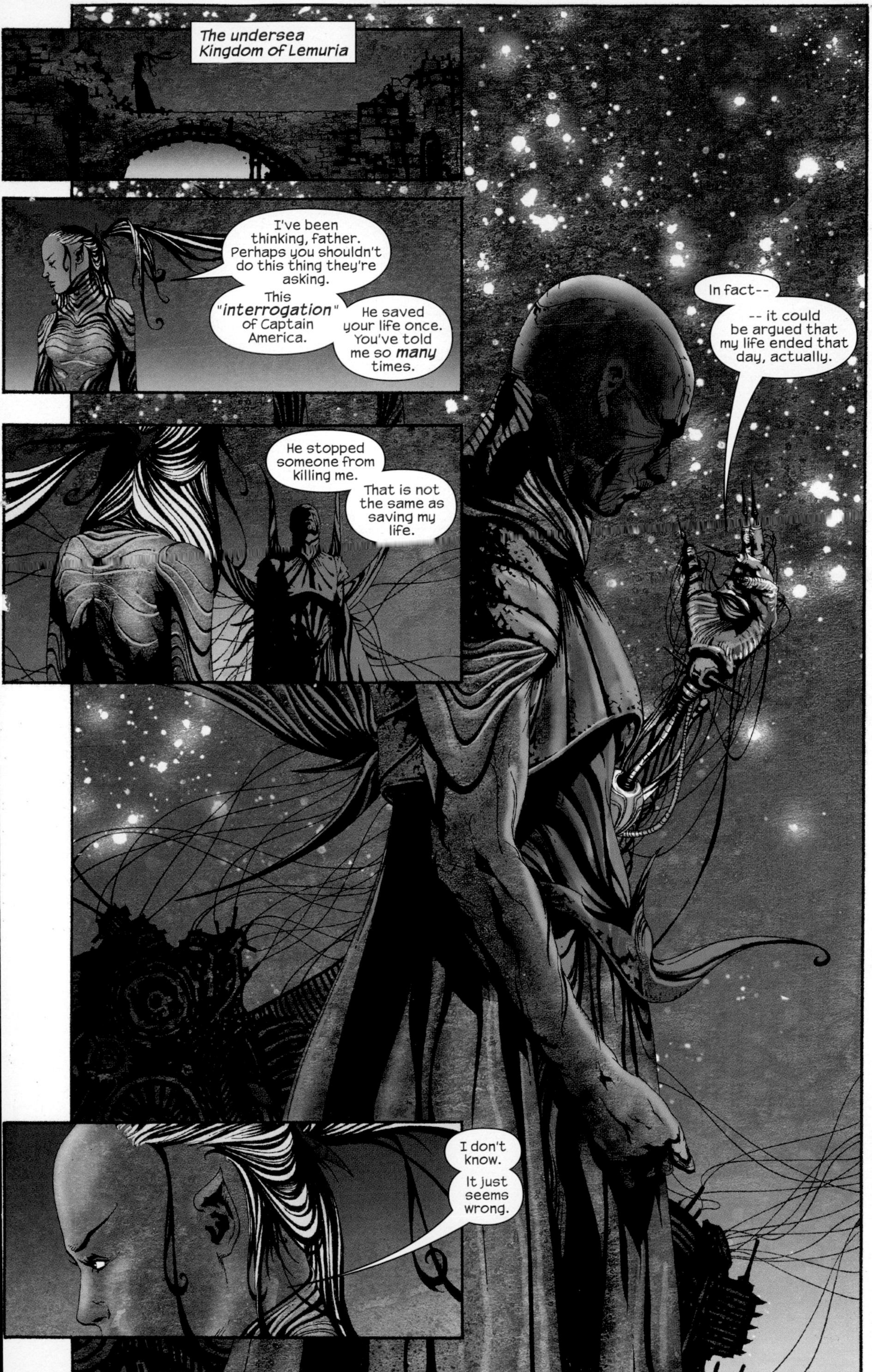
The undersea Kingdom of Lemuria
I've been thinking, father. Perhaps you shouldn't do this thing they're asking.
This "interrogation" of Captain America.
He saved your life once. You've told me so many times.
In fact--
-- it could be argued that my life ended that day, actually.
He stopped someone from killing me.
That is not the same as saving my life.
I don't know.
It just seems wrong.

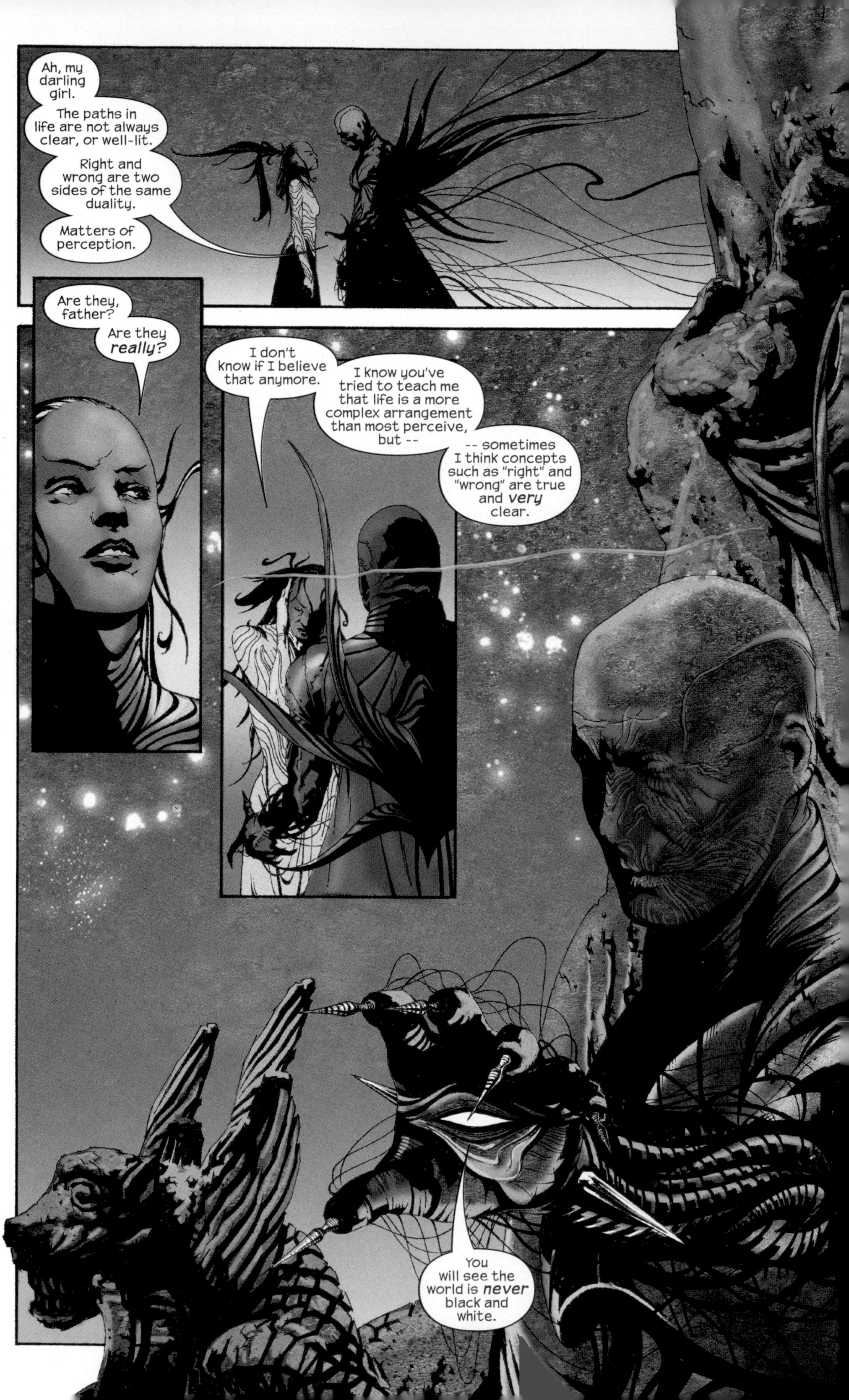
Ah, my darling girl.
The paths in life are not always clear, or well-lit.
Right and wrong are two sides of the same duality.
Matters of perception.
Are they, father?
Are they *really?*
I don't know if I believe that anymore.
I know you've tried to teach me that life is a more complex arrangement than most perceive, but --
-- sometimes I think concepts such as "right" and "wrong" are true and *very* clear.
You will see the world is *never* black and white.

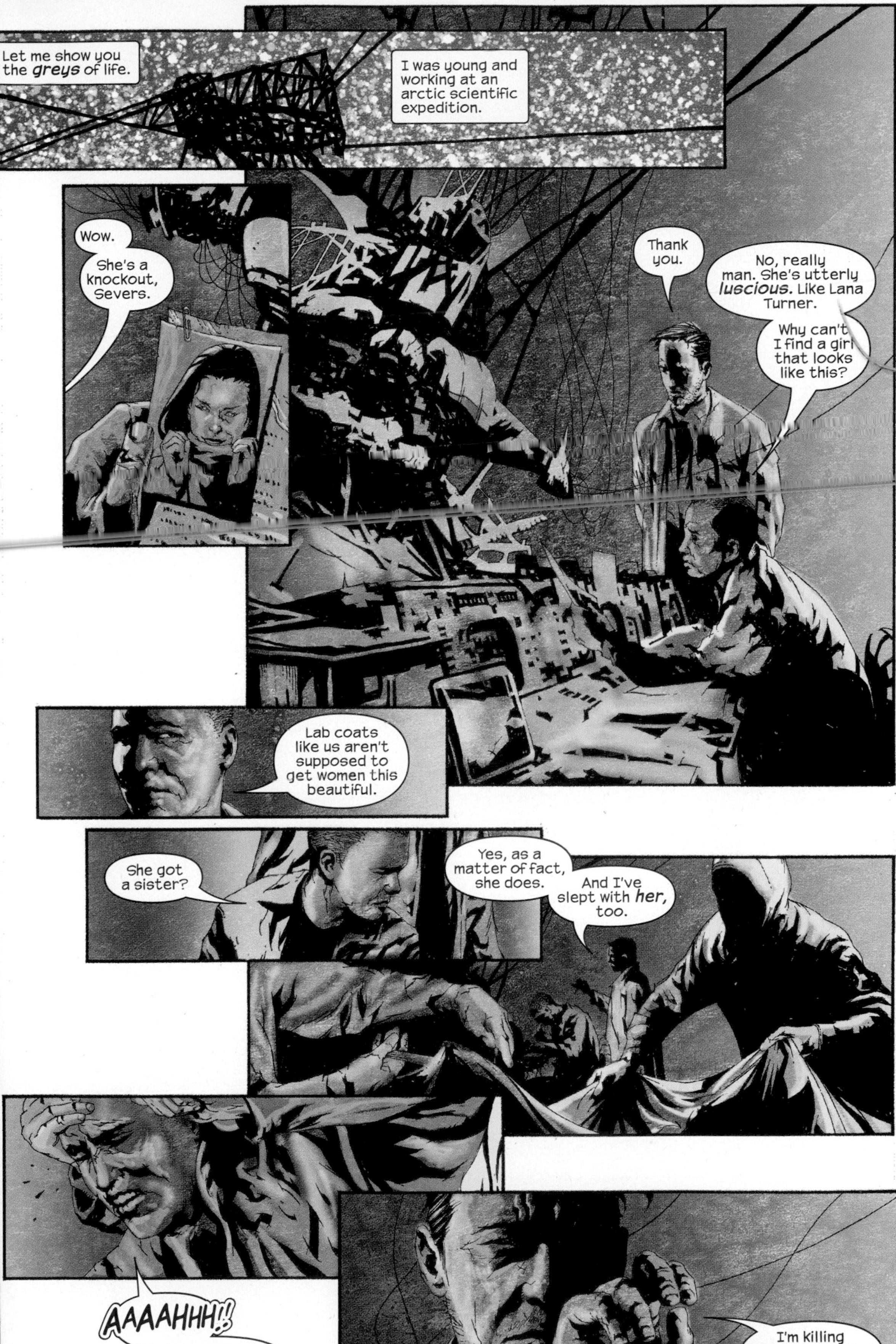
Let me show you the *greys* of life.
I was young and working at an arctic scientific expedition.
Wow.
She's a knockout, Severs.
Thank you.
No, really man. She's utterly *luscious.* Like Lana Turner.
Why can't I find a girl that looks like this?
Lab coats like us aren't supposed to get women this beautiful.
She got a sister?
Yes, as a matter of fact, she does.
And I've slept with *her,* too.
AAAAHHH!!
What the hell *are* you doing to meeeee...
I'm killing you and stealing our discoveries, you idiot.

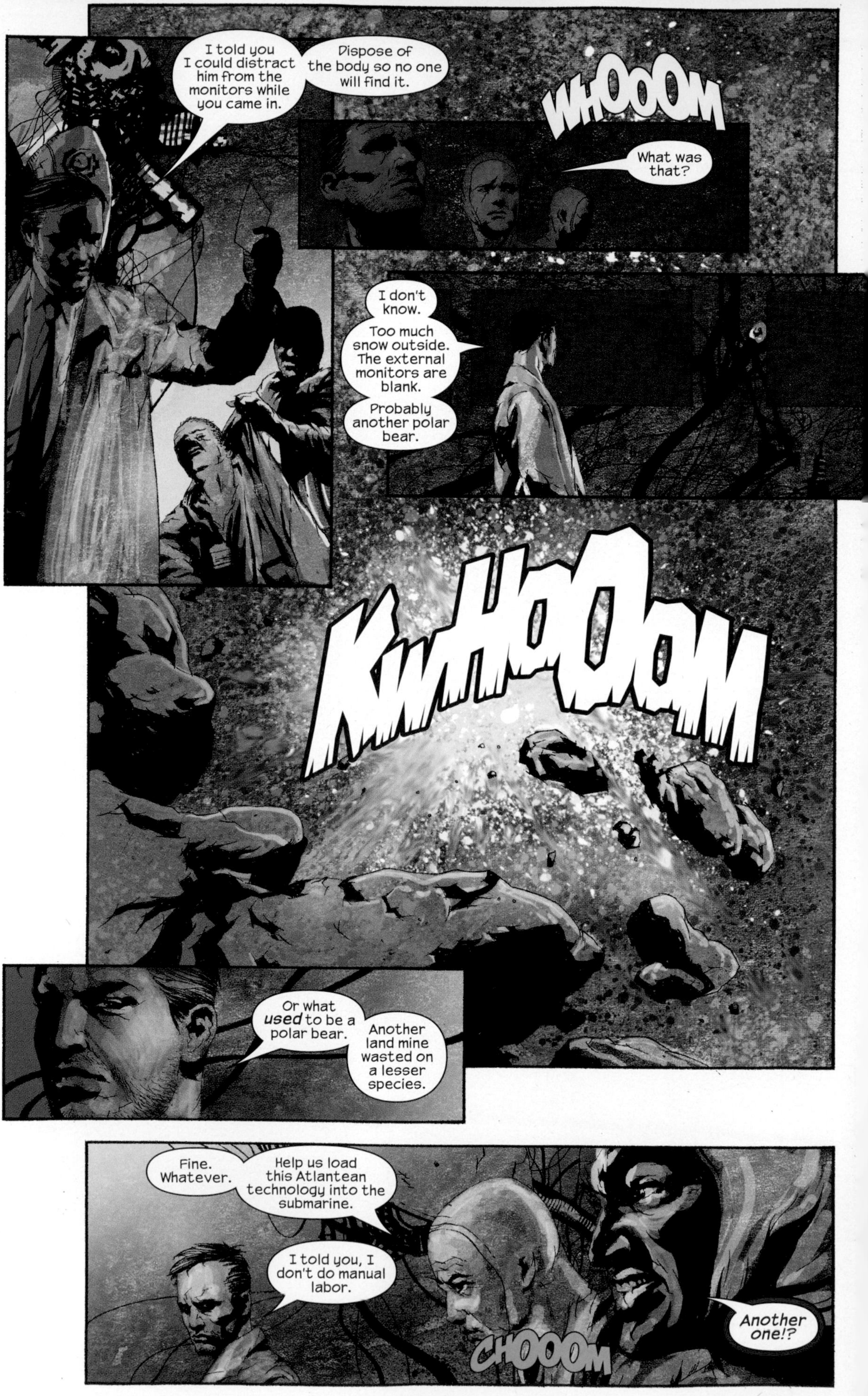

I told you I could distract him from the monitors while you came in.
Dispose of the body so no one will find it.
WHOOOM
What was that?
I don't know.
Too much snow outside. The external monitors are blank.
Probably another polar bear.
KuHOOOM
Or what *used* to be a polar bear.
Another land mine wasted on a lesser species.
Fine. Whatever.
Help us load this Atlantean technology into the submarine.
I told you, I don't do manual labor.
CHOOOM
Another one!?

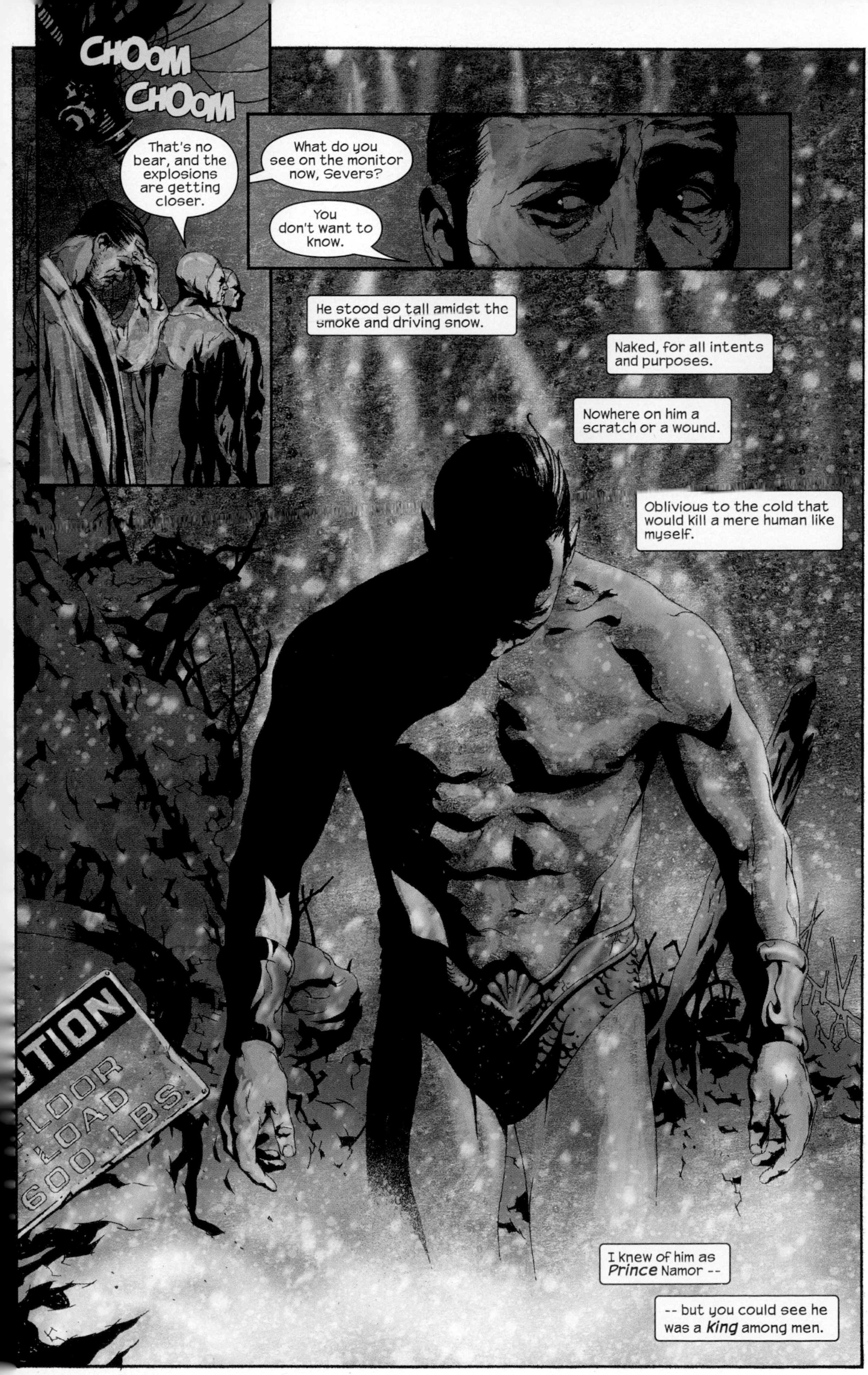
CHOOM
CHOOM
That's no bear, and the explosions are getting closer.
What do you see on the monitor now, Severs?
You don't want to know.
He stood so tall amidst the smoke and driving snow.
Naked, for all intents and purposes.
Nowhere on him a scratch or a wound.
Oblivious to the cold that would kill a mere human like myself.
CAUTION
FLOOR
LOAD
600 LBS
I knew of him as *Prince* Namor --
-- but you could see he was a *king* among men.

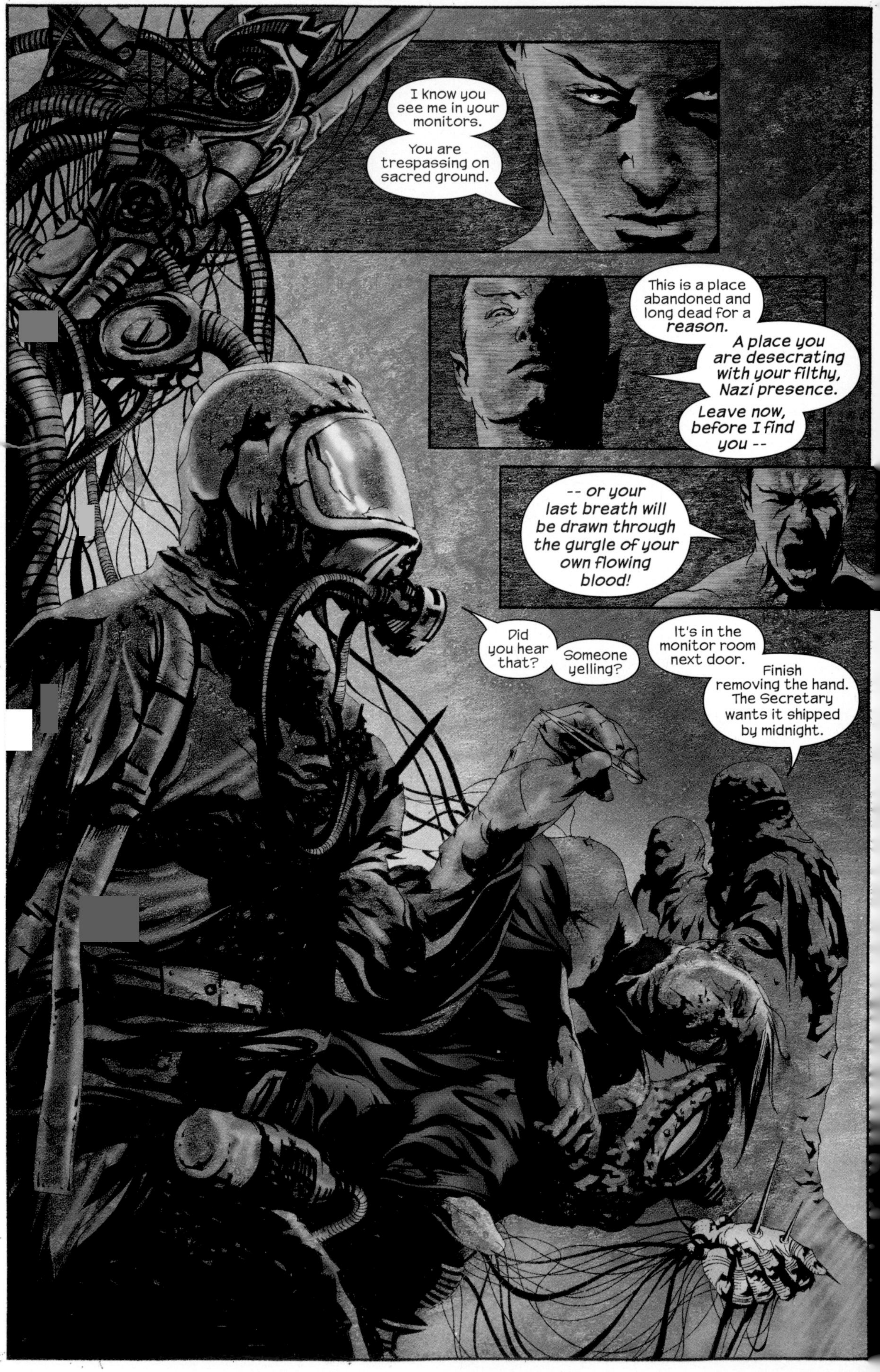
I know you see me in your monitors.
You are trespassing on sacred ground.
This is a place abandoned and long dead for a *reason.*
A place you are desecrating with your filthy, Nazi presence.
Leave now, before I find you --
-- or your last breath will be drawn through the gurgle of your own flowing blood!
Did you hear that?
Someone yelling?
It's in the monitor room next door.
Finish removing the hand. The Secretary wants it shipped by midnight.

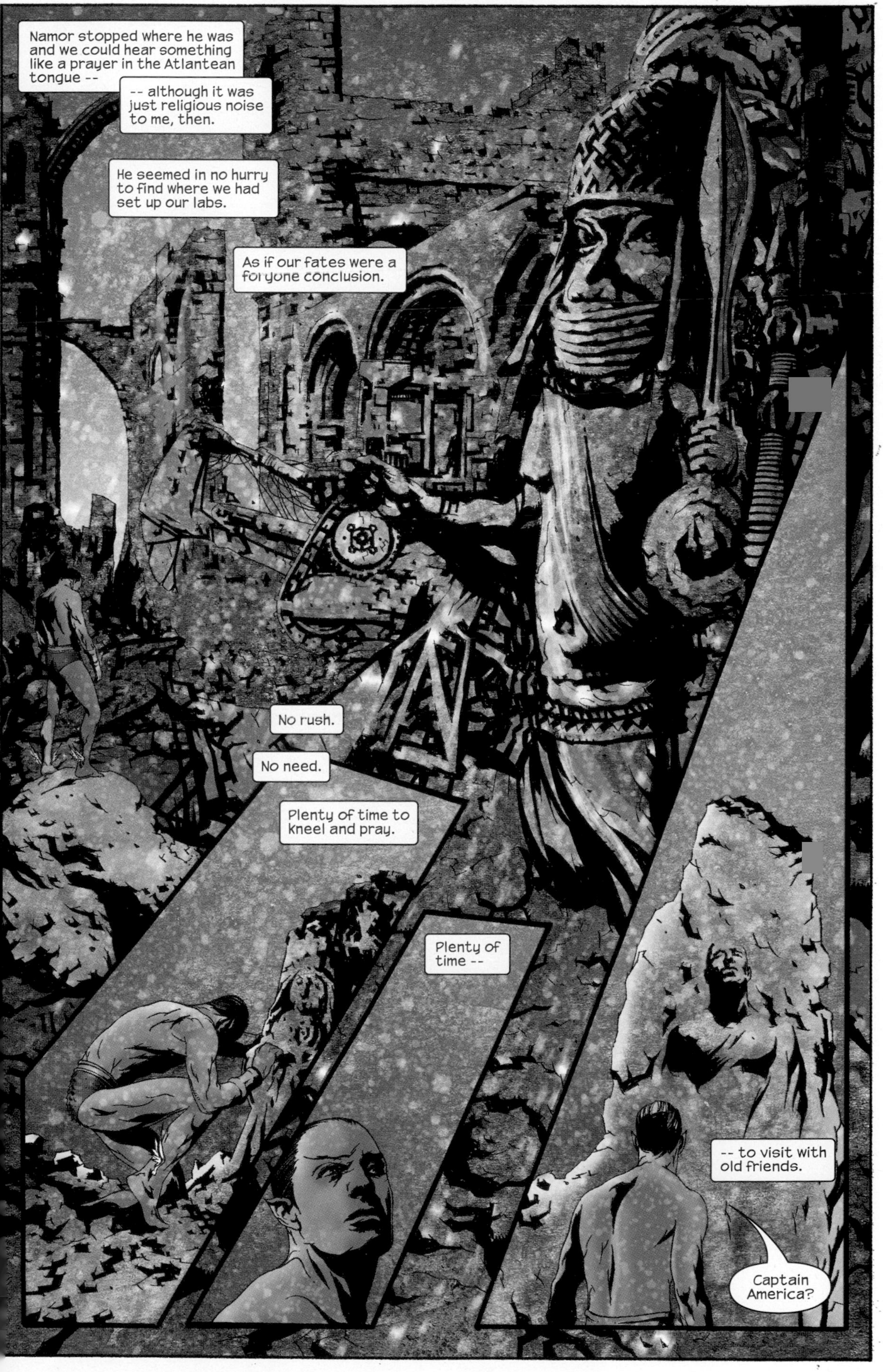
Namor stopped where he was and we could hear something like a prayer in the Atlantean tongue --
-- although it was just religious noise to me, then.
He seemed in no hurry to find where we had set up our labs.
As if our fates were a foregone conclusion.
No rush.
No need.
Plenty of time to kneel and pray.
Plenty of time --
-- to visit with old friends.
Captain America?

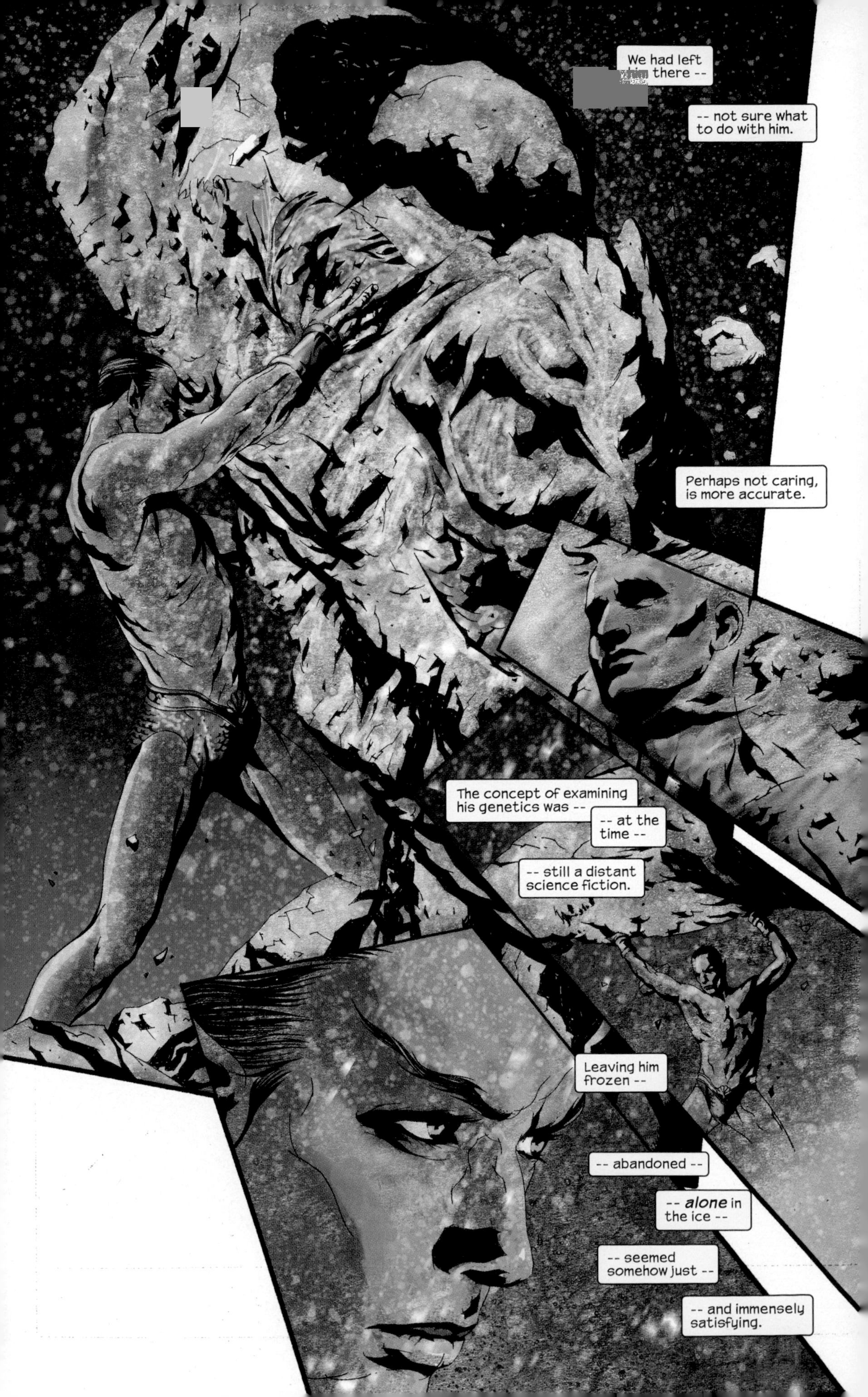
We had left him there --
-- not sure what to do with him.
Perhaps not caring, is more accurate.
The concept of examining his genetics was --
-- at the time --
-- still a distant science fiction.
Leaving him frozen --
-- abandoned --
-- *alone* in the ice --
-- seemed somehow just --
-- and immensely satisfying.

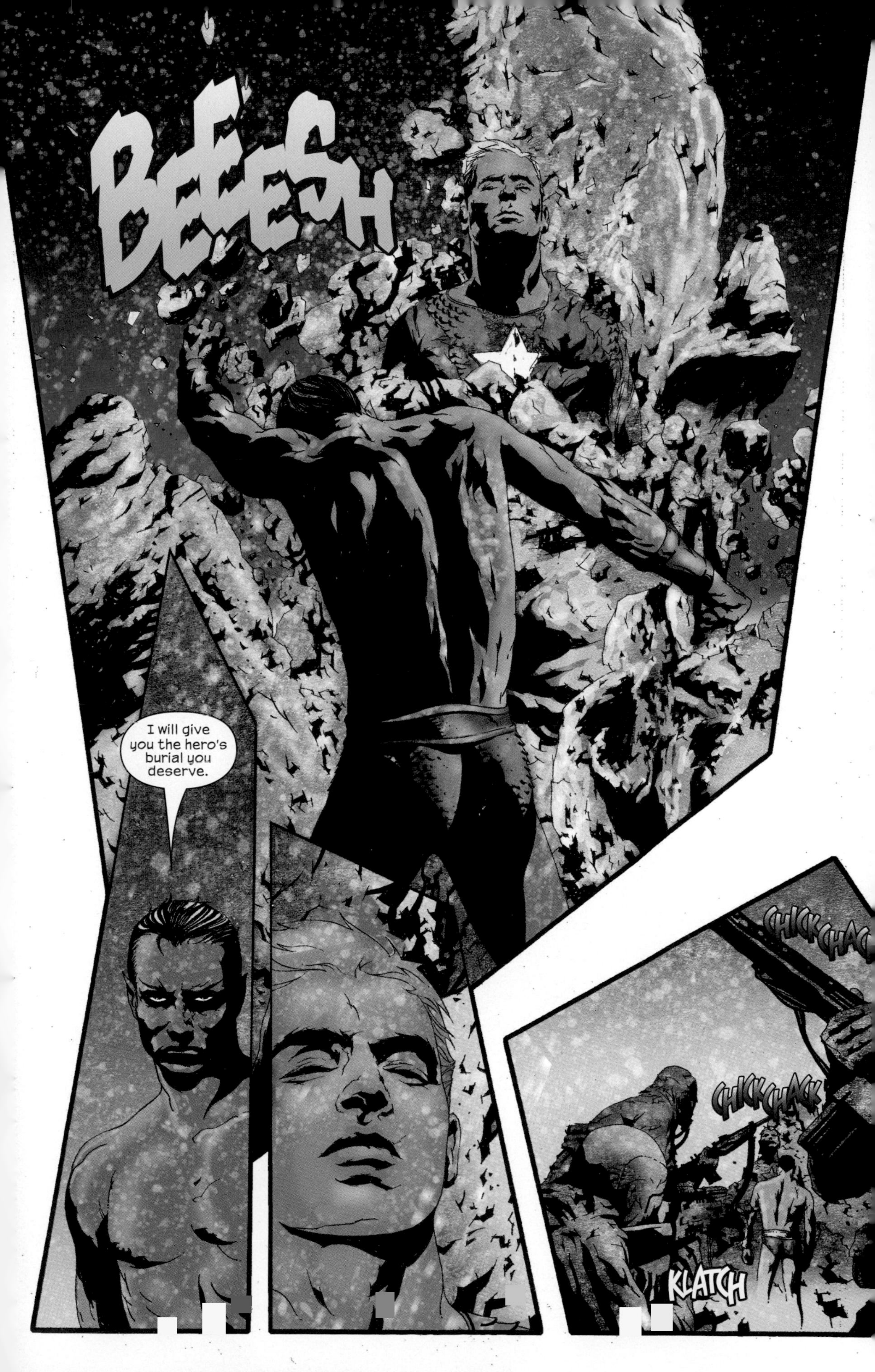
BOOSH
I will give you the hero's burial you deserve.
CHICKCHACK
CHICKCHACK
KLATCH

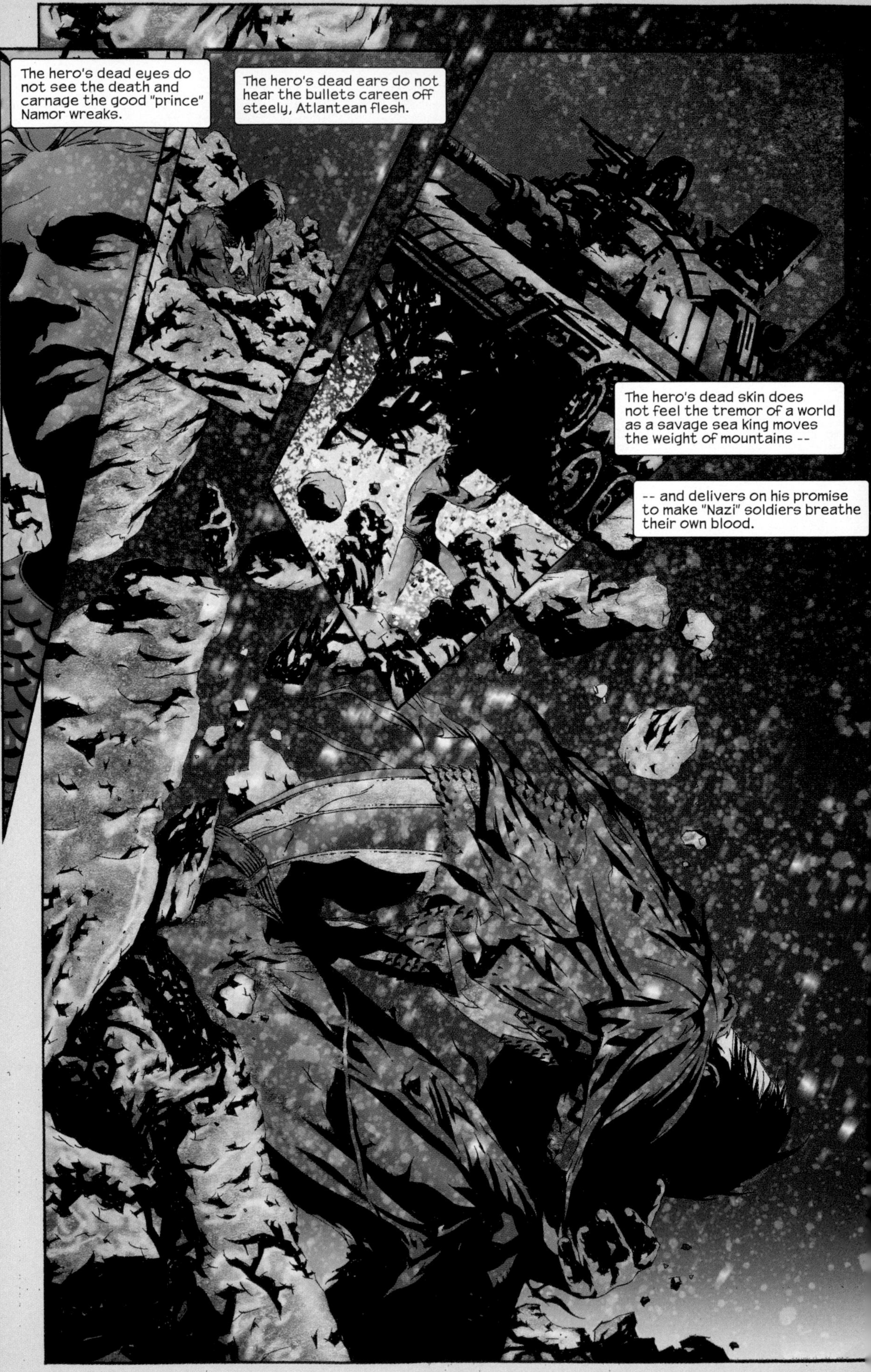
The hero's dead eyes do not see the death and carnage the good "prince" Namor wreaks.
The hero's dead ears do not hear the bullets careen off steely, Atlantean flesh.
The hero's dead skin does not feel the tremor of a world as a savage sea king moves the weight of mountains --
-- and delivers on his promise to make "Nazi" soldiers breathe their own blood.

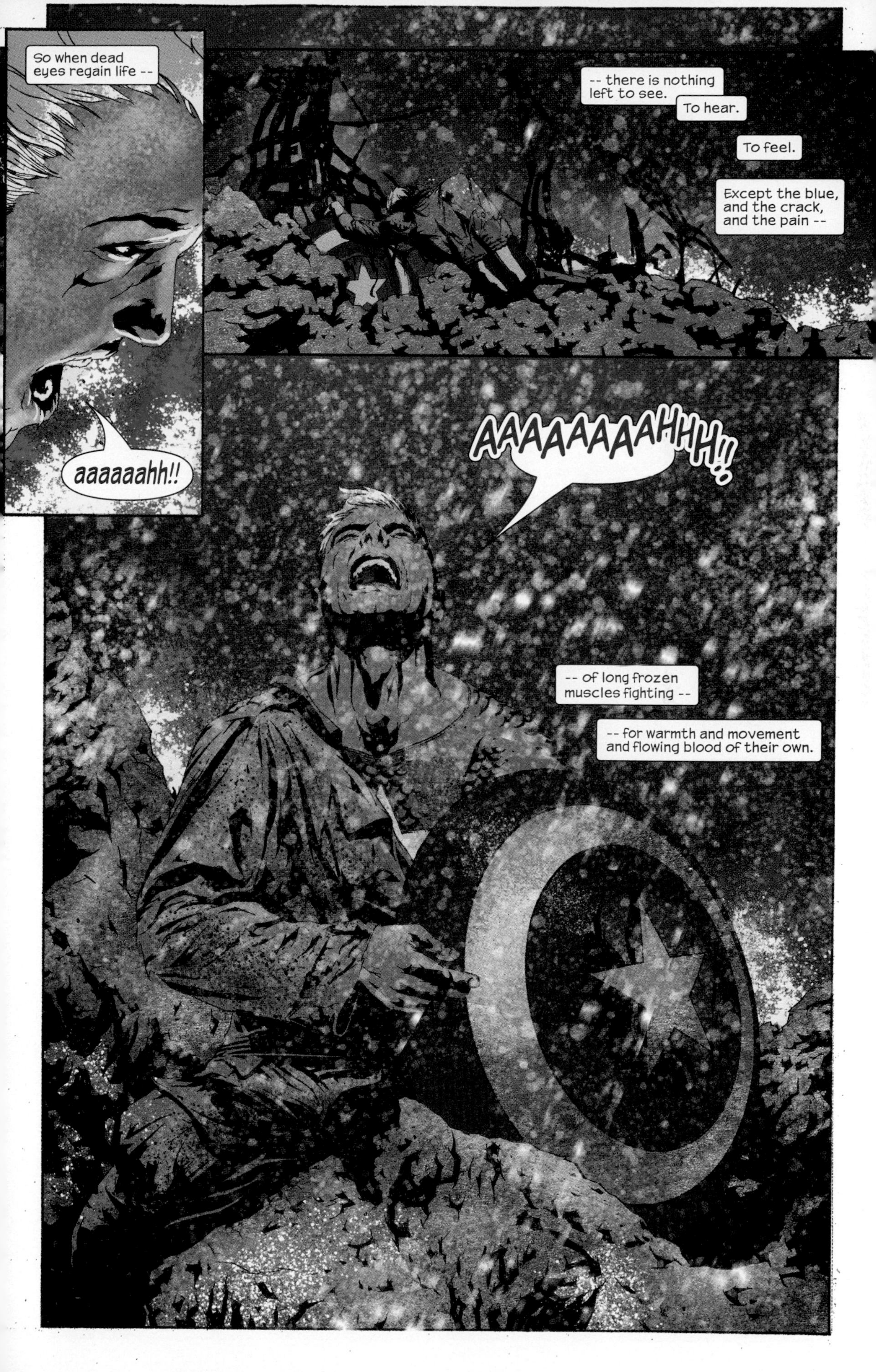
So when dead eyes regain life --
-- there is nothing left to see.
To hear.
To feel.
Except the blue, and the crack, and the pain --
aaaaaahh!!
AAAAAAAAAHHH!!
-- of long frozen muscles fighting --
-- for warmth and movement and flowing blood of their own.

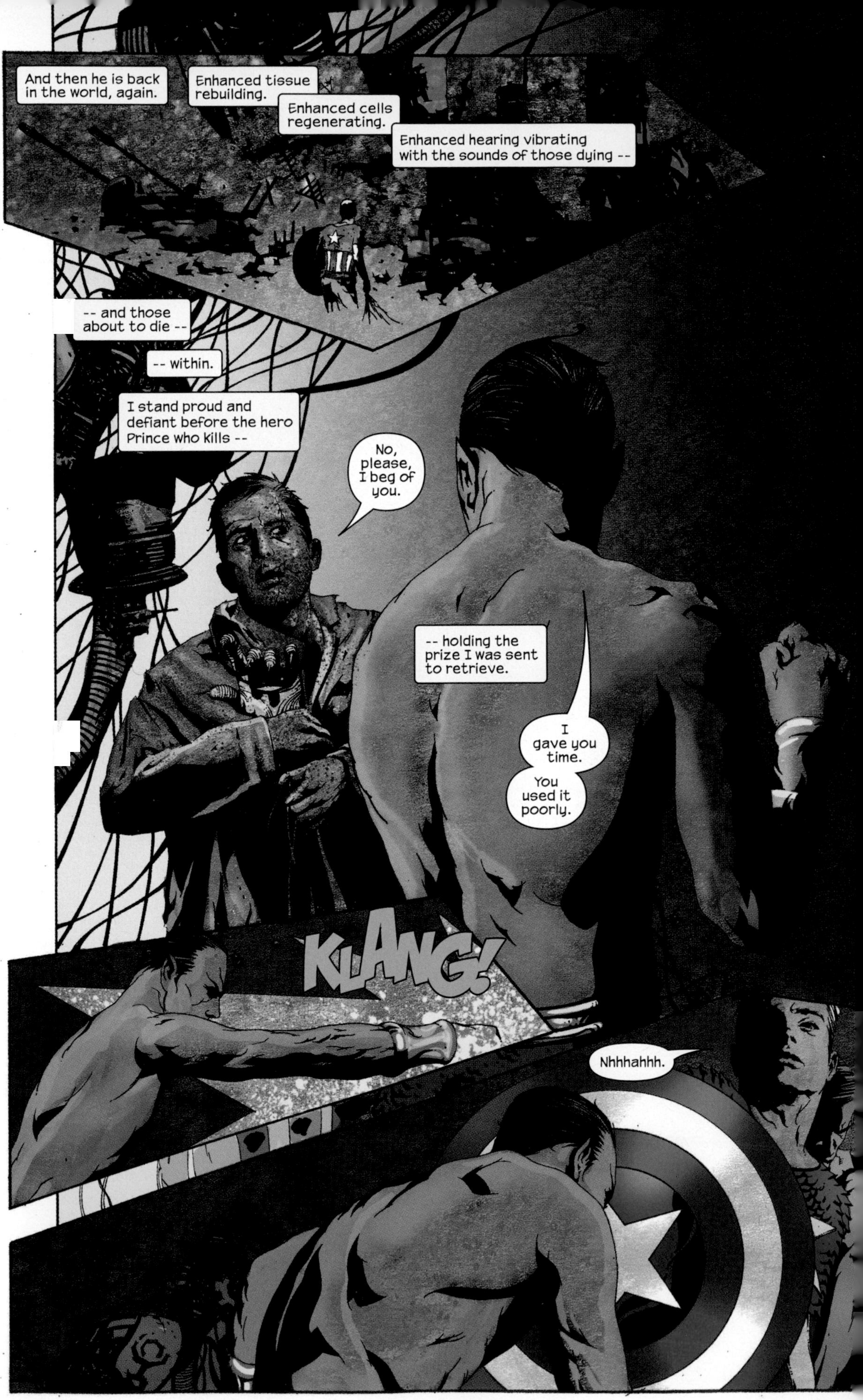
And then he is back in the world, again.
Enhanced tissue rebuilding.
Enhanced cells regenerating.
Enhanced hearing vibrating with the sounds of those dying --
-- and those about to die --
-- within.
I stand proud and defiant before the hero Prince who kills --
No, please, I beg of you.
-- holding the prize I was sent to retrieve.
I gave you time.
You used it poorly.
KLANG!
Nhhhahhh.

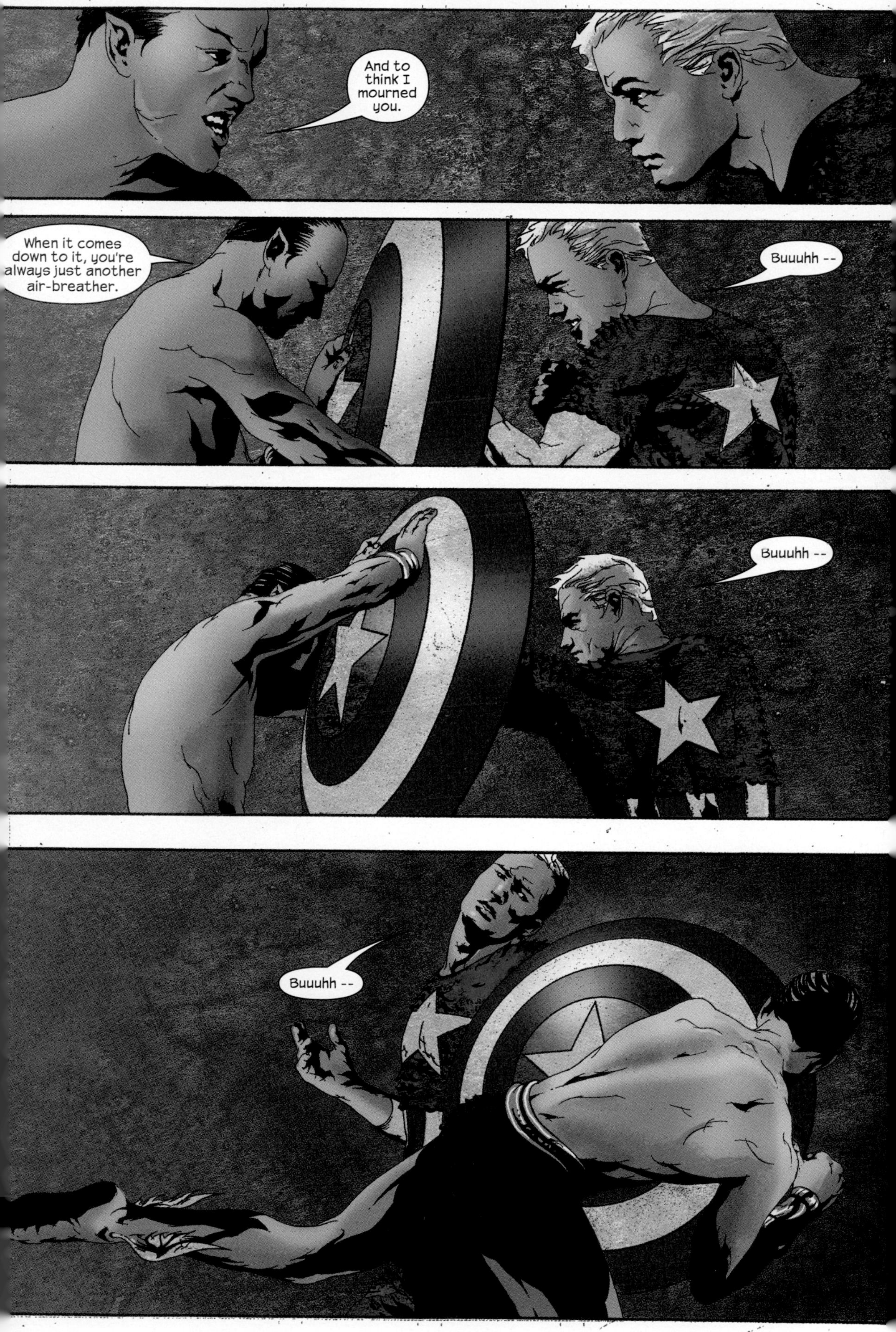
And to think I mourned you.
When it comes down to it, you're always just another air-breather.
Buuuhh --
Buuuhh --
Buuuhh --

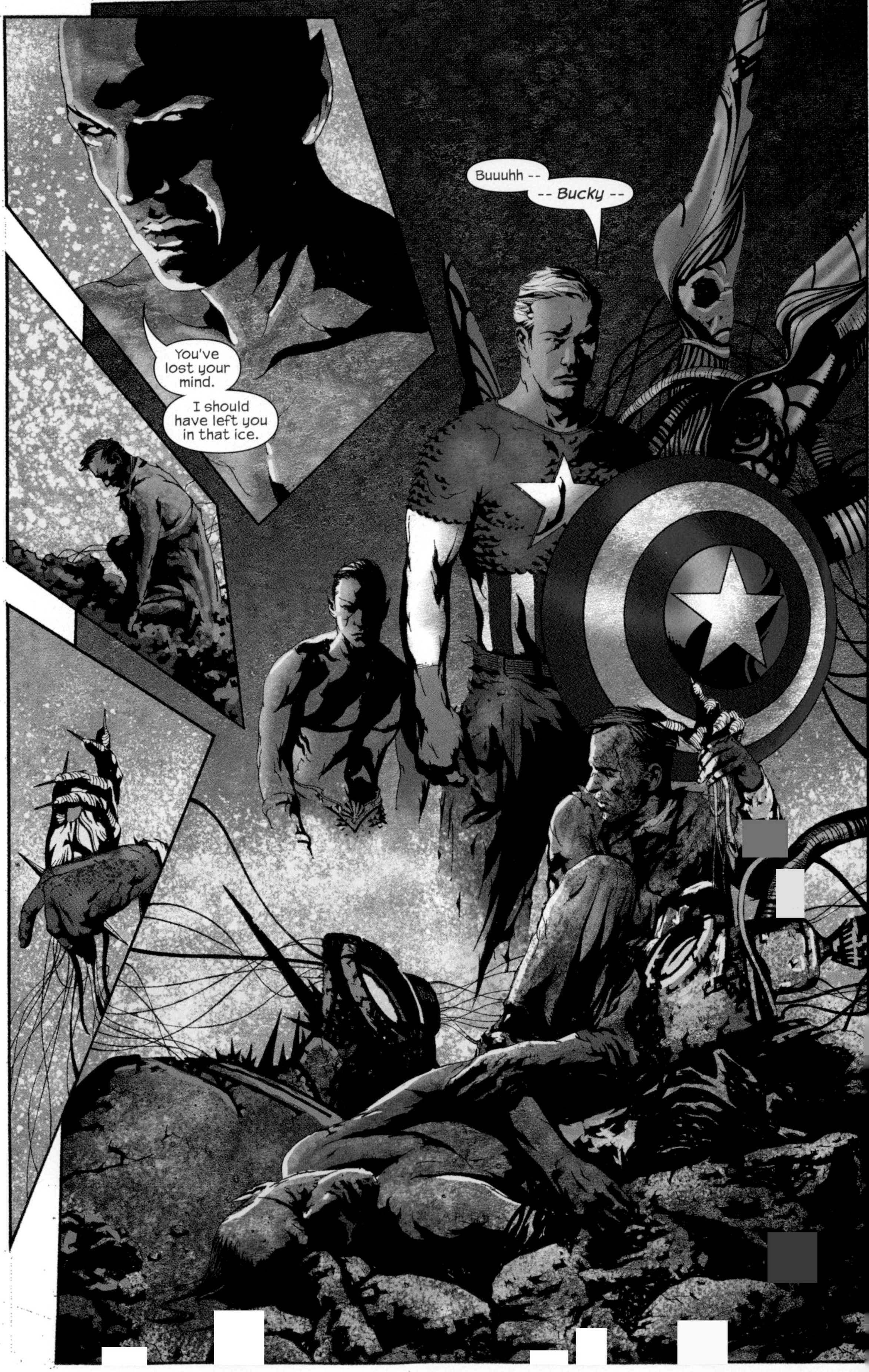
You've lost your mind.
I should have left you in that ice.
Buuuhh --
-- Bucky --

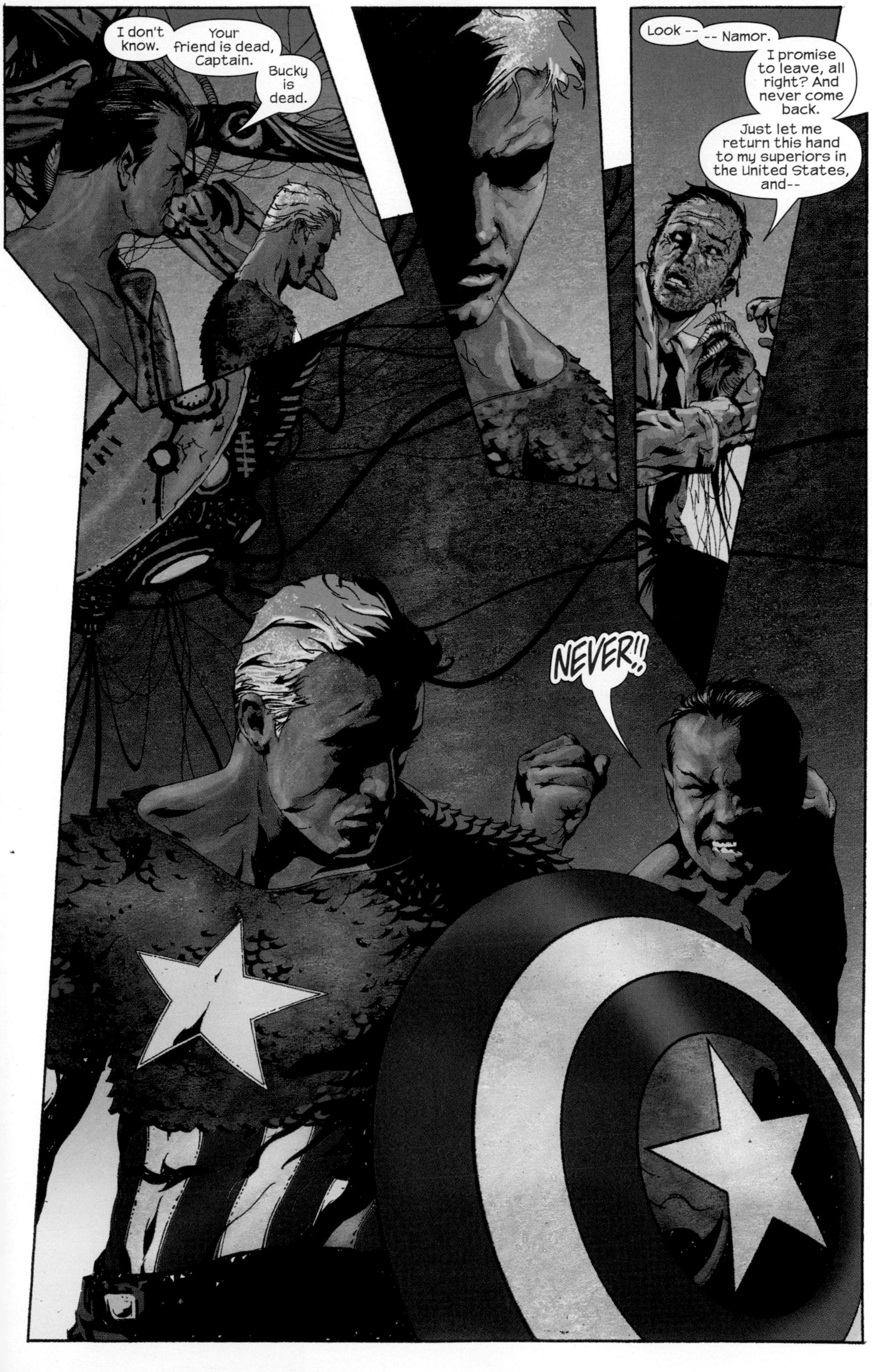
I don't know.
Your friend is dead, Captain.
Bucky is dead.
Look --
-- Namor.
I promise to leave, all right? And never come back.
Just let me return this hand to my superiors in the United States, and--
NEVER!!

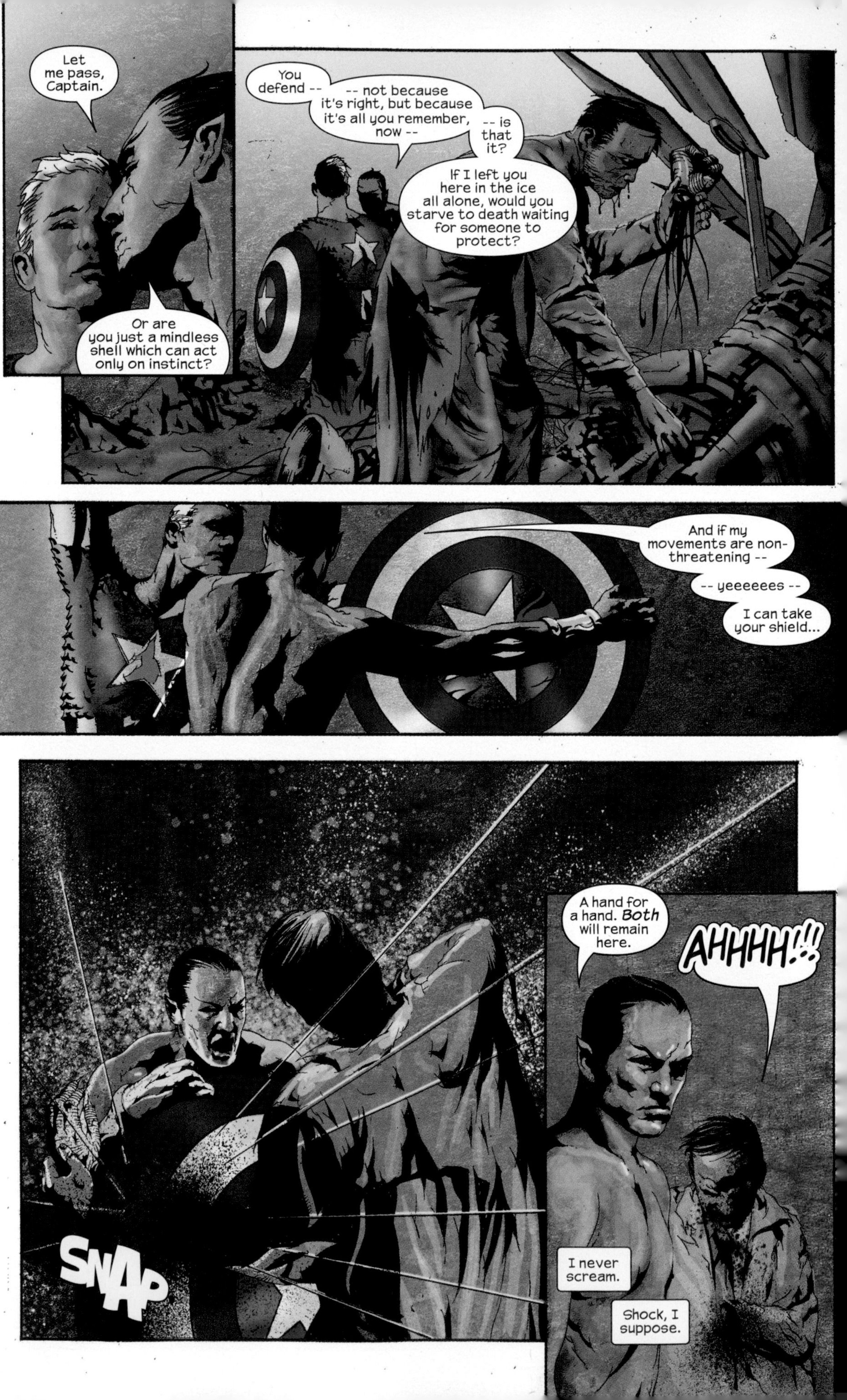
Let me pass, Captain.
Or are you just a mindless shell which can act only on instinct?
You defend --
-- not because it's right, but because it's all you remember, now --
-- is that it?
If I left you here in the ice all alone, would you starve to death waiting for someone to protect?
And if my movements are non-threatening --
-- yeeeeees --
I can take your shield...
SNAP
A hand for a hand. *Both* will remain here.
AHHHH!!!
I never scream.
Shock, I suppose.

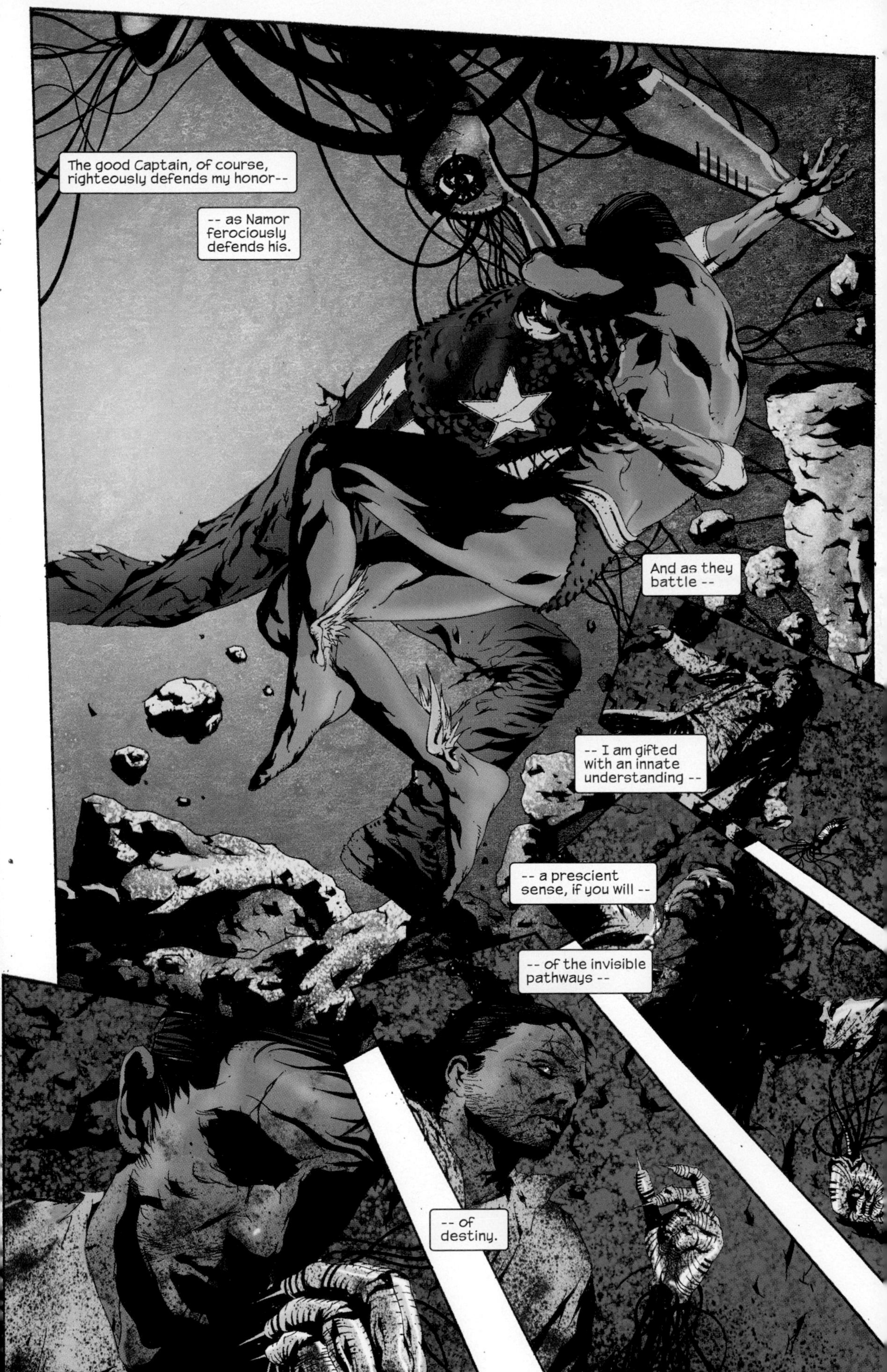
The good Captain, of course, righteously defends my honor--
-- as Namor ferociously defends his.
And as they battle --
-- I am gifted with an innate understanding --
-- a prescient sense, if you will --
-- of the invisible pathways --
-- of destiny.

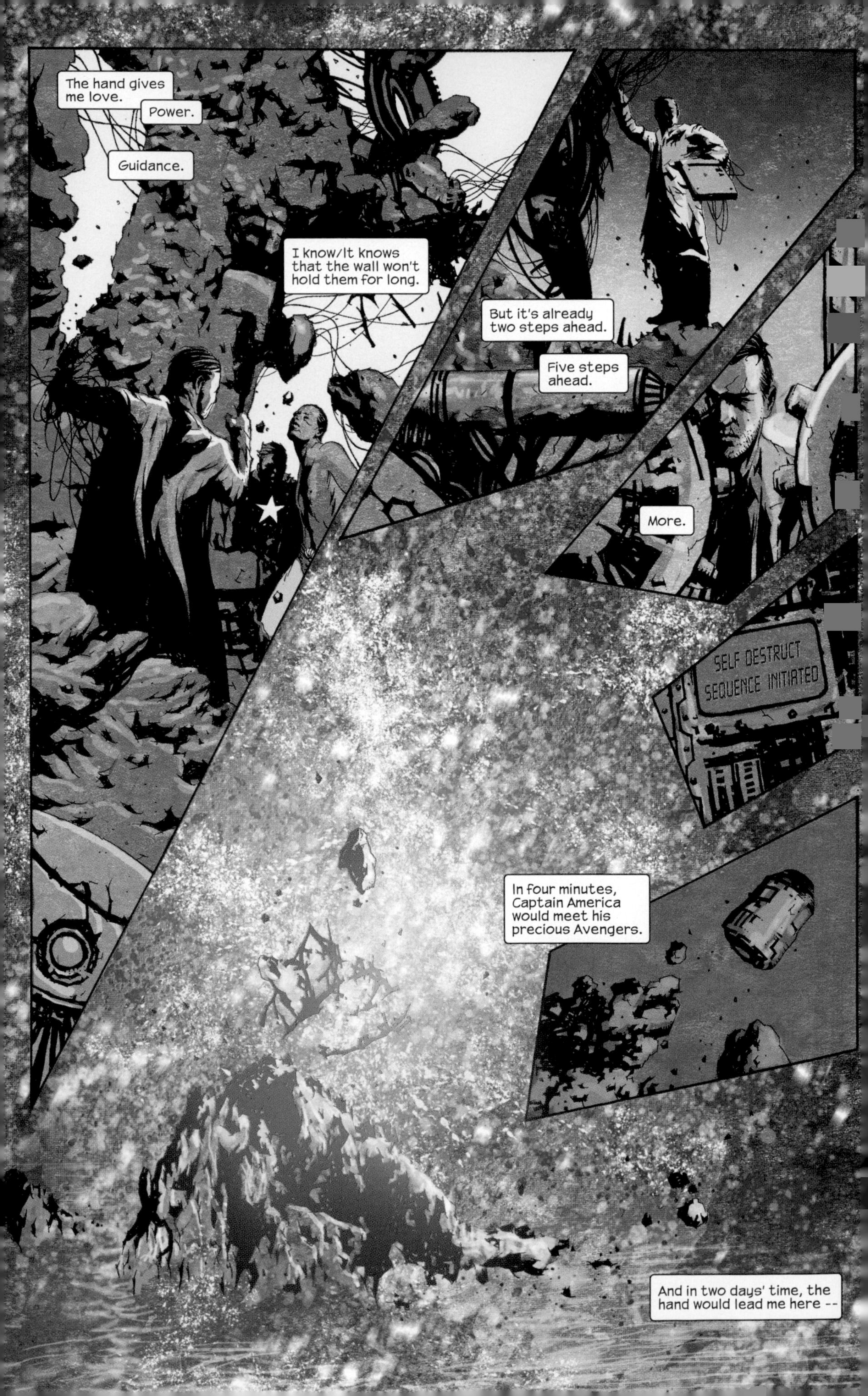
The hand gives me love.
Power.
Guidance.
I know/It knows that the wall won't hold them for long.
But it's already two steps ahead.
Five steps ahead.
More.
SELF DESTRUCT SEQUENCE INITIATED
In four minutes, Captain America would meet his precious Avengers.
And in two days' time, the hand would lead me here --

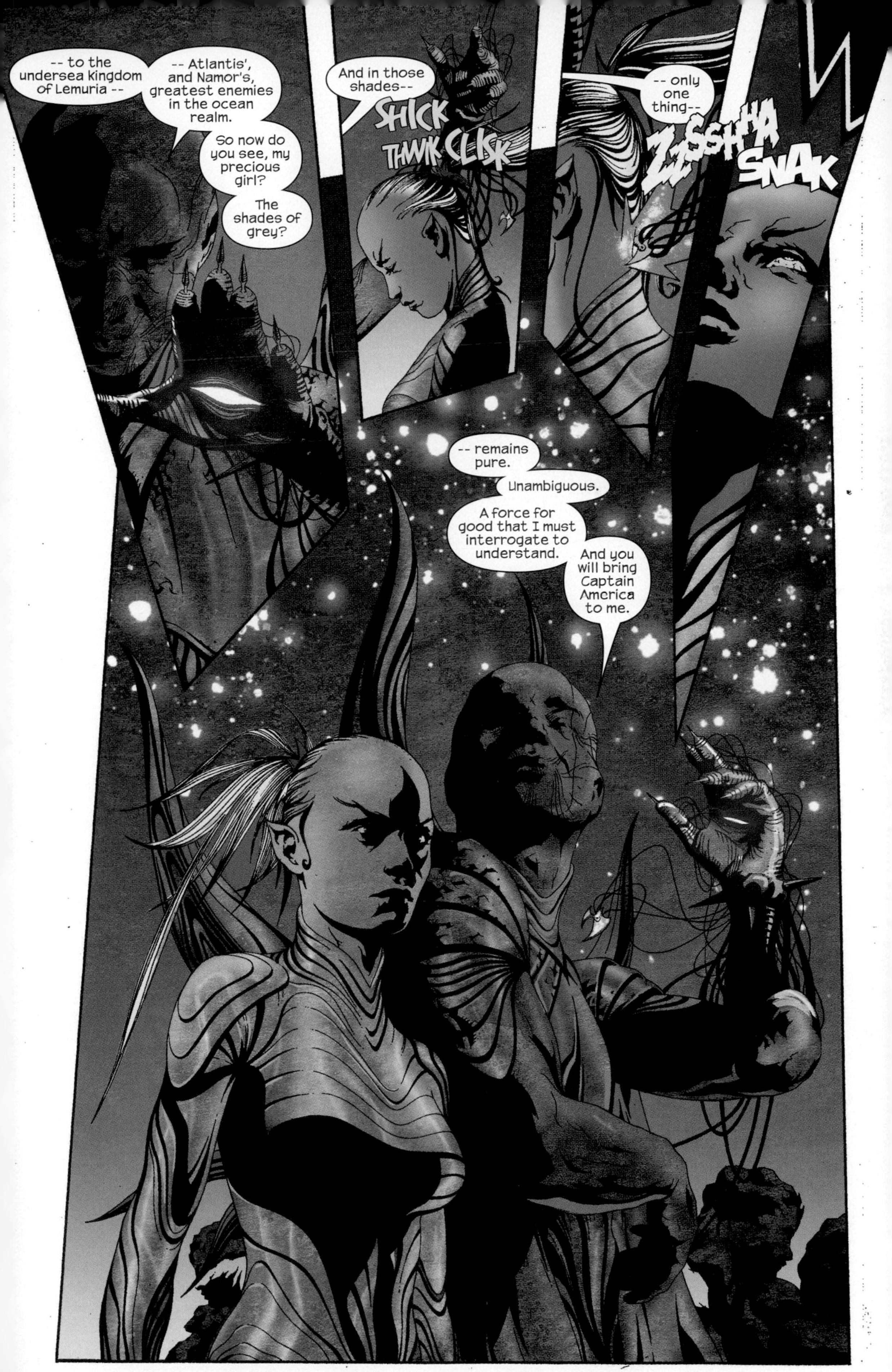
-- to the undersea kingdom of Lemuria --
-- Atlantis', and Namor's, greatest enemies in the ocean realm.
So now do you see, my precious girl?
The shades of grey?
And in those shades--
SHICK
THWIK CLISK
-- only one thing--
ZISSHHA
SNAK
-- remains pure.
Unambiguous.
A force for good that I must interrogate to understand.
And you will bring Captain America to me.

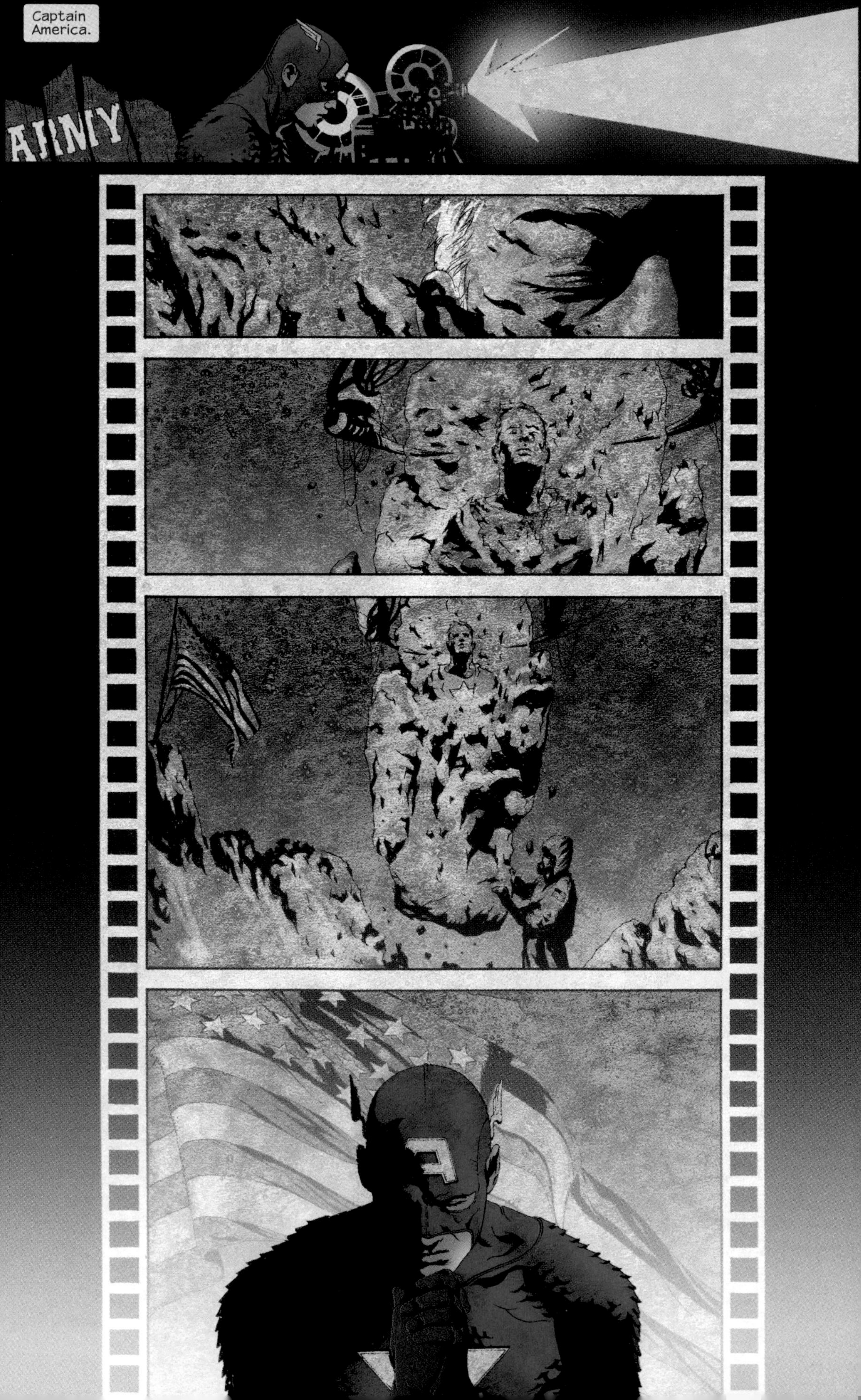
Captain
America.
ARMY

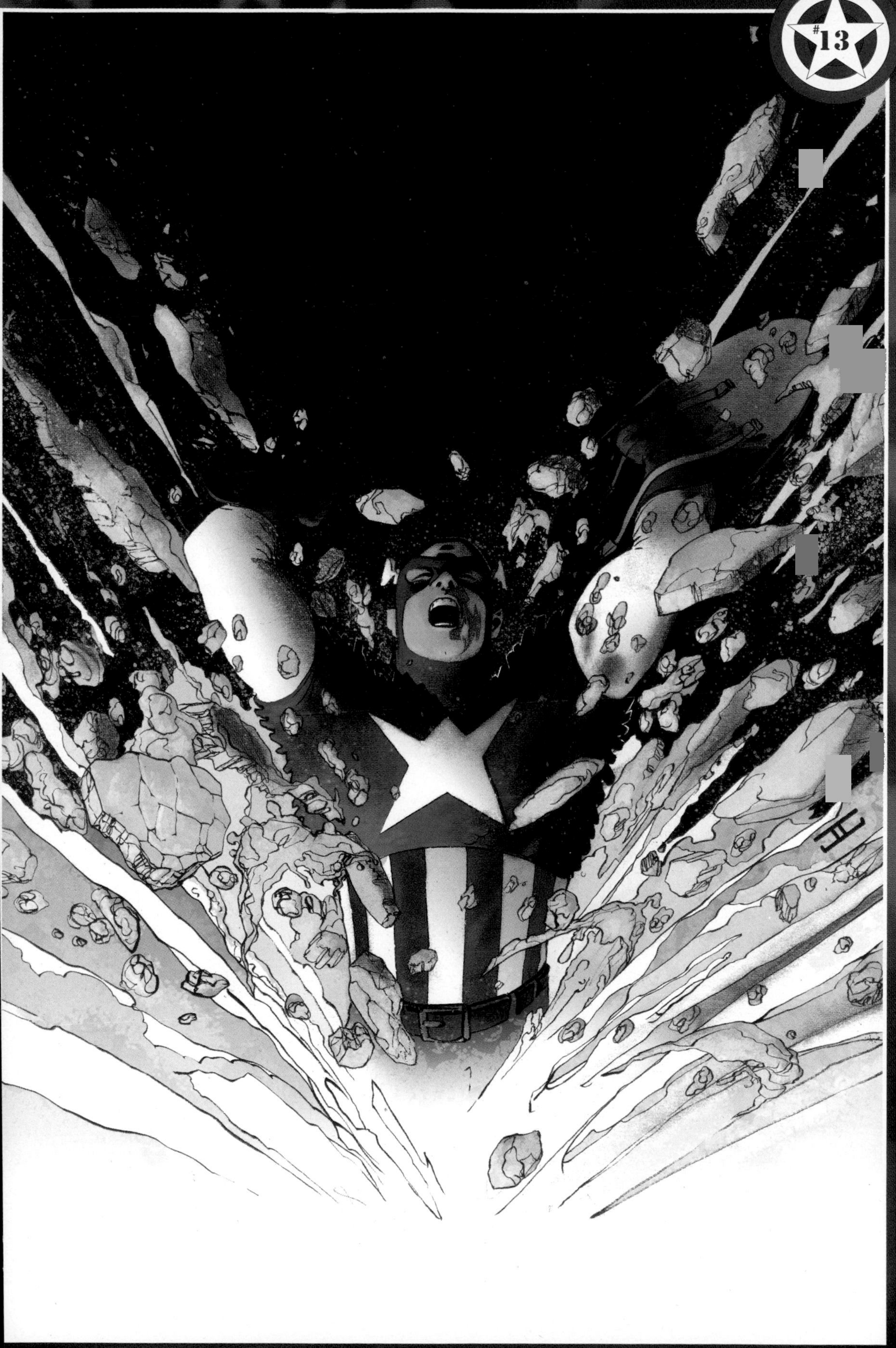
#13

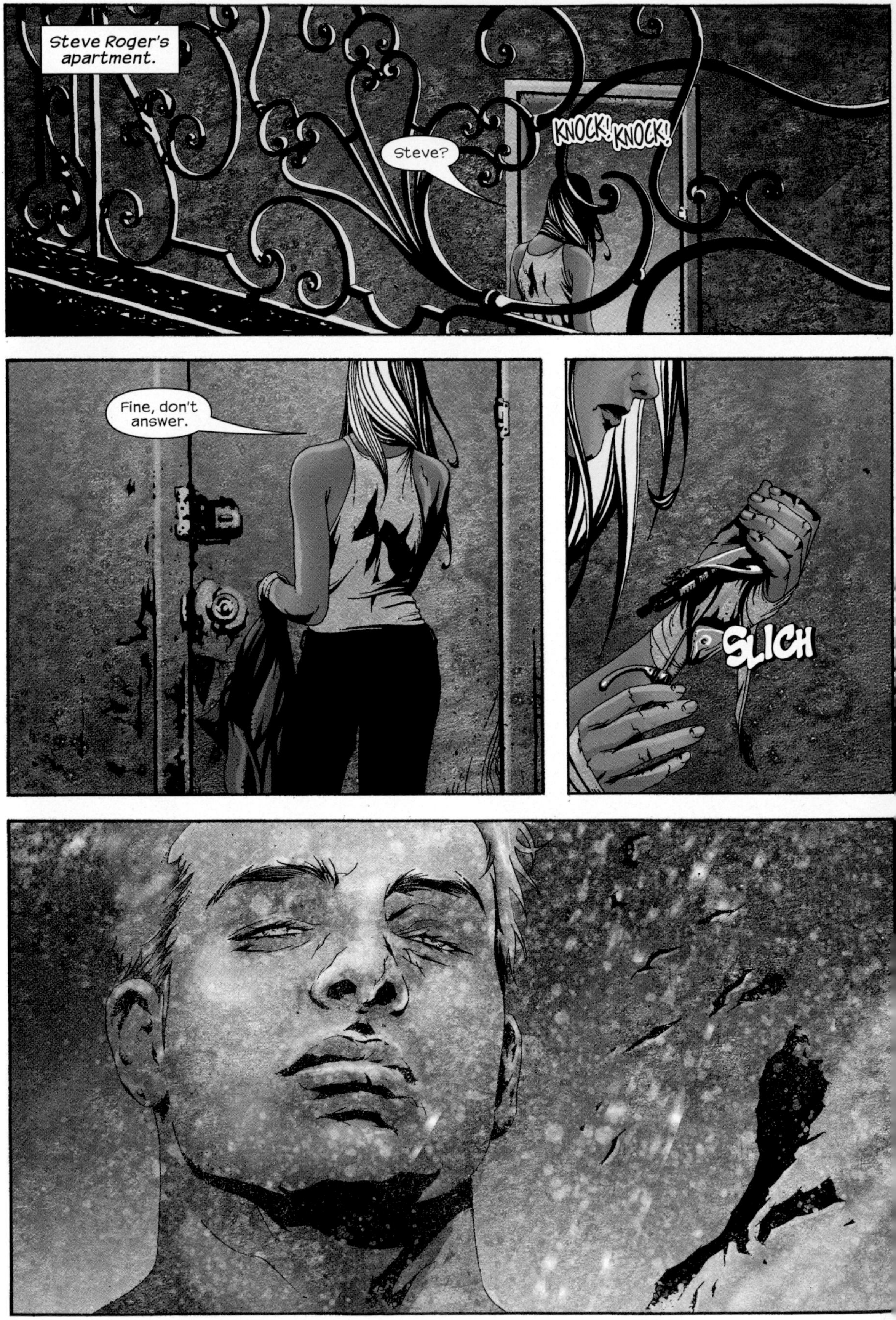
Steve Roger's apartment.
Steve?
KNOCK! KNOCK!
Fine, don't answer.
SLICH

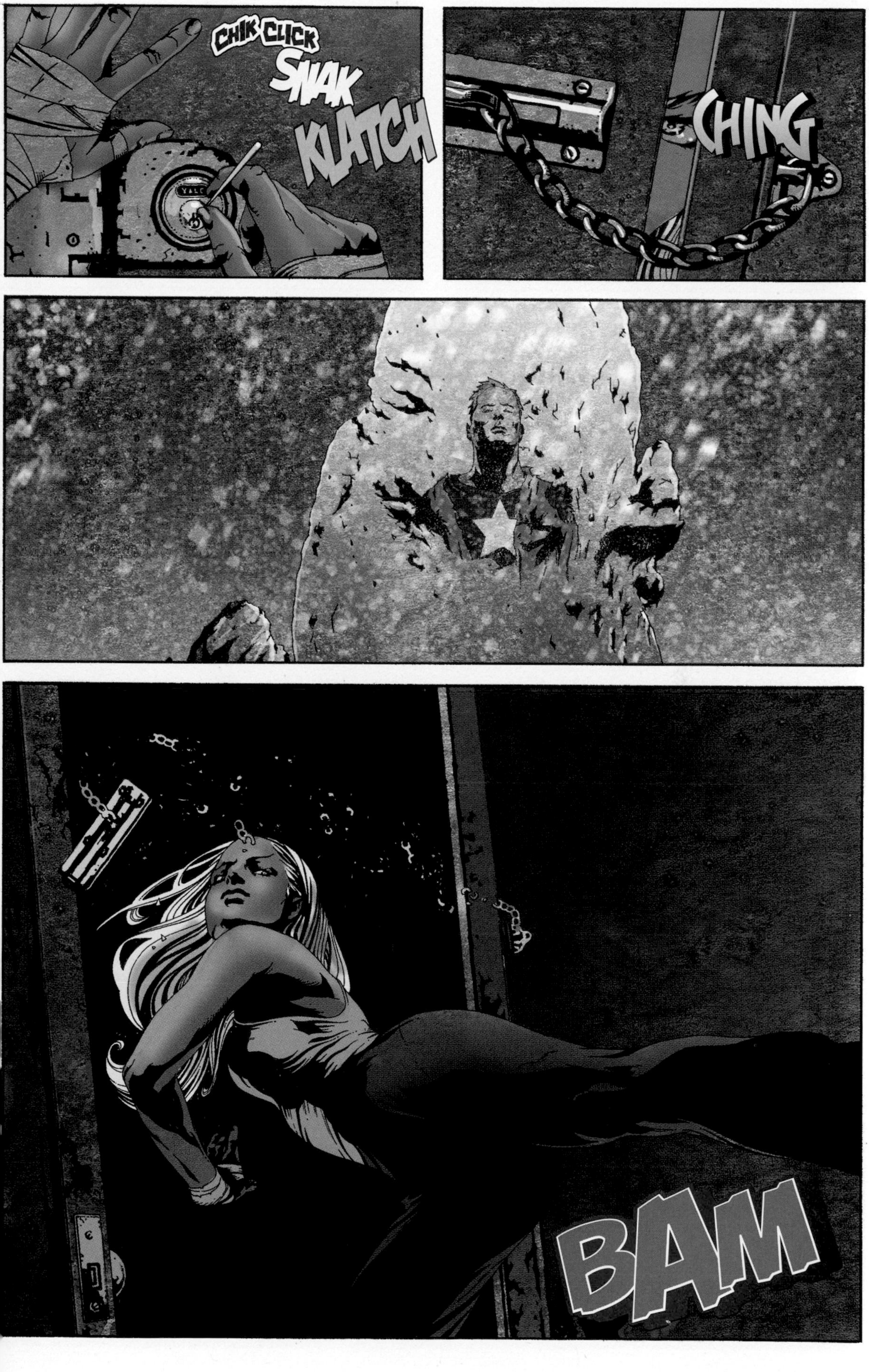
CHIK CLICK
SNAK
KLATCH
YALE
CHING
BAM

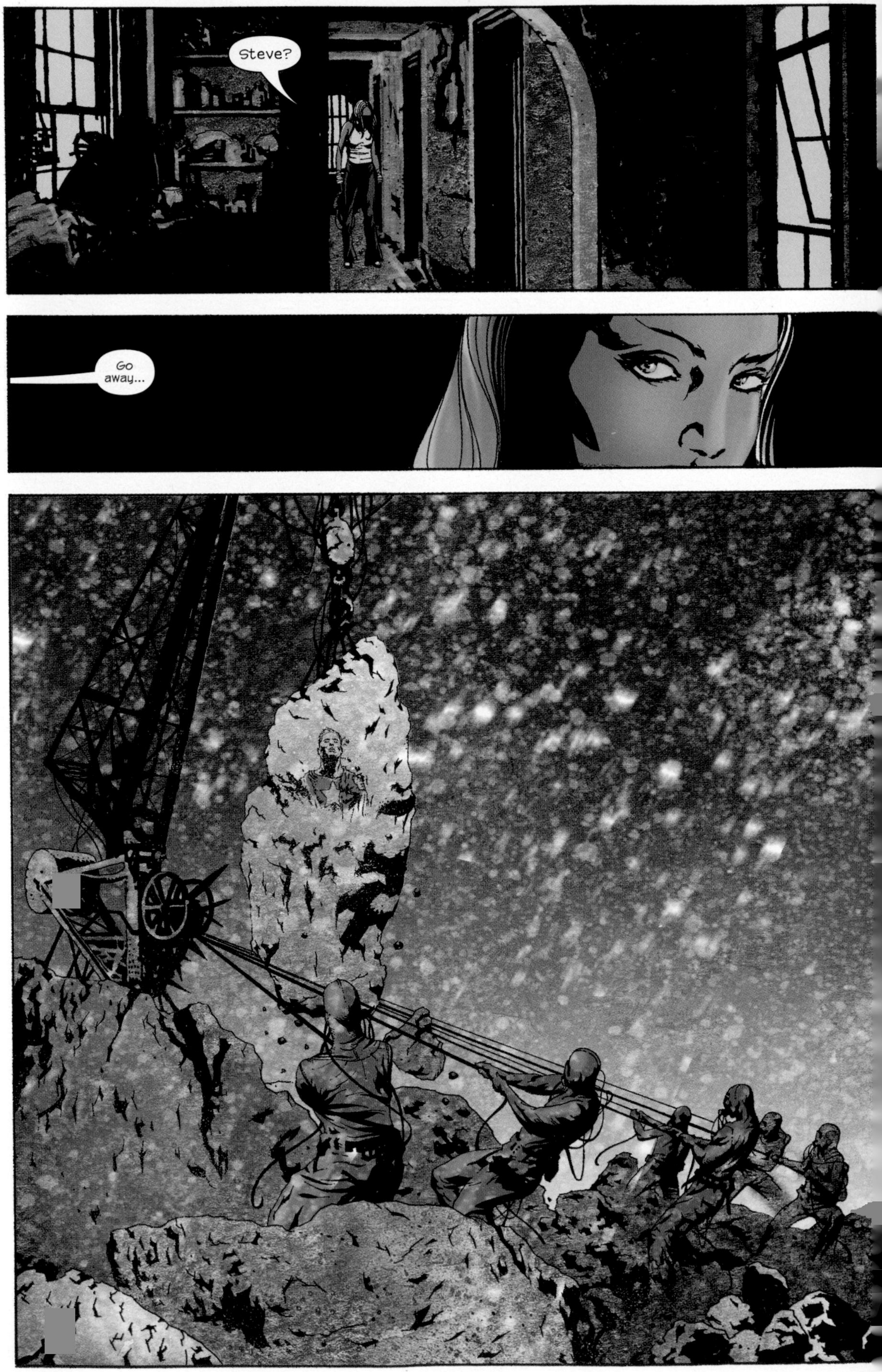
Steve?
Go away...

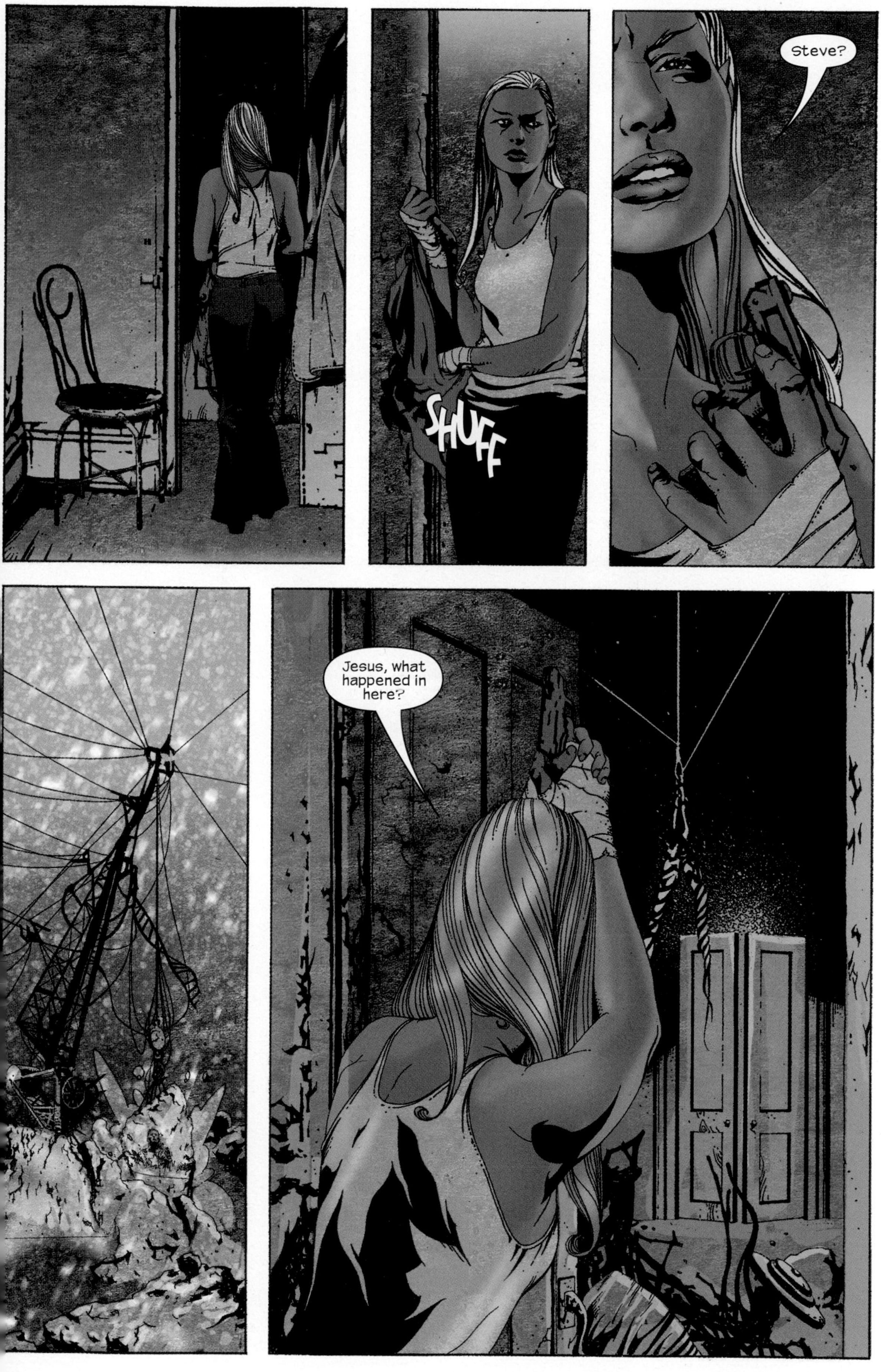
SHUFF
Steve?
Jesus, what happened in here?

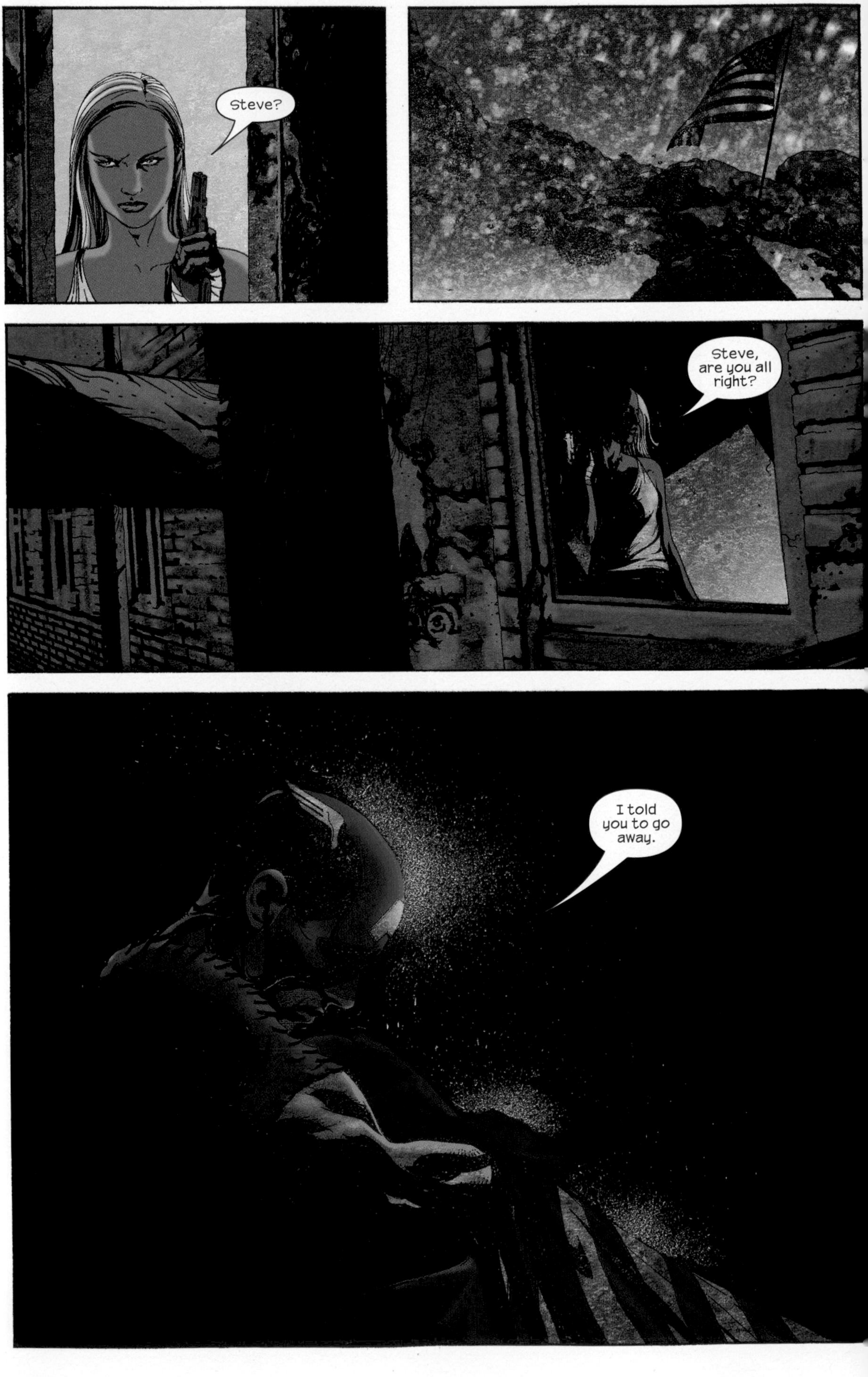
Steve?
Steve, are you all right?
I told you to go away.

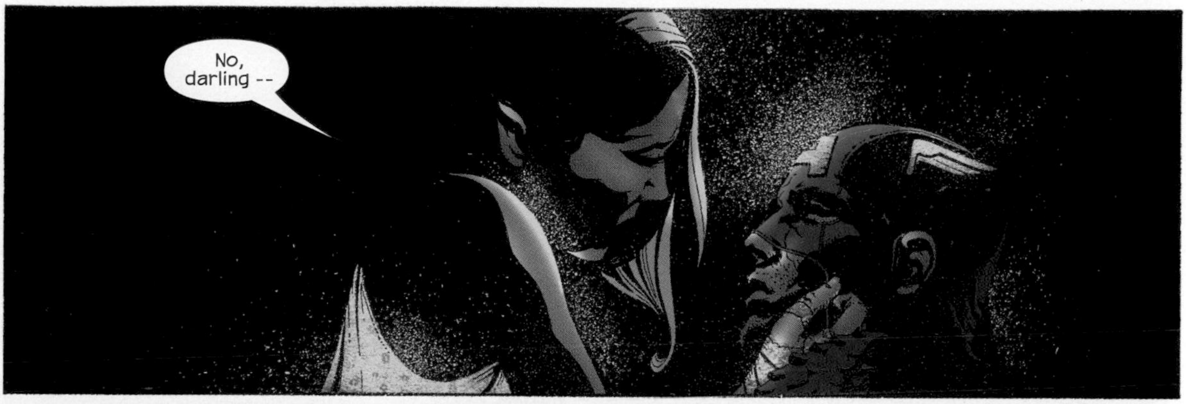
No, darling --

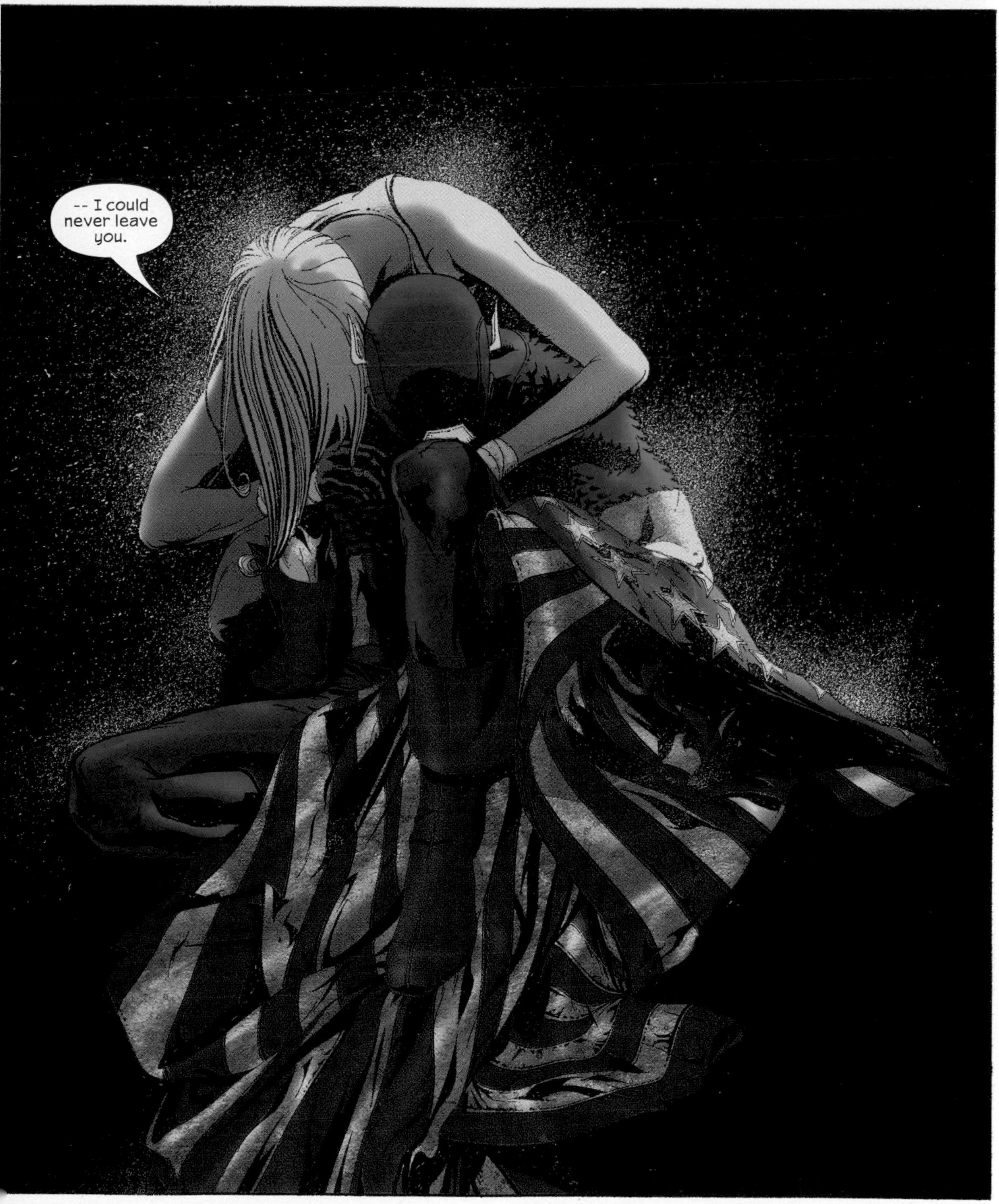
-- I could never leave you.

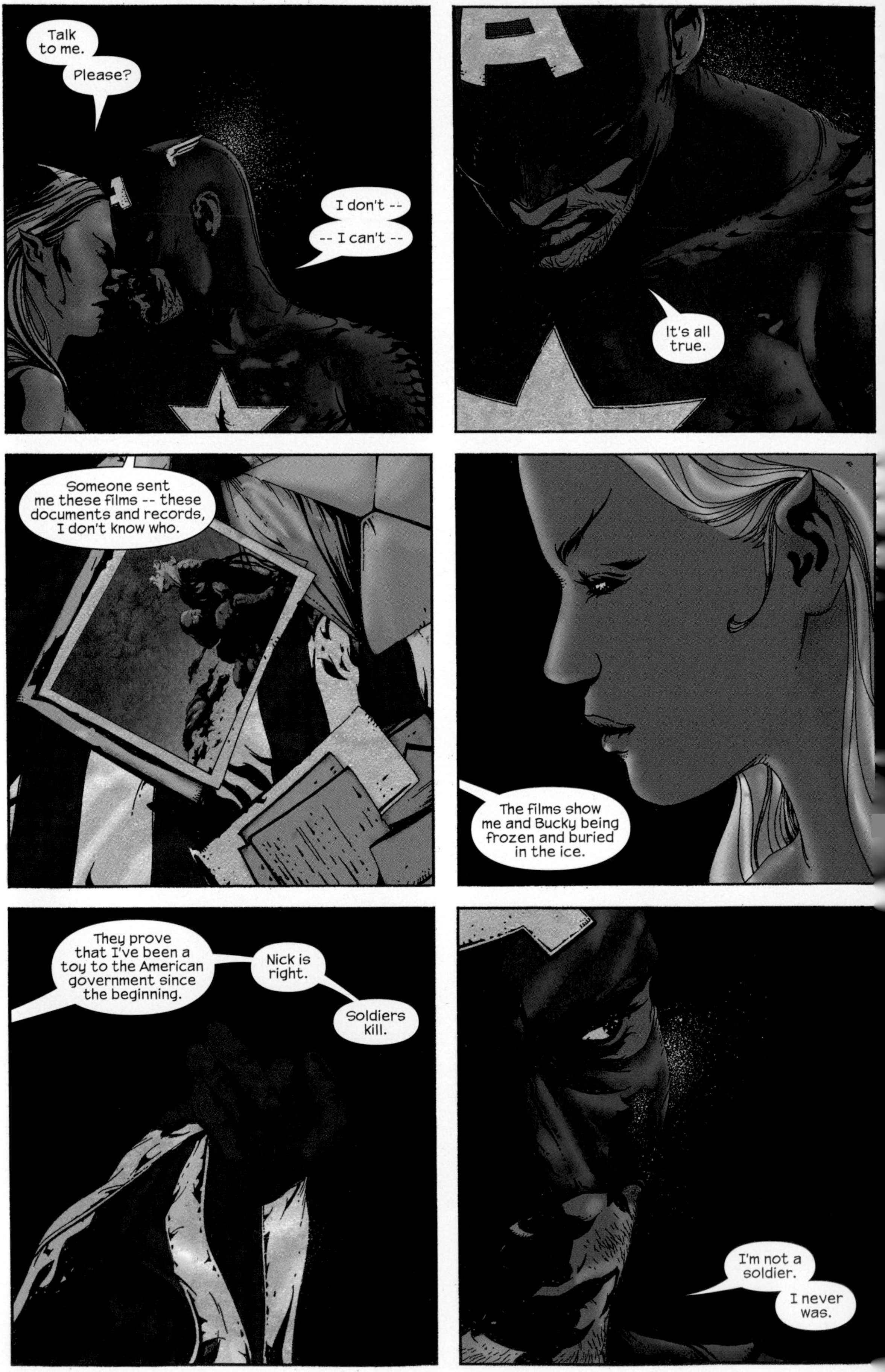
Talk to me.
Please?
I don't --
-- I can't --
It's all true.
Someone sent me these films -- these documents and records, I don't know who.
The films show me and Bucky being frozen and buried in the ice.
They prove that I've been a toy to the American government since the beginning.
Nick is right.
Soldiers kill.
I'm not a soldier.
I never was.

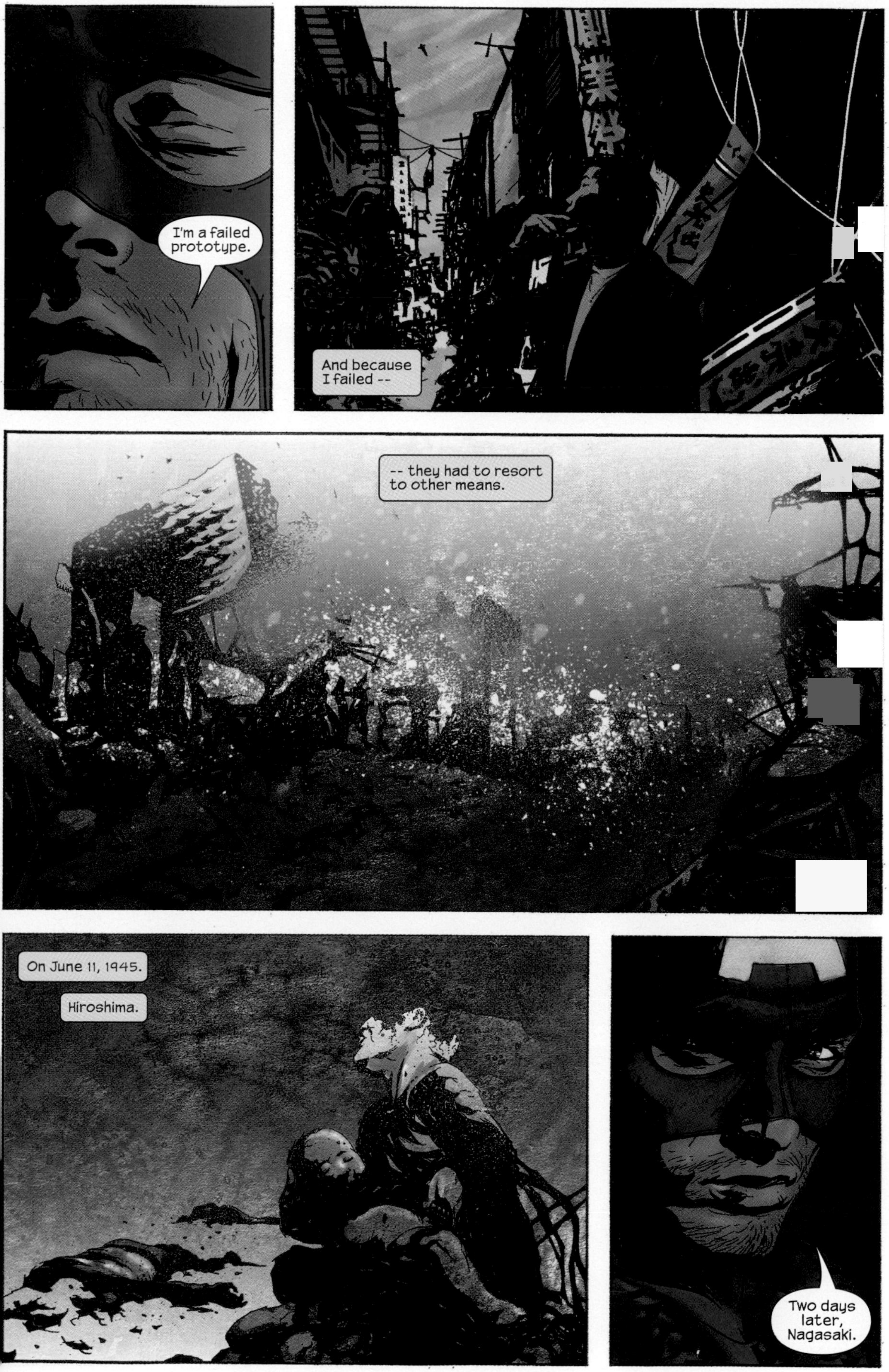
I'm a failed prototype.
And because I failed --
-- they had to resort to other means.
On June 11, 1945.
Hiroshima.
Two days later, Nagasaki.

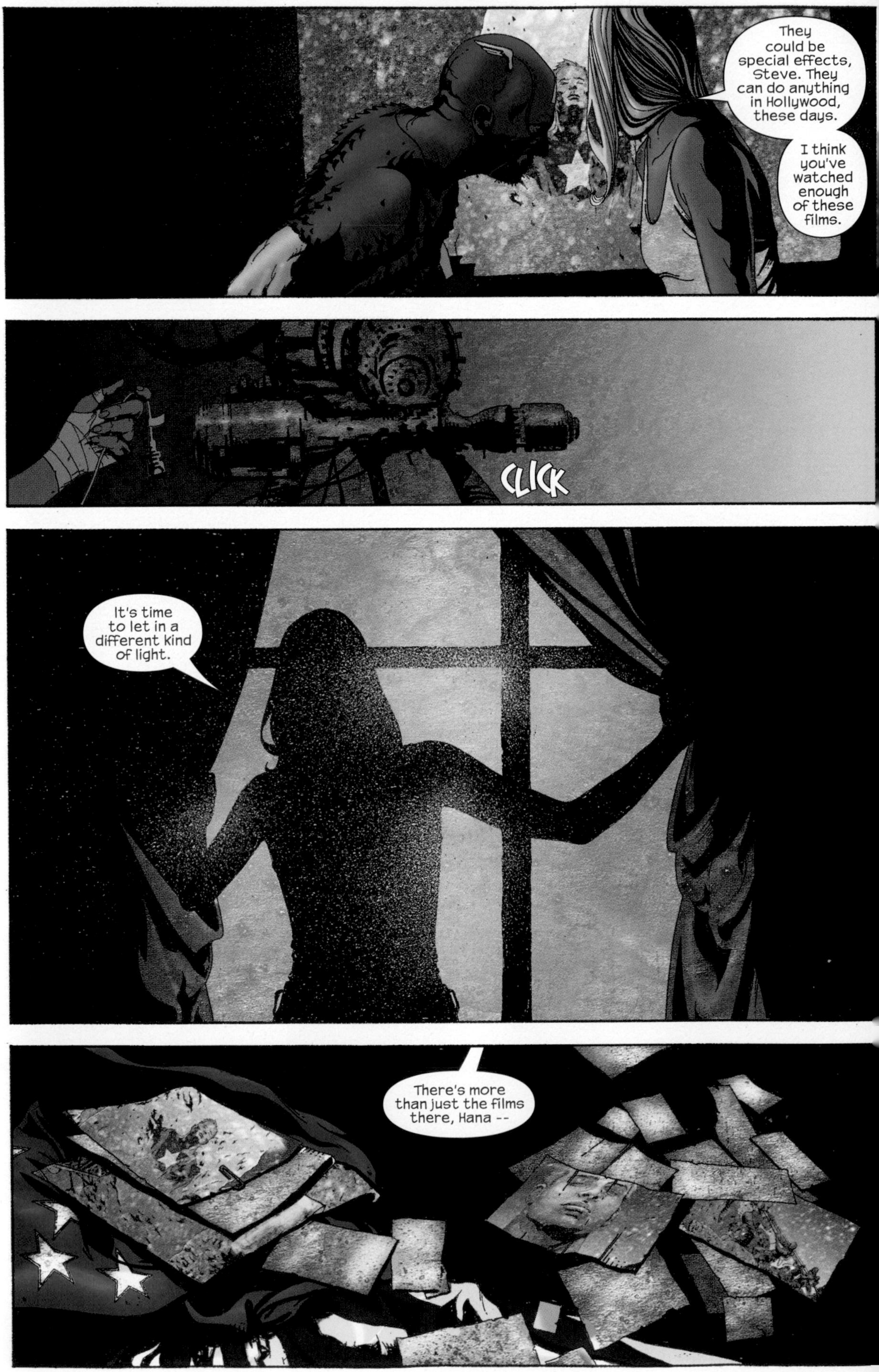
They could be special effects, Steve. They can do anything in Hollywood, these days.
I think you've watched enough of these films.
CLICK
It's time to let in a different kind of light.
There's more than just the films there, Hana --

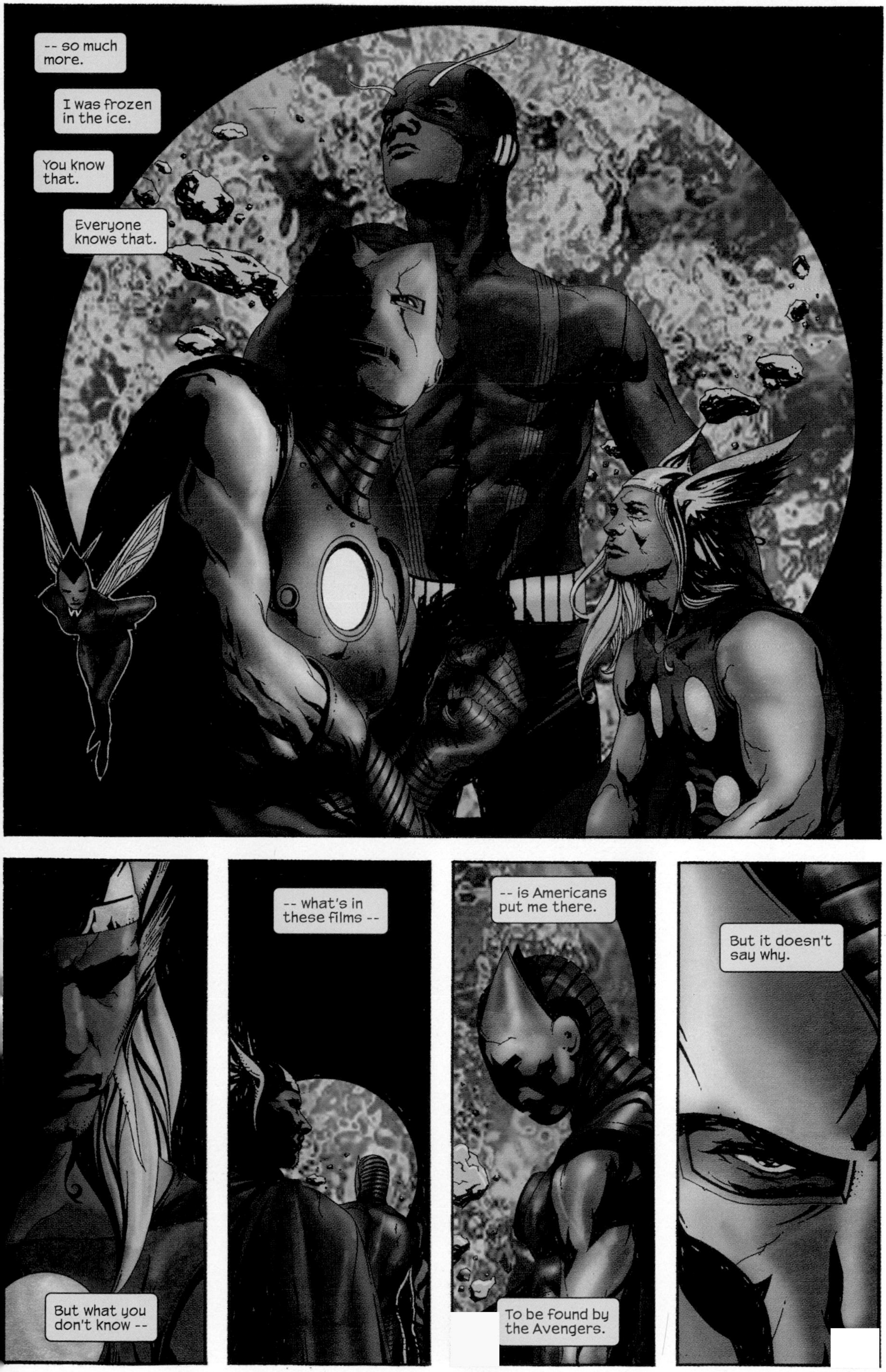
-- so much more.
I was frozen in the ice.
You know that.
Everyone knows that.
But what you don't know --
-- what's in these films --
-- is Americans put me there.
To be found by the Avengers.
But it doesn't say why.

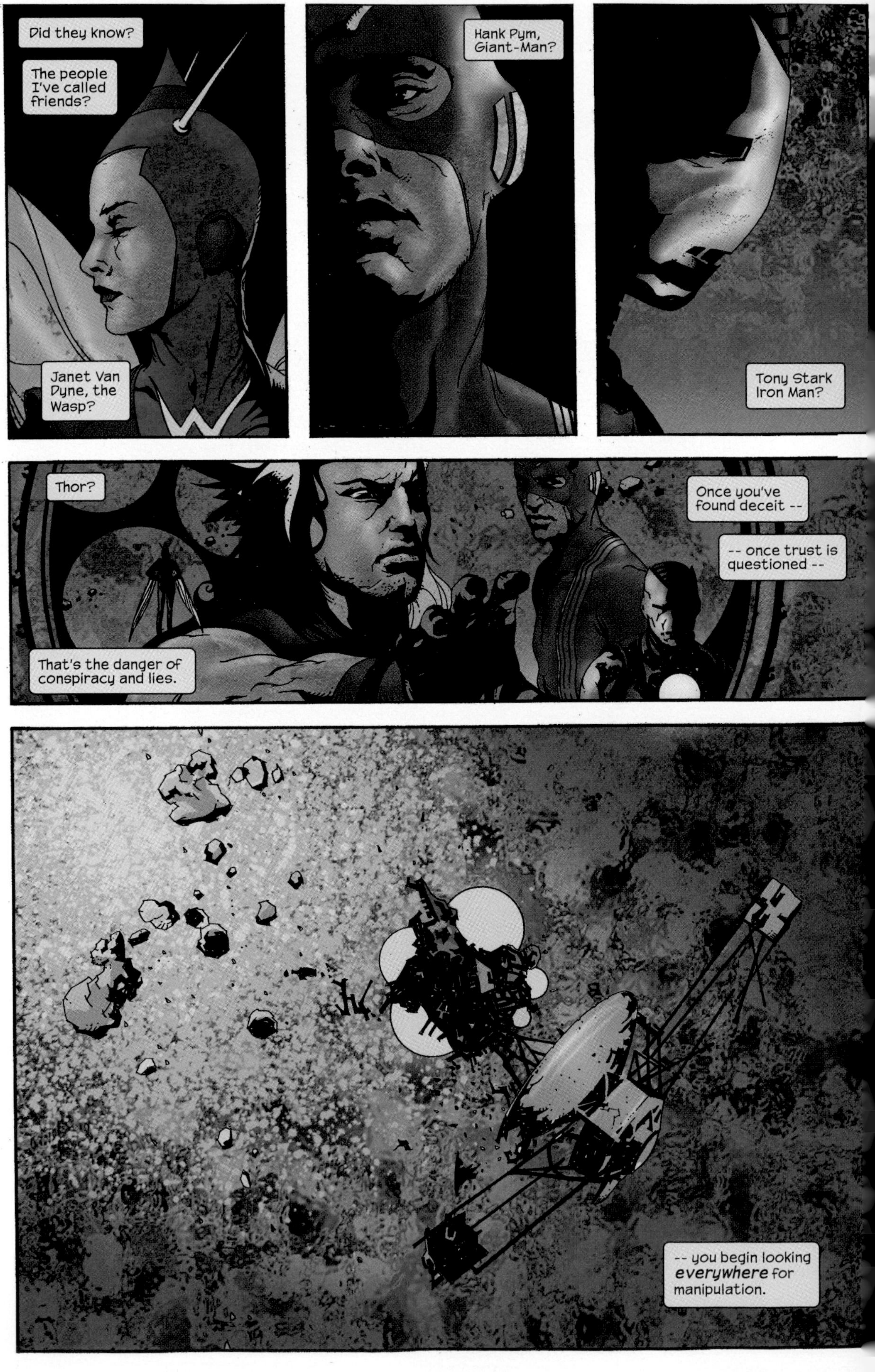
Did they know?
The people I've called friends?
Janet Van Dyne, the Wasp?
Hank Pym, Giant-Man?
Tony Stark Iron Man?
Thor?
Once you've found deceit --
-- once trust is questioned --
That's the danger of conspiracy and lies.
-- you begin looking *everywhere* for manipulation.

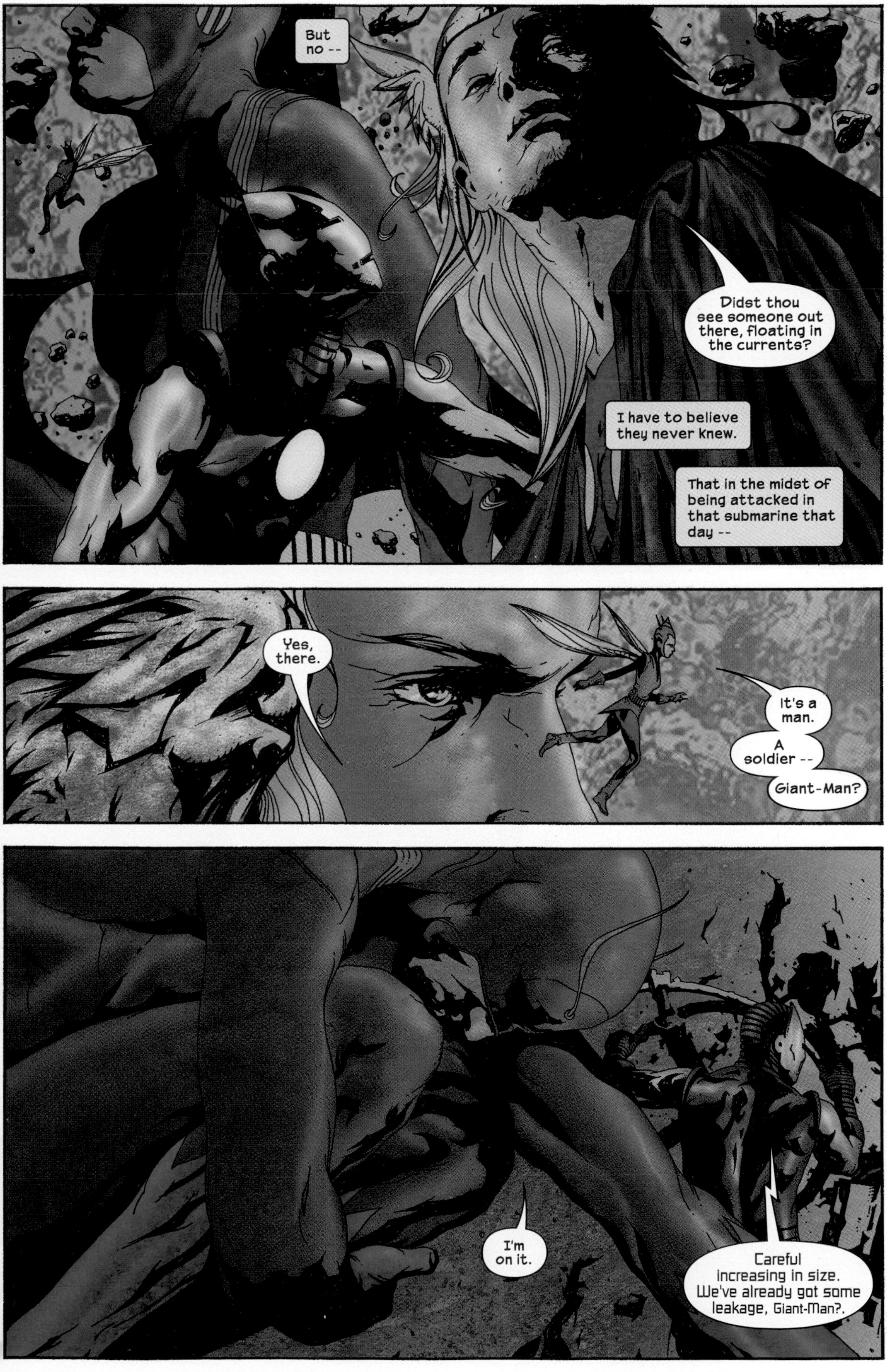

But no --
Didst thou see someone out there, floating in the currents?
I have to believe they never knew.
That in the midst of being attacked in that submarine that day --
Yes, there.
It's a man.
A soldier --
Giant-Man?
I'm on it.
Careful increasing in size. We've already got some leakage, Giant-Man?.

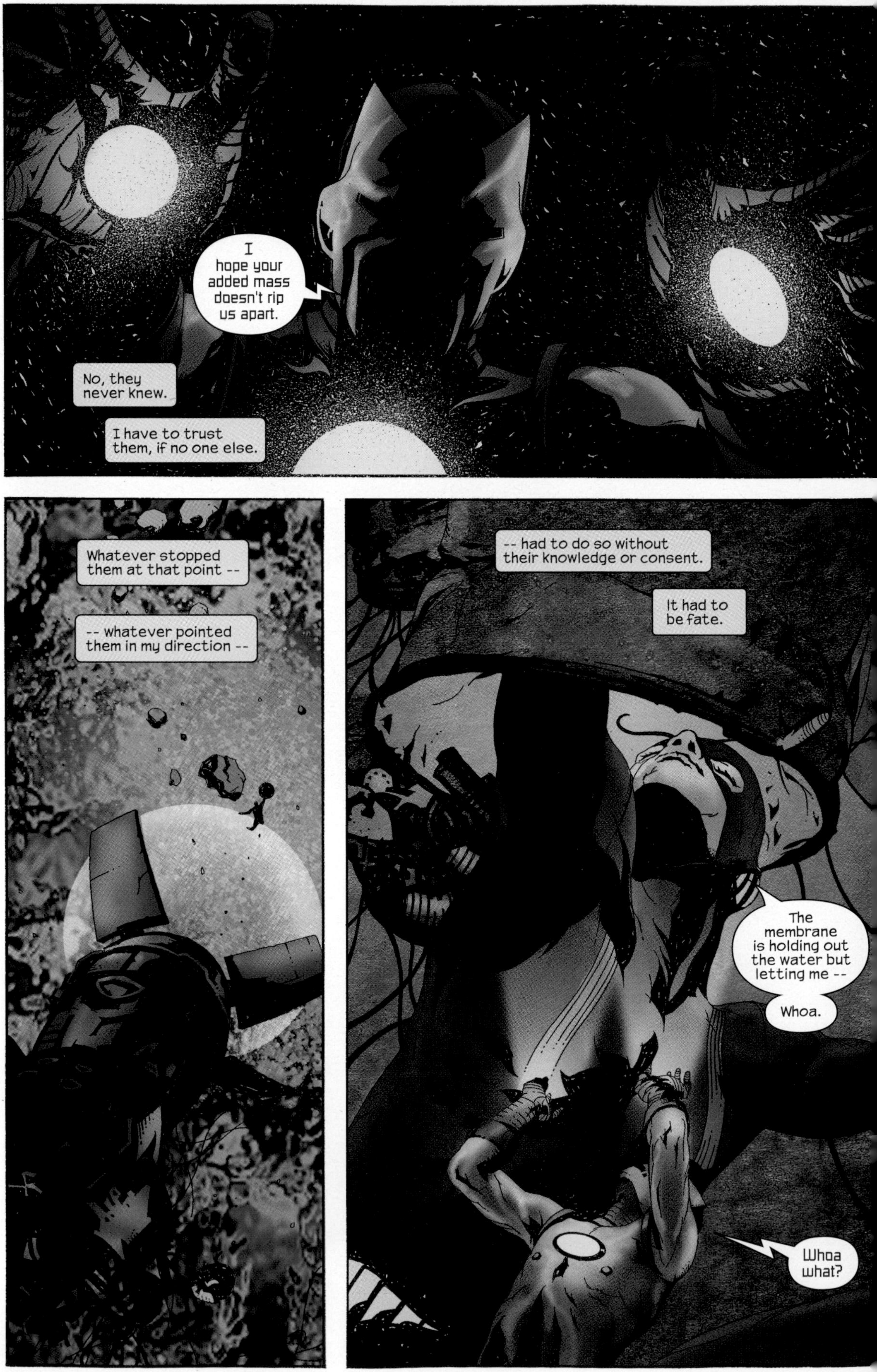
I hope your added mass doesn't rip us apart.
No, they never knew.
I have to trust them, if no one else.
Whatever stopped them at that point --
-- whatever pointed them in my direction --
-- had to do so without their knowledge or consent.
It had to be fate.
The membrane is holding out the water but letting me --
Whoa.
Whoa what?

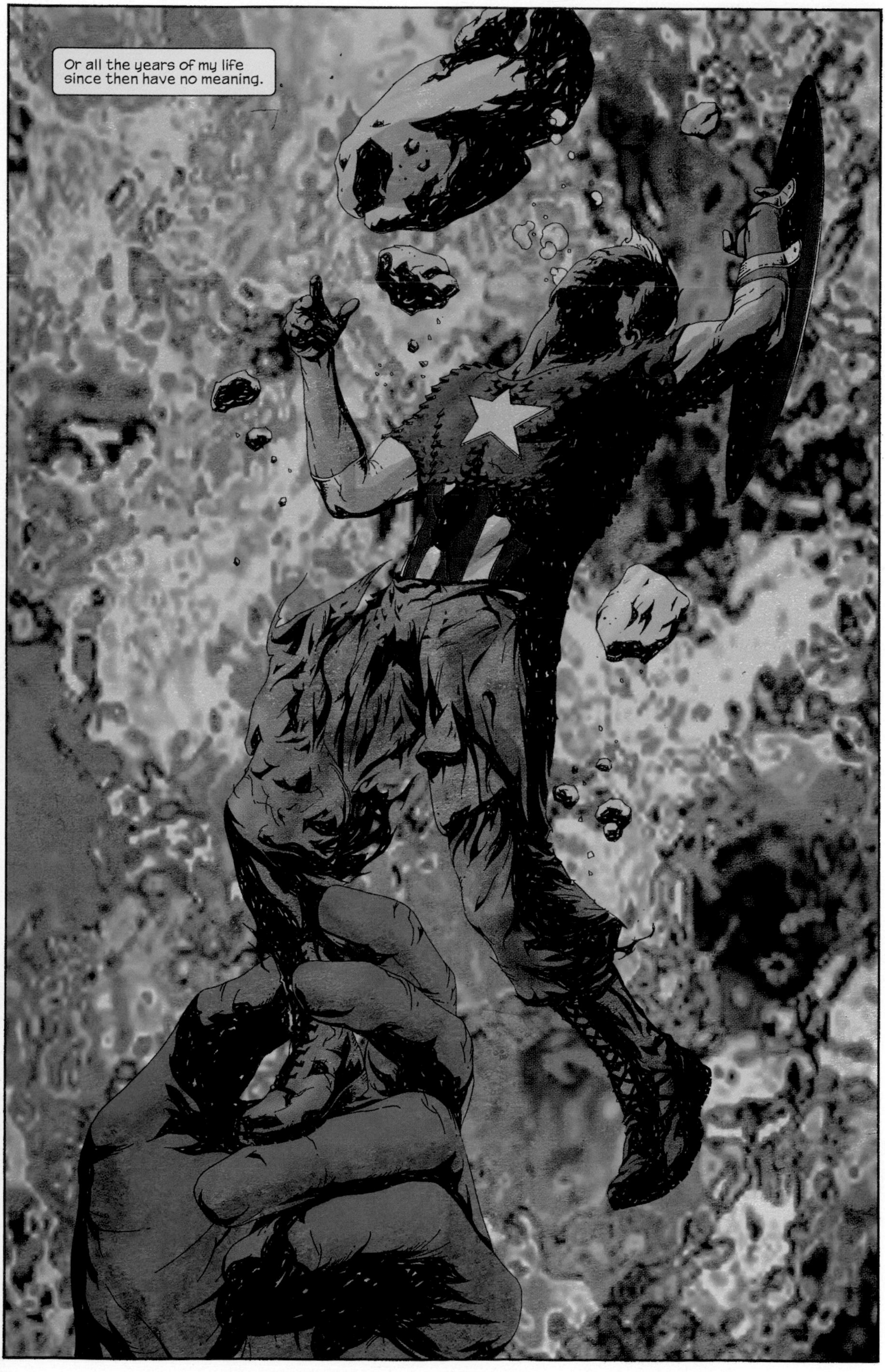
Or all the years of my life since then have no meaning.

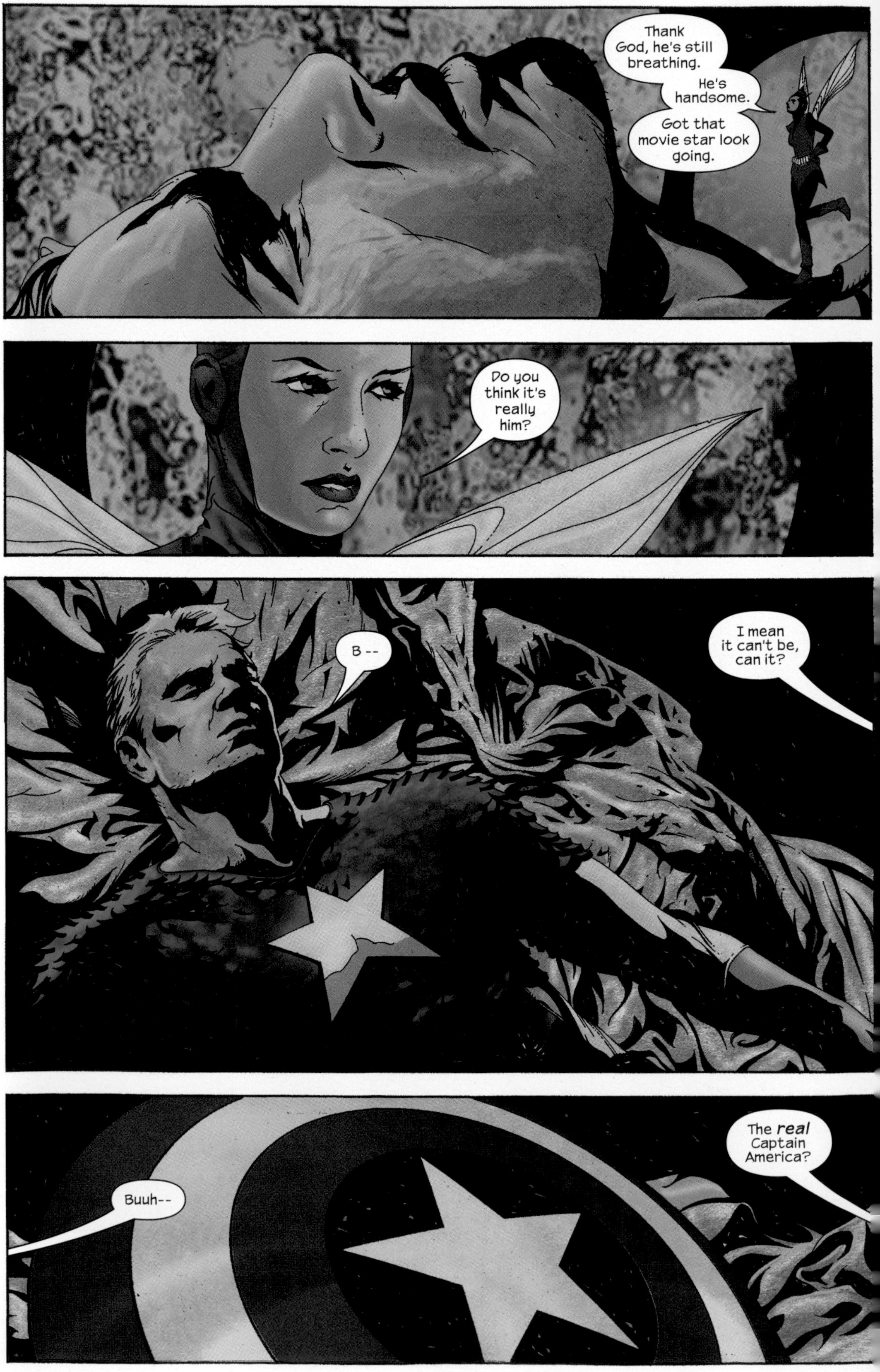
Thank God, he's still breathing.
He's handsome.
Got that movie star look going.
Do you think it's really him?
B --
I mean it can't be, can it?
The *real* Captain America?
Buuh--

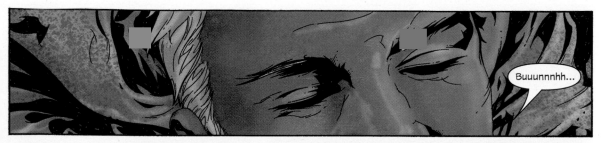

Buuunnnhh...

Buuuc--

Why would they keep me frozen for so many years --

-- only to reawaken me again in an age of gods?

BUCKY!

When it was too late for me to change both.

Too late for me to offer another option.

Or is that *why*? To stop *me* from stopping *them*?

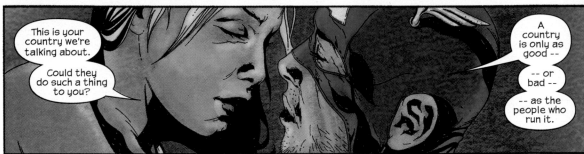

This is your country we're talking about.

Could they do such a thing to you?

A country is only as good --

-- or bad --

-- as the people who run it.

Wouldn't it have been easier to kill you?

I don't know. No one's ever been able to.

Maybe they tried.

Here. I think you need this.

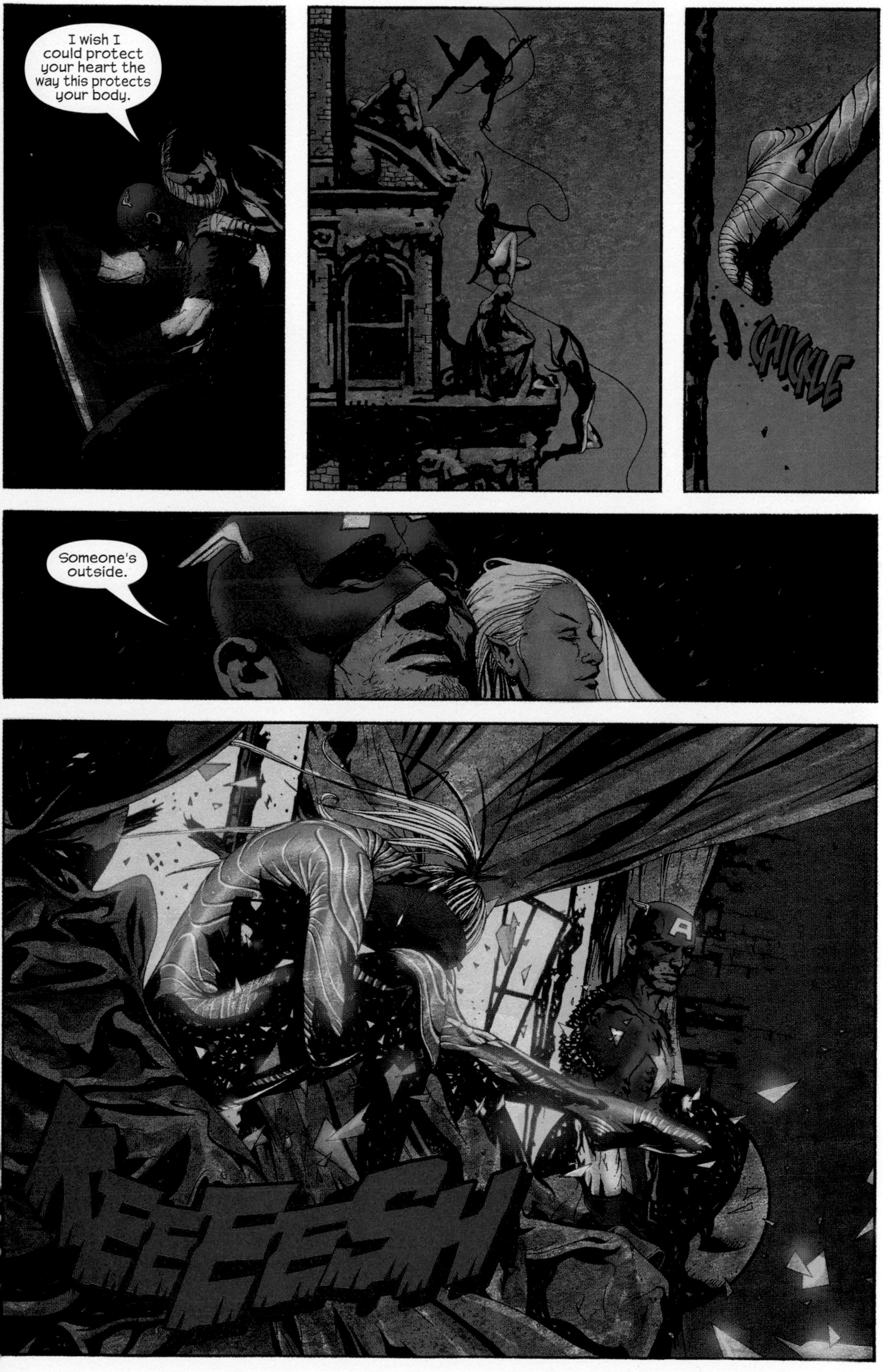
I wish I could protect your heart the way this protects your body.
CHICKLE
Someone's outside.

Three of them move as one.

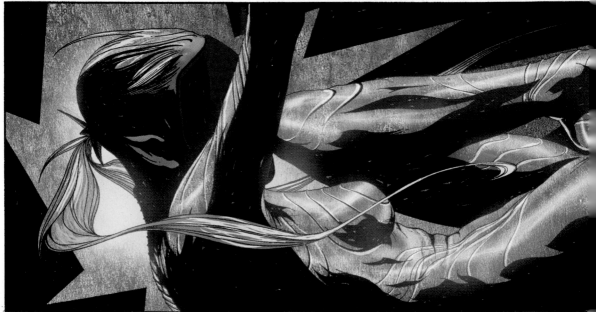

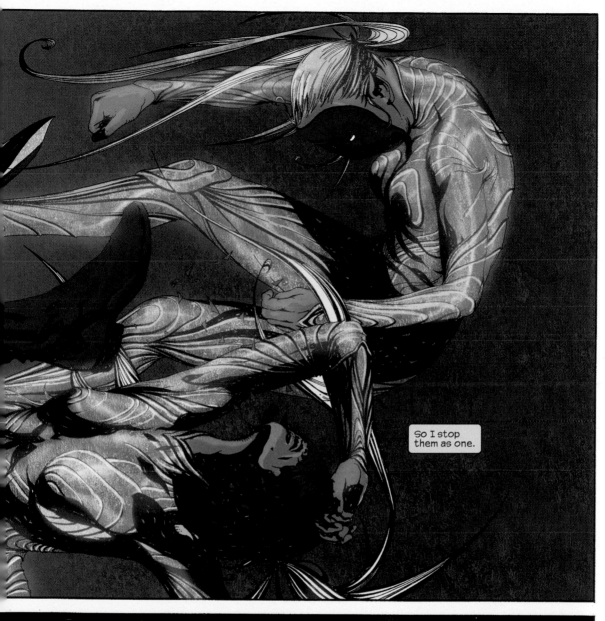

So I stop
them as one.

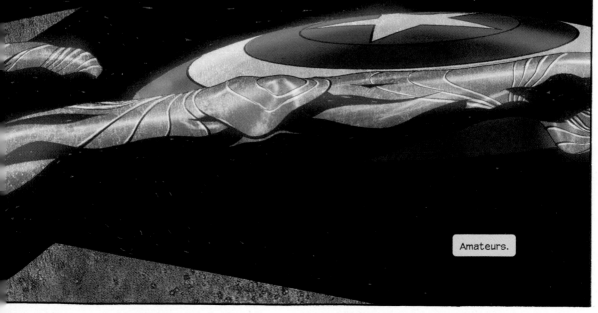

Amateurs.

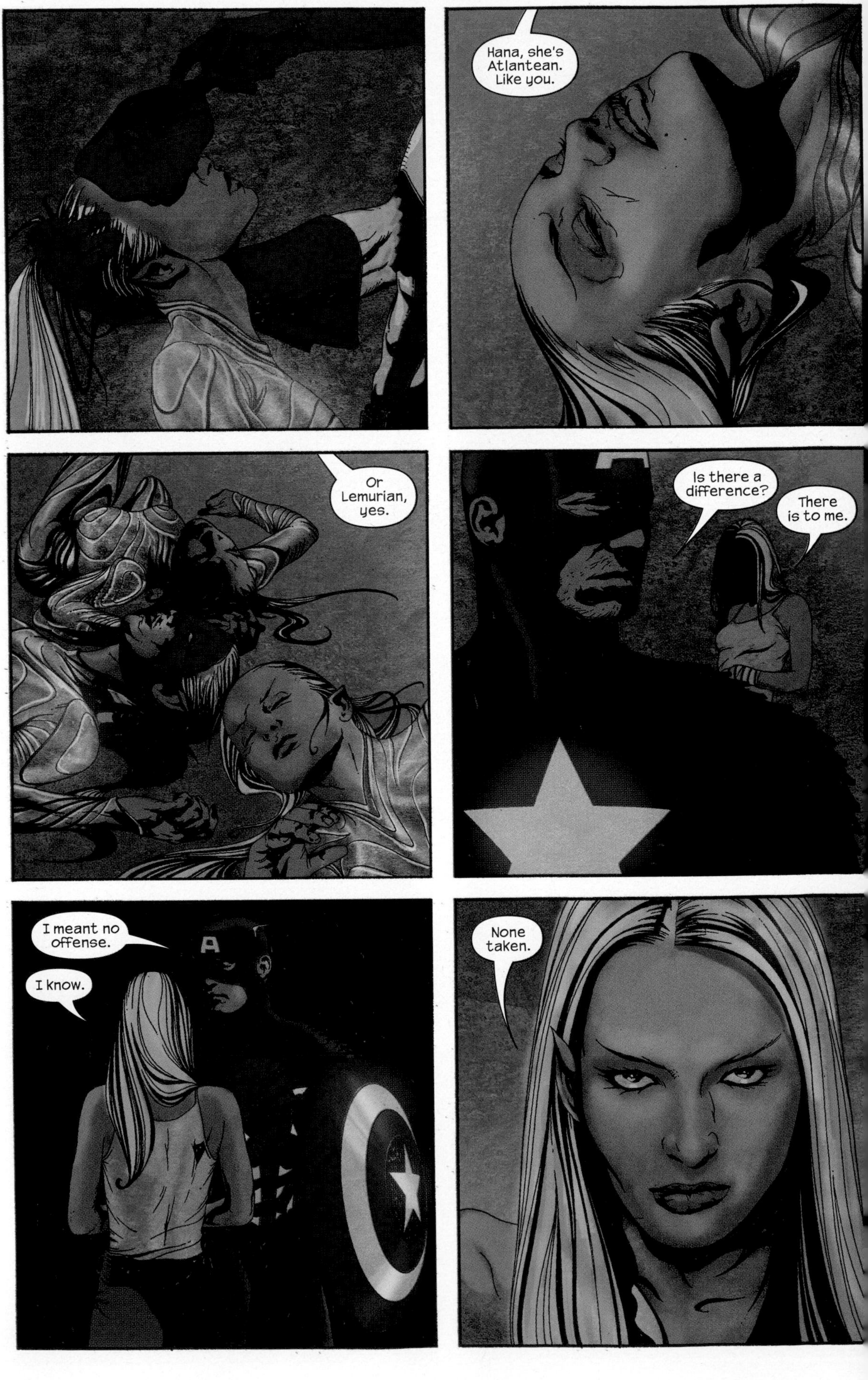

Hana, she's Atlantean. Like you.
Or Lemurian, yes.
Is there a difference?
There is to me.
I meant no offense.
I know.
None taken.

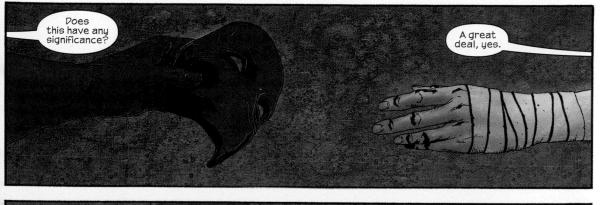

Does this have any significance?

A great deal, yes.

It is the mask of the Assassins Guild.

They may be hired to kidnap, assault --

-- or kill.

It is mostly ceremonial.

It is usually only used for parties, or celebrations, now.

Although originally it was obviously meant to be worn to intimidate your prey --

"-- once they were clearly in your sights."

14

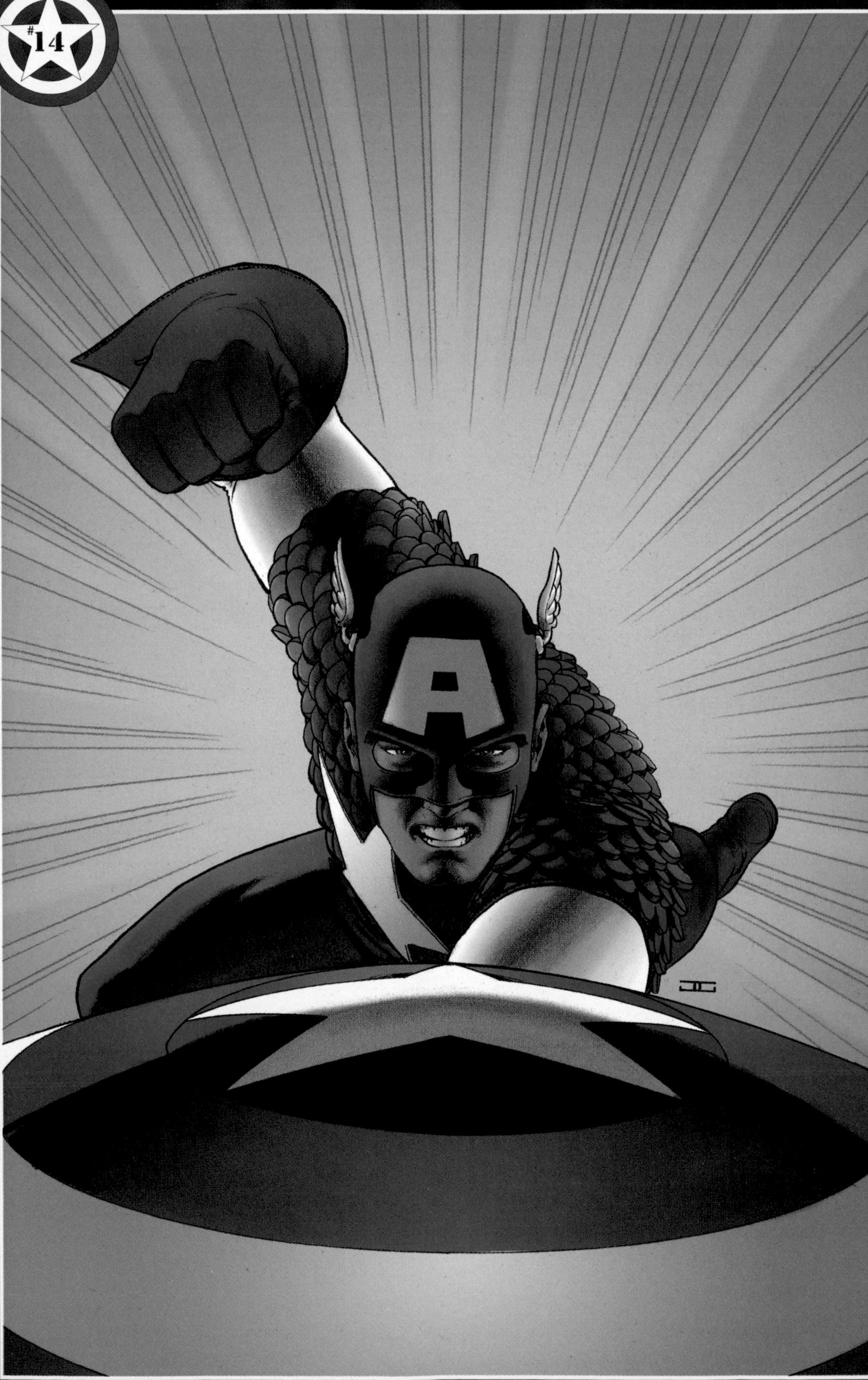

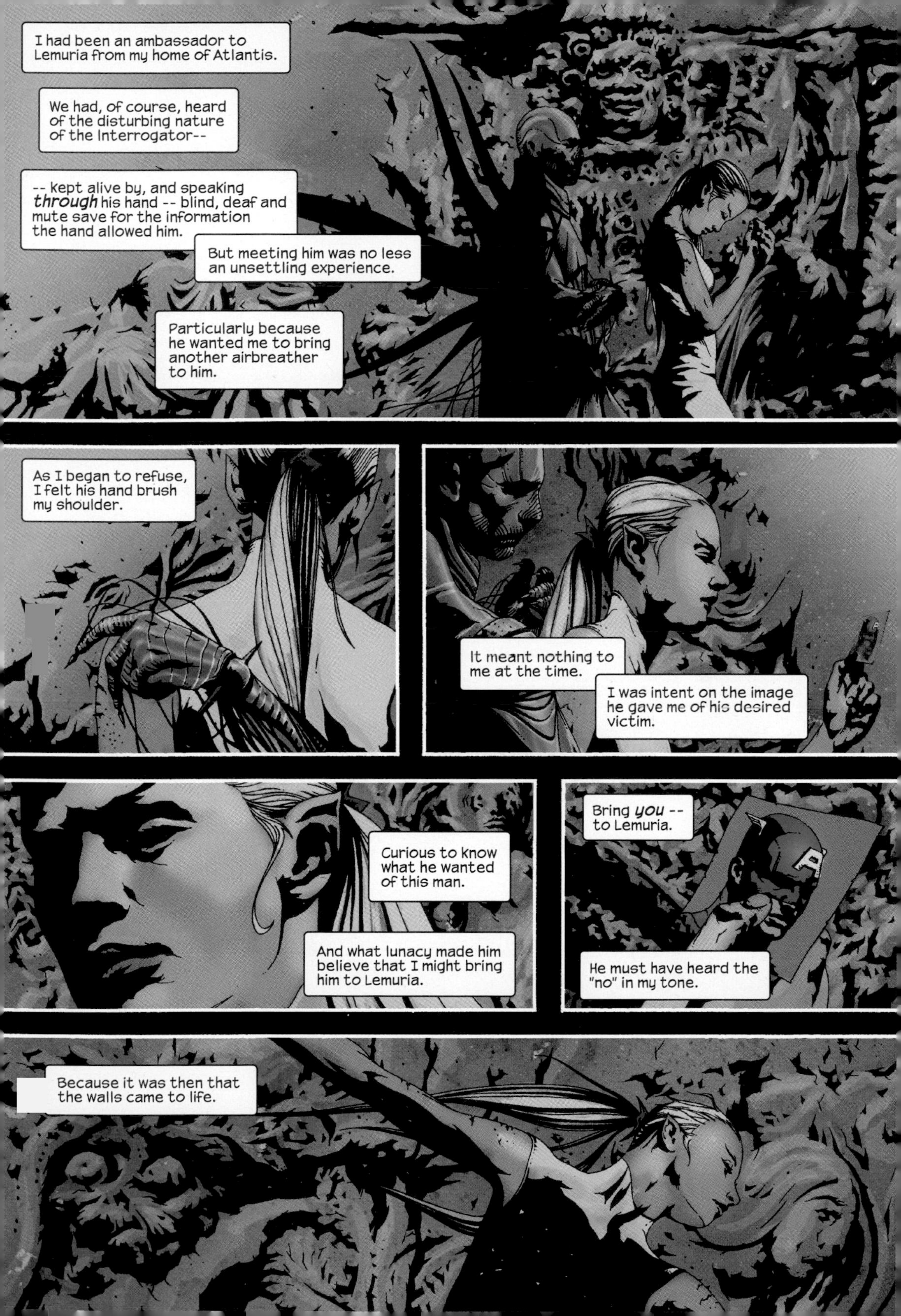
I had been an ambassador to Lemuria from my home of Atlantis.
We had, of course, heard of the disturbing nature of the Interrogator--
-- kept alive by, and speaking *through* his hand -- blind, deaf and mute save for the information the hand allowed him.
But meeting him was no less an unsettling experience.
Particularly because he wanted me to bring another airbreather to him.
As I began to refuse, I felt his hand brush my shoulder.
It meant nothing to me at the time.
I was intent on the image he gave me of his desired victim.
Curious to know what he wanted of this man.
And what lunacy made him believe that I might bring him to Lemuria.
Bring *you* -- to Lemuria.
He must have heard the "no" in my tone.
Because it was then that the walls came to life.

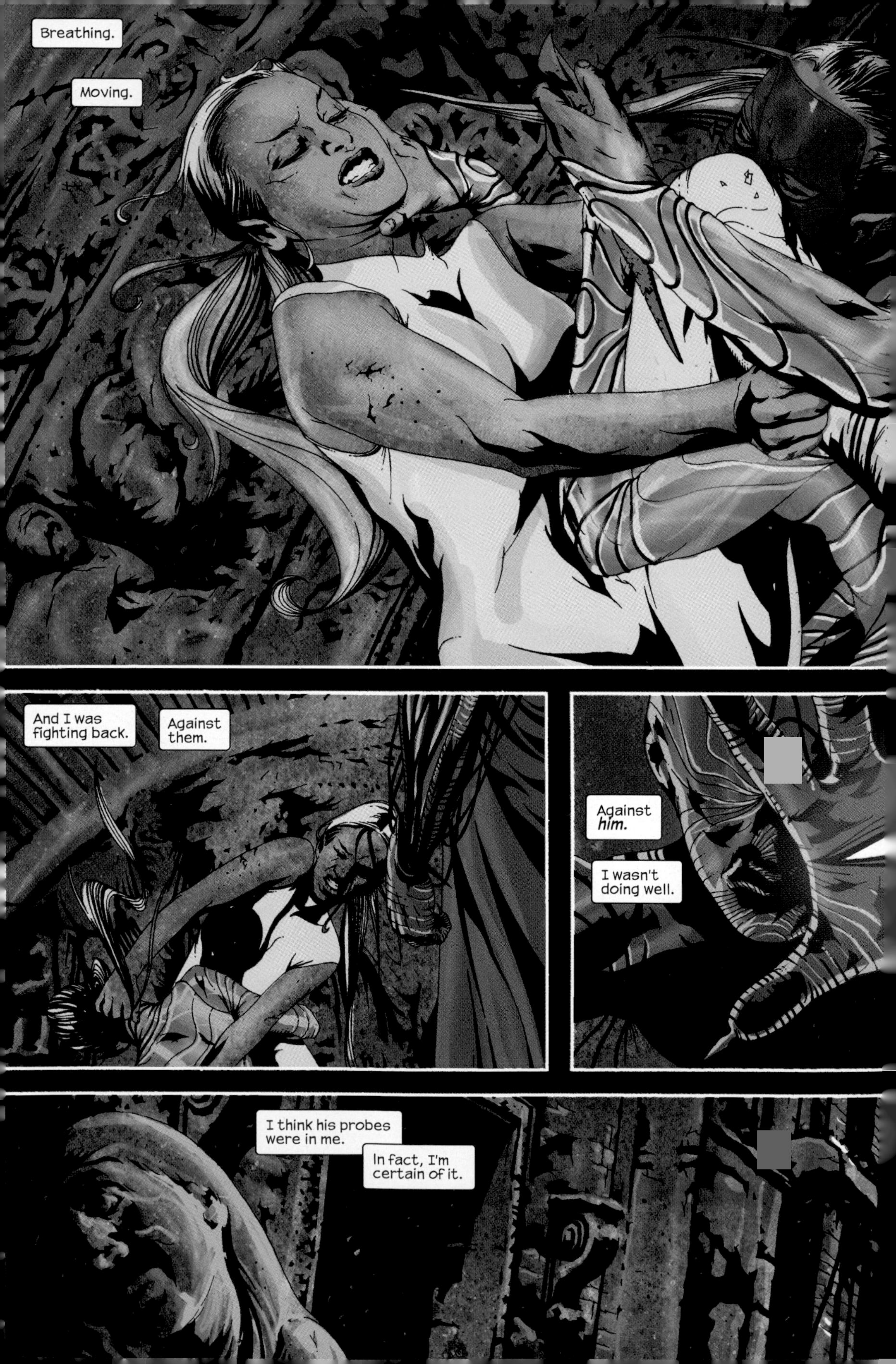
Breathing.
Moving.
And I was fighting back.
Against them.
Against *him.*
I wasn't doing well.
I think his probes were in me.
In fact, I'm certain of it.

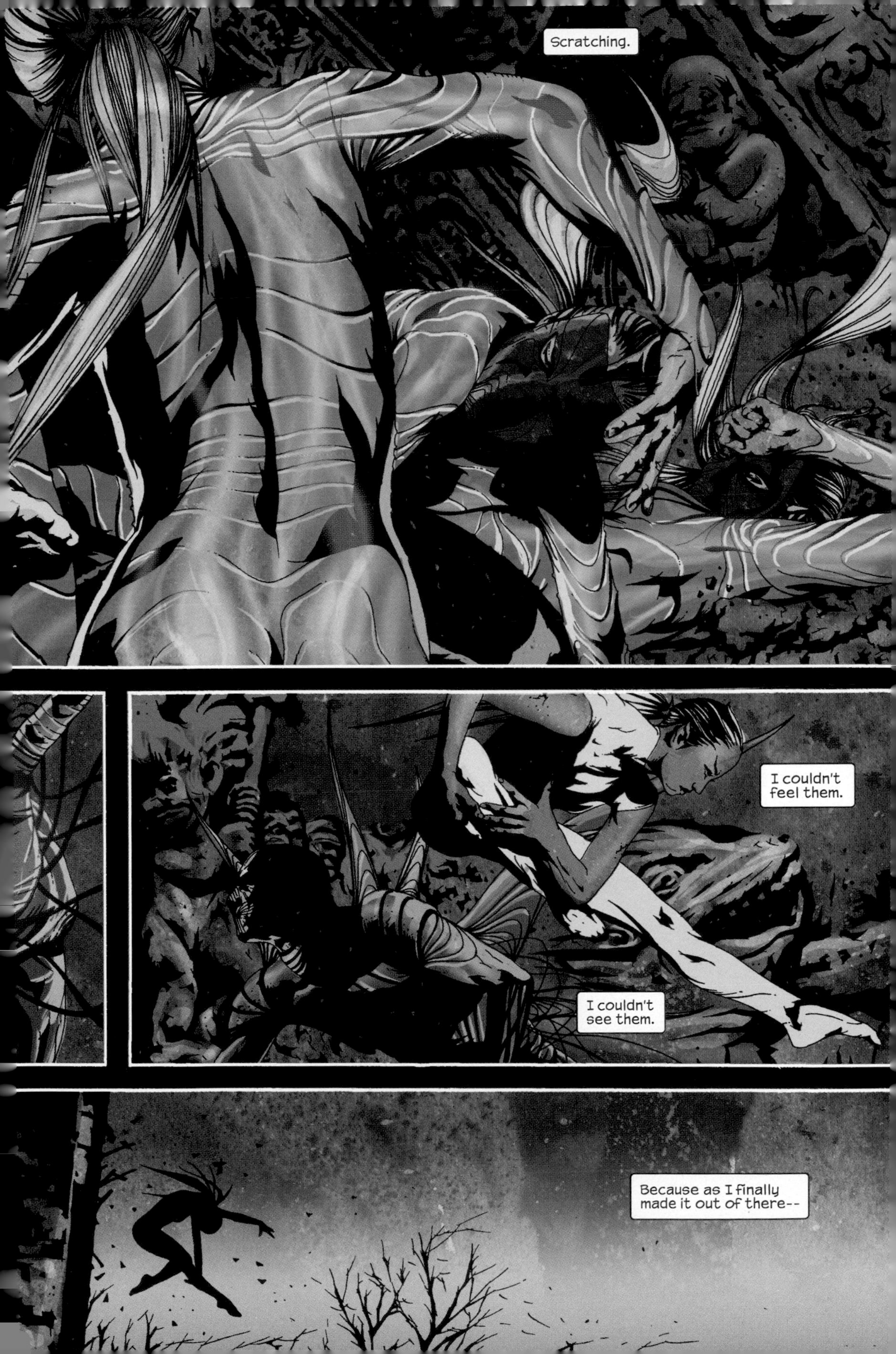
Scratching.
I couldn't feel them.
I couldn't see them.
Because as I finally made it out of there--

My mind went back to that moment, so vividly --

-- so powerfully that for a moment I believed I was there --

-- in that beautiful instant --

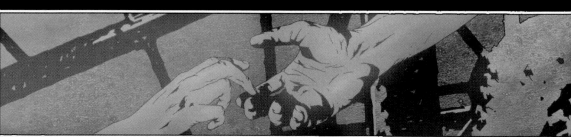

-- when I first felt love for you.

And I decided I wanted to be with you --

-- to help you --

-- to stand by you --

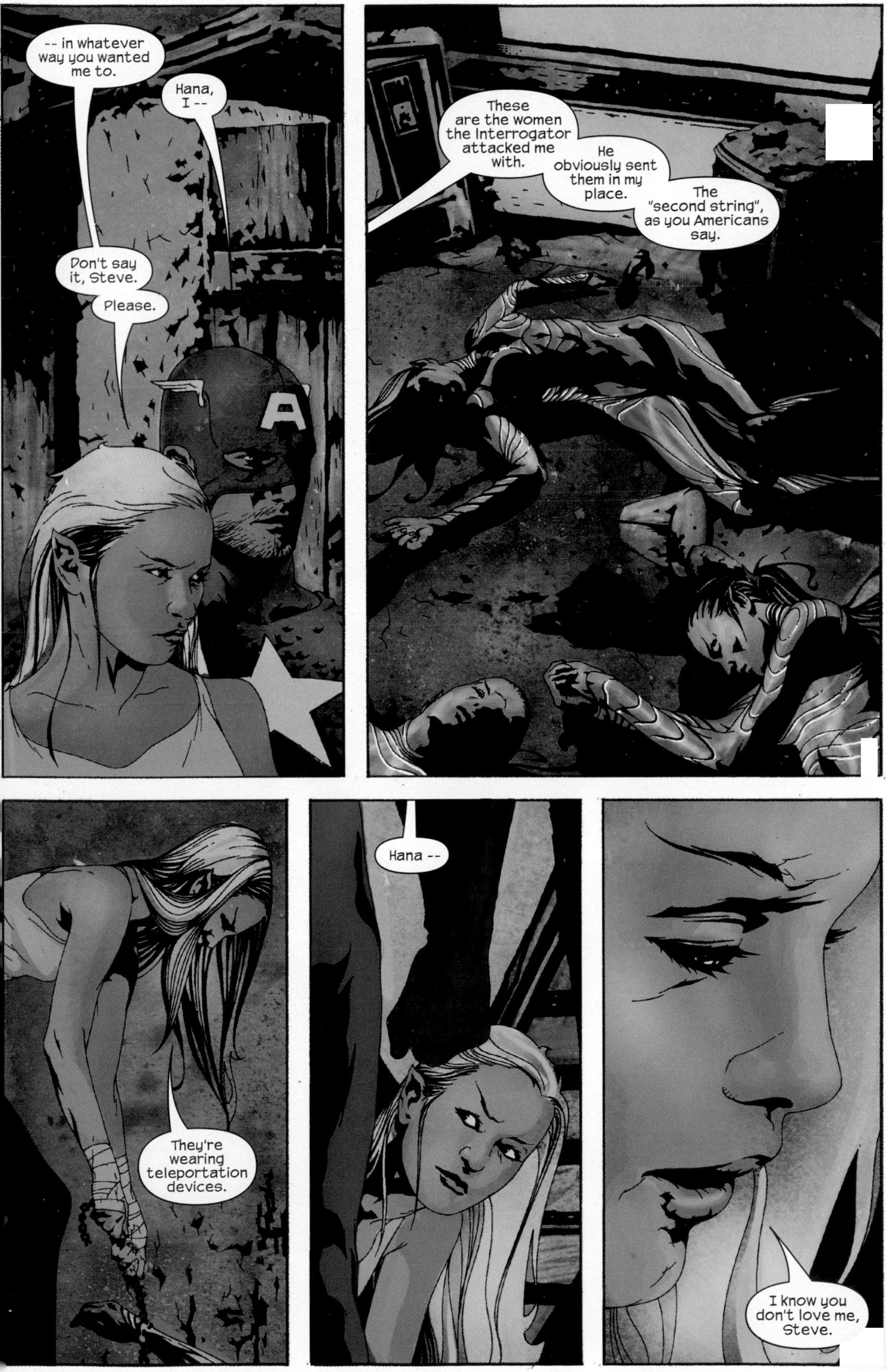
-- in whatever way you wanted me to.
Hana, I --
Don't say it, Steve.
Please.
These are the women the Interrogator attacked me with.
He obviously sent them in my place.
The "second string", as you Americans say.
They're wearing teleportation devices.
Hana --
I know you don't love me, Steve.

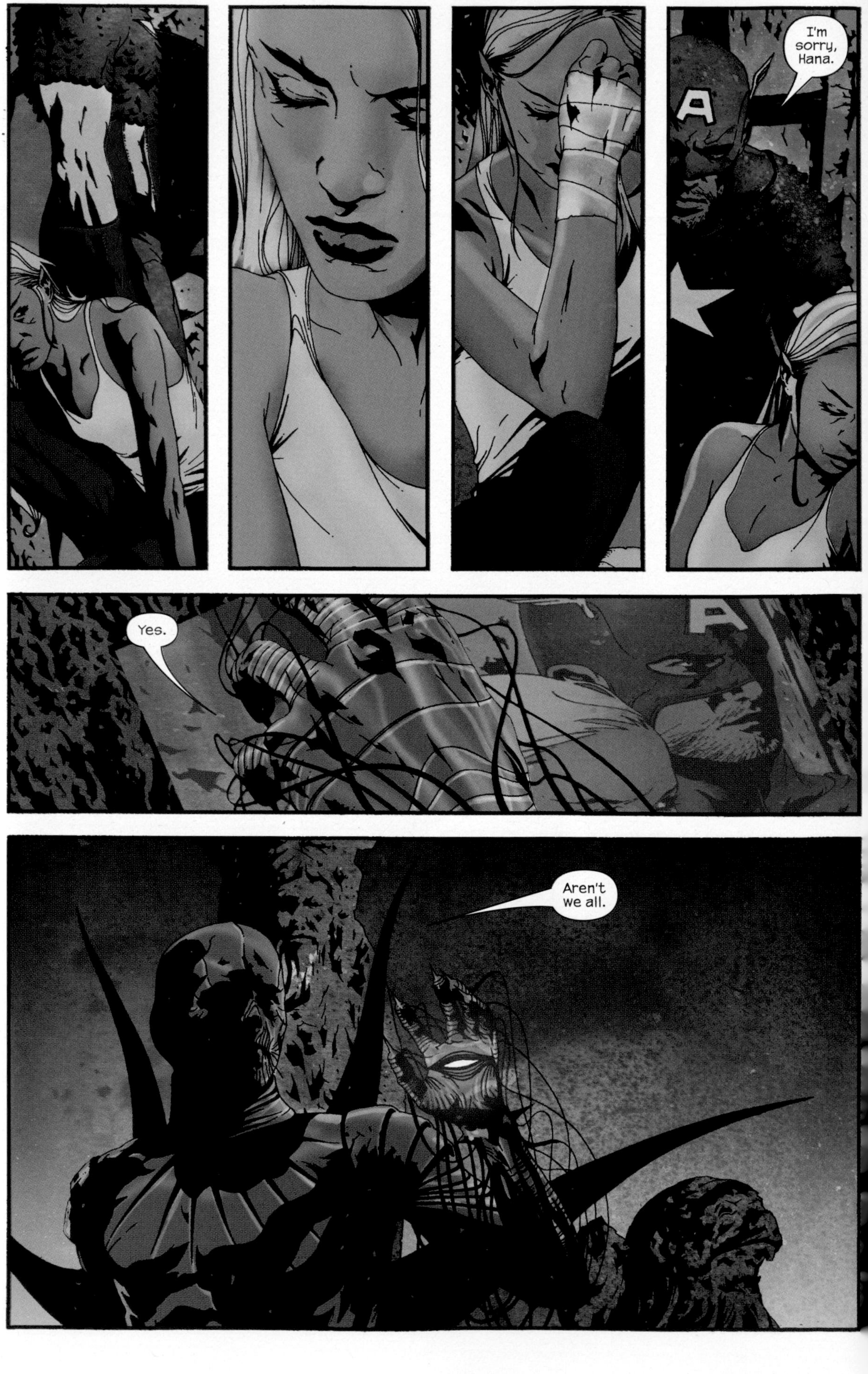
I'm sorry, Hana.
Yes.
Aren't we all.

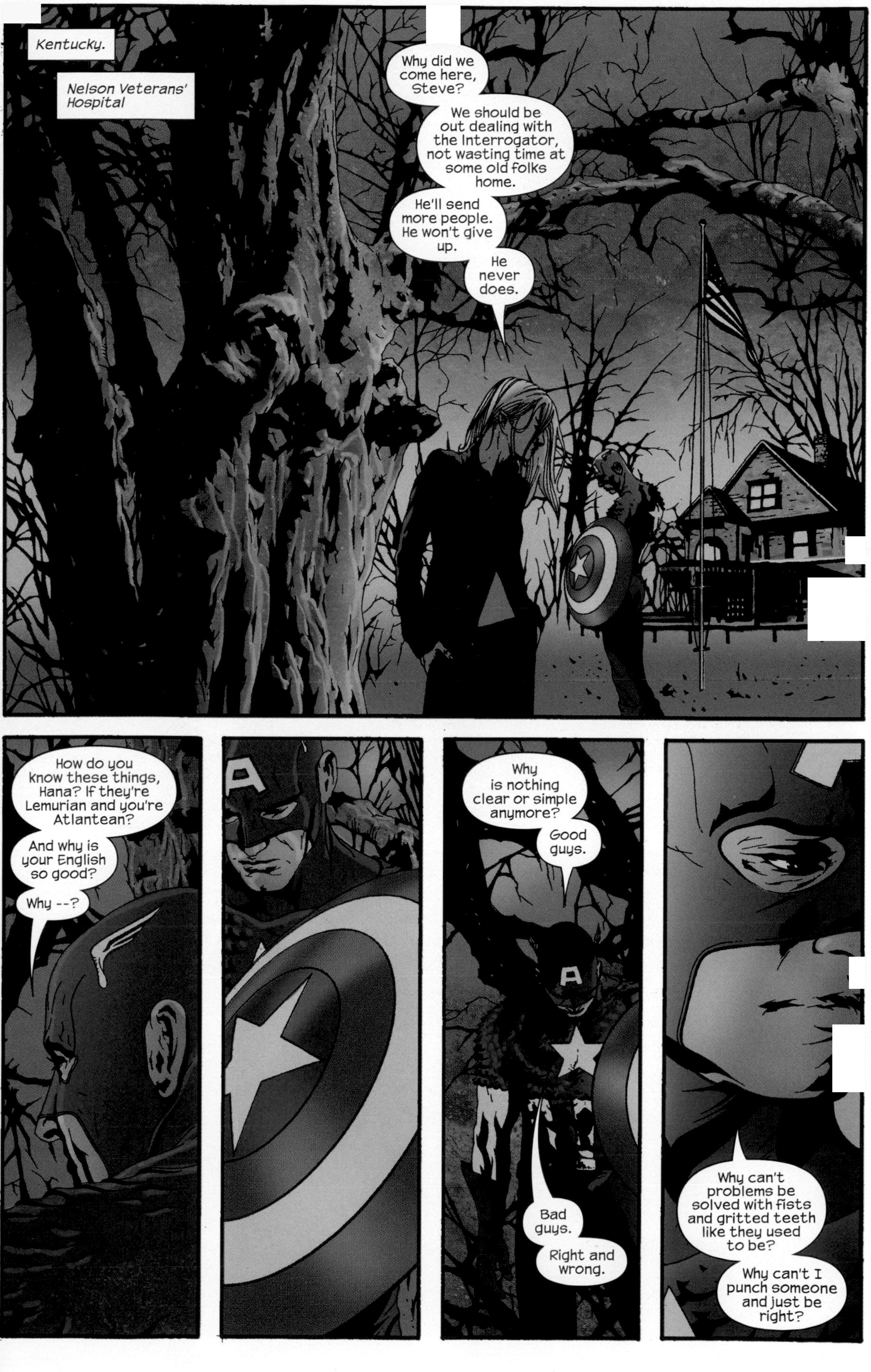
Kentucky.
Nelson Veterans' Hospital
Why did we come here, Steve?
We should be out dealing with the Interrogator, not wasting time at some old folks home.
He'll send more people. He won't give up.
He never does.
How do you know these things, Hana? If they're Lemurian and you're Atlantean?
And why is your English so good?
Why --?
Why is nothing clear or simple anymore?
Good guys.
Bad guys.
Right and wrong.
Why can't problems be solved with fists and gritted teeth like they used to be?
Why can't I punch someone and just be right?

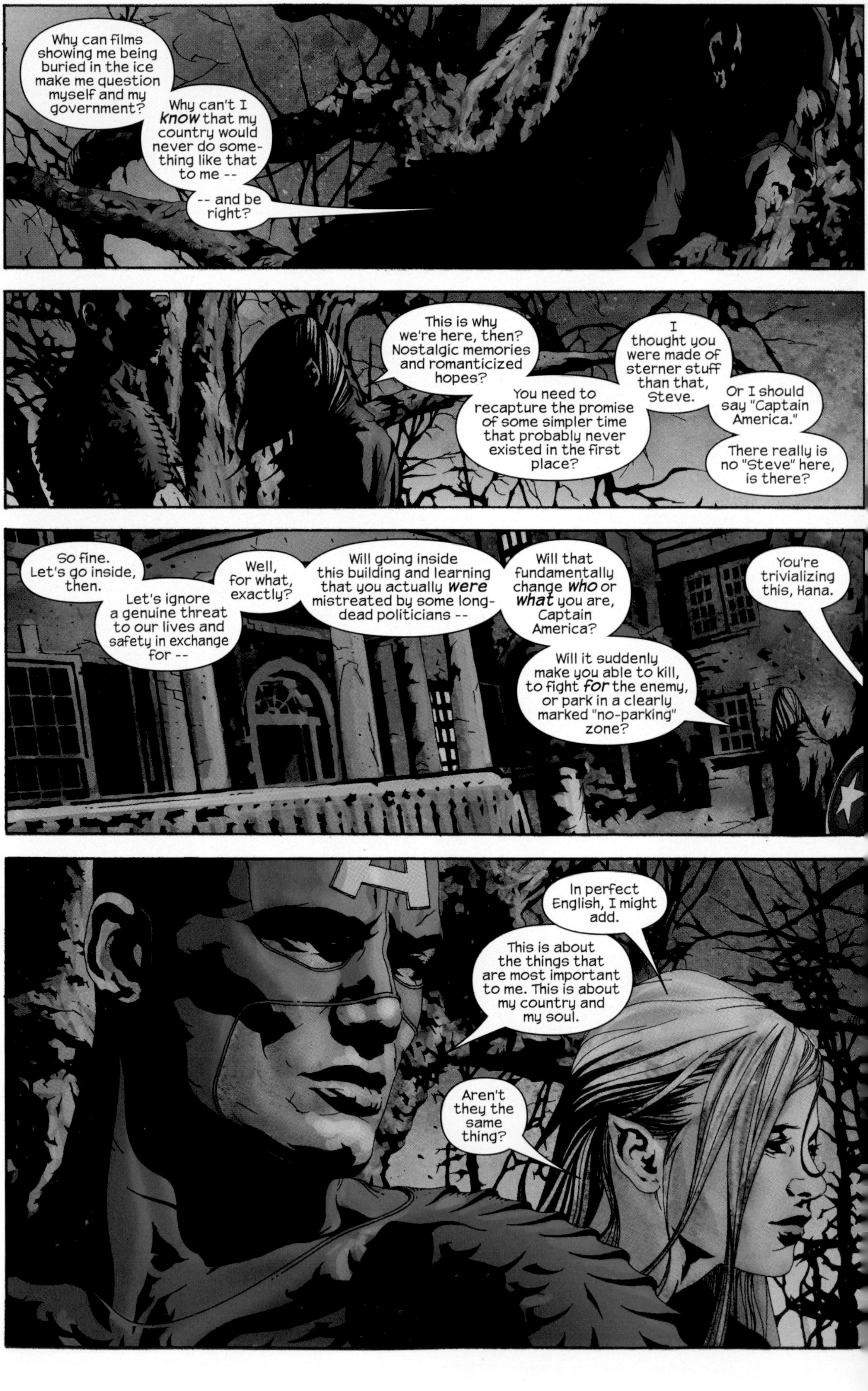

Why can films showing me being buried in the ice make me question myself and my government?
Why can't I *know* that my country would never do something like that to me --
-- and be right?
This is why we're here, then? Nostalgic memories and romanticized hopes?
You need to recapture the promise of some simpler time that probably never existed in the first place?
I thought you were made of sterner stuff than that, Steve.
Or I should say "Captain America."
There really is no "Steve" here, is there?
So fine. Let's go inside, then.
Let's ignore a genuine threat to our lives and safety in exchange for --
Well, for what, exactly?
Will going inside this building and learning that you actually *were* mistreated by some long-dead politicians --
Will that fundamentally change *who* or *what* you are, Captain America?
Will it suddenly make you able to kill, to fight *for* the enemy, or park in a clearly marked "no-parking" zone?
You're trivializing this, Hana.
In perfect English, I might add.
This is about the things that are most important to me. This is about my country and my soul.
Aren't they the same thing?

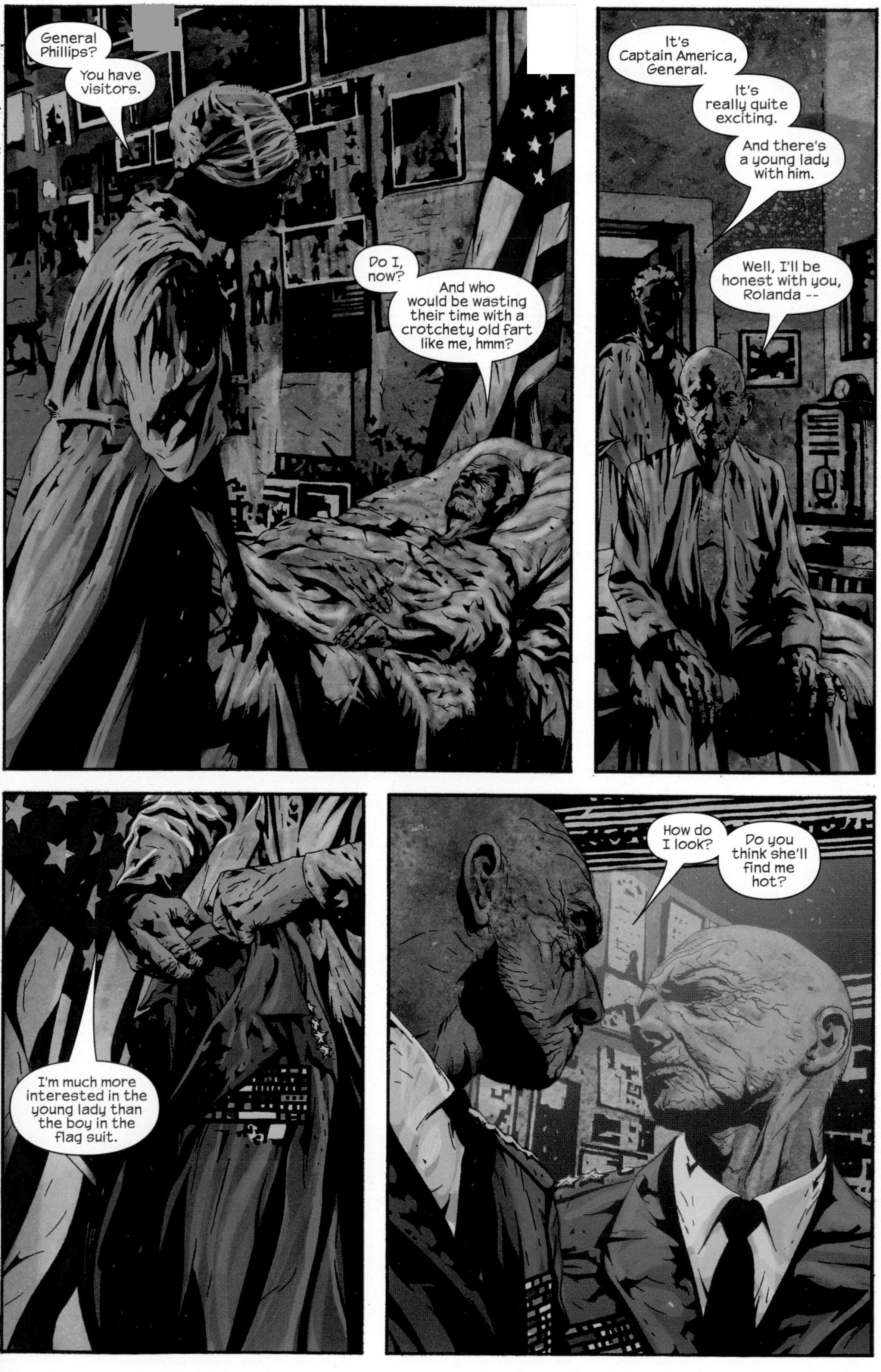
General Phillips?
You have visitors.
Do I, now?
And who would be wasting their time with a crotchety old fart like me, hmm?
It's Captain America, General.
It's really quite exciting.
And there's a young lady with him.
Well, I'll be honest with you, Rolanda --
I'm much more interested in the young lady than the boy in the flag suit.
How do I look?
Do you think she'll find me hot?

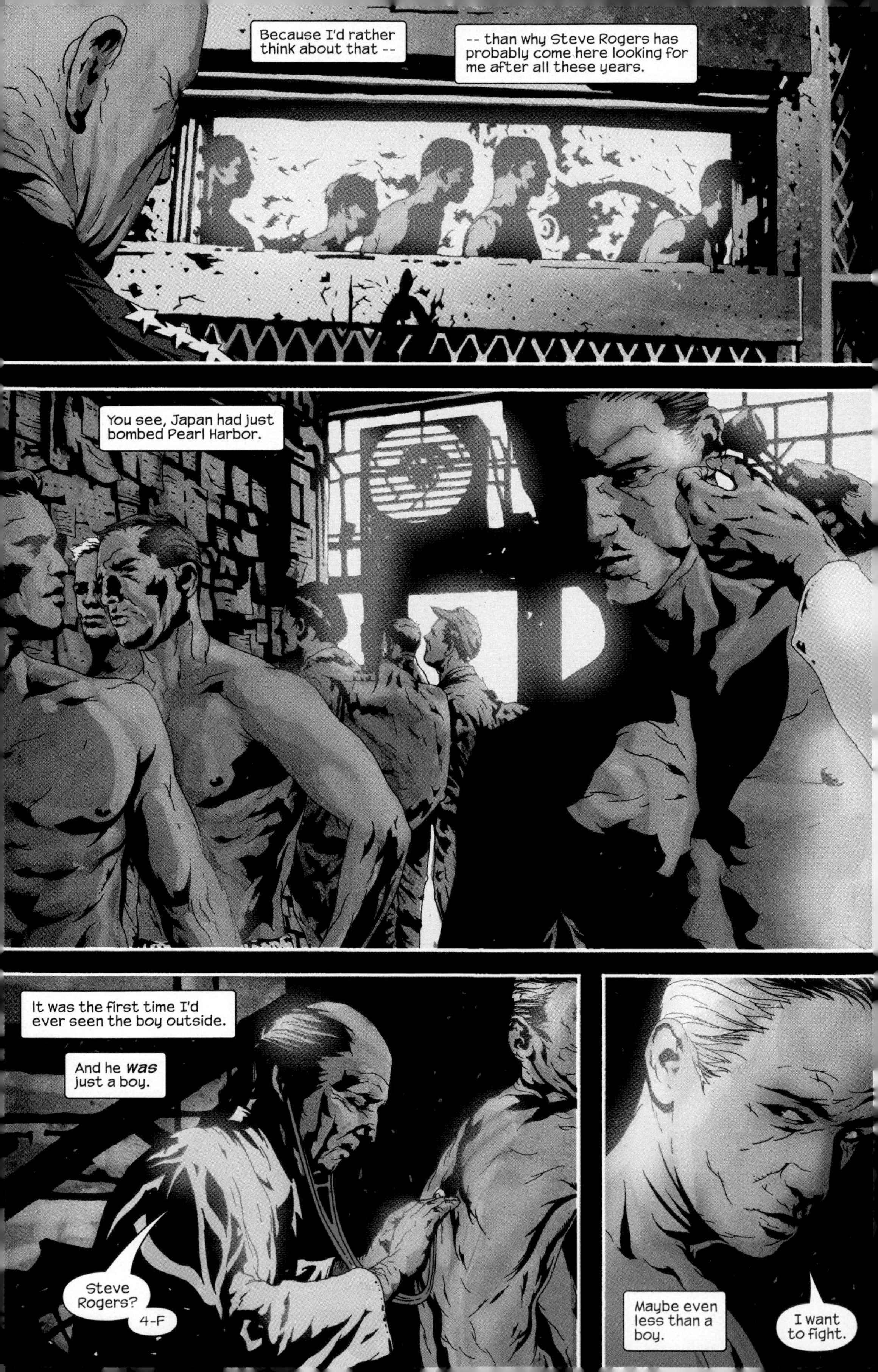
Because I'd rather think about that --
-- than why Steve Rogers has probably come here looking for me after all these years.
You see, Japan had just bombed Pearl Harbor.
It was the first time I'd ever seen the boy outside.
And he *was* just a boy.
Steve Rogers?
4-F
Maybe even less than a boy.
I want to fight.

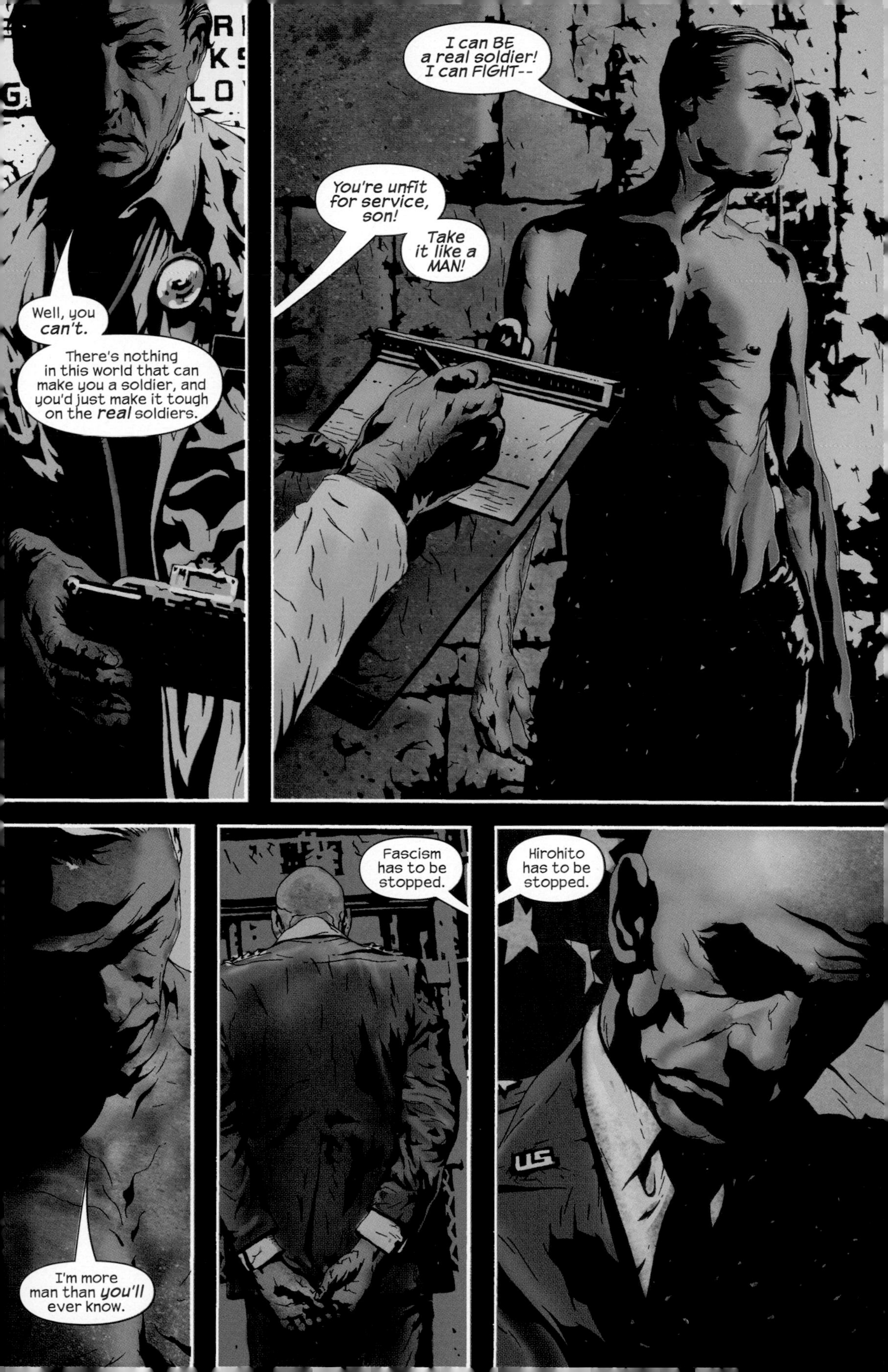
I can BE a real soldier! I can FIGHT--
Well, you can't.
There's nothing in this world that can make you a soldier, and you'd just make it tough on the real soldiers.
You're unfit for service, son!
Take it like a MAN!
I'm more man than you'll ever know.
Fascism has to be stopped.
Hirohito has to be stopped.

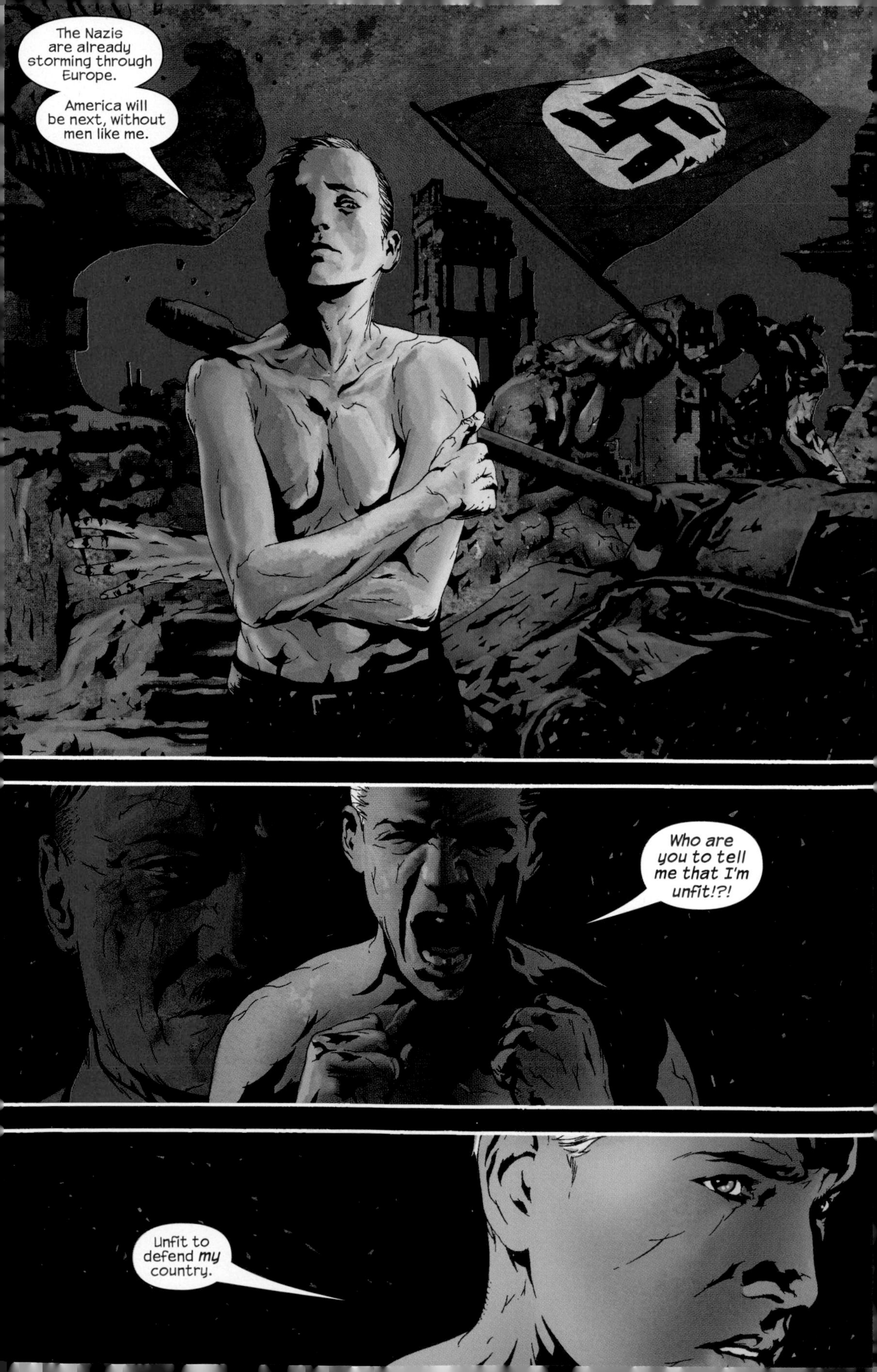
The Nazis are already storming through Europe.
America will be next, without men like me.
Who are you to tell me that I'm unfit!?!
Unfit to defend *my* country.

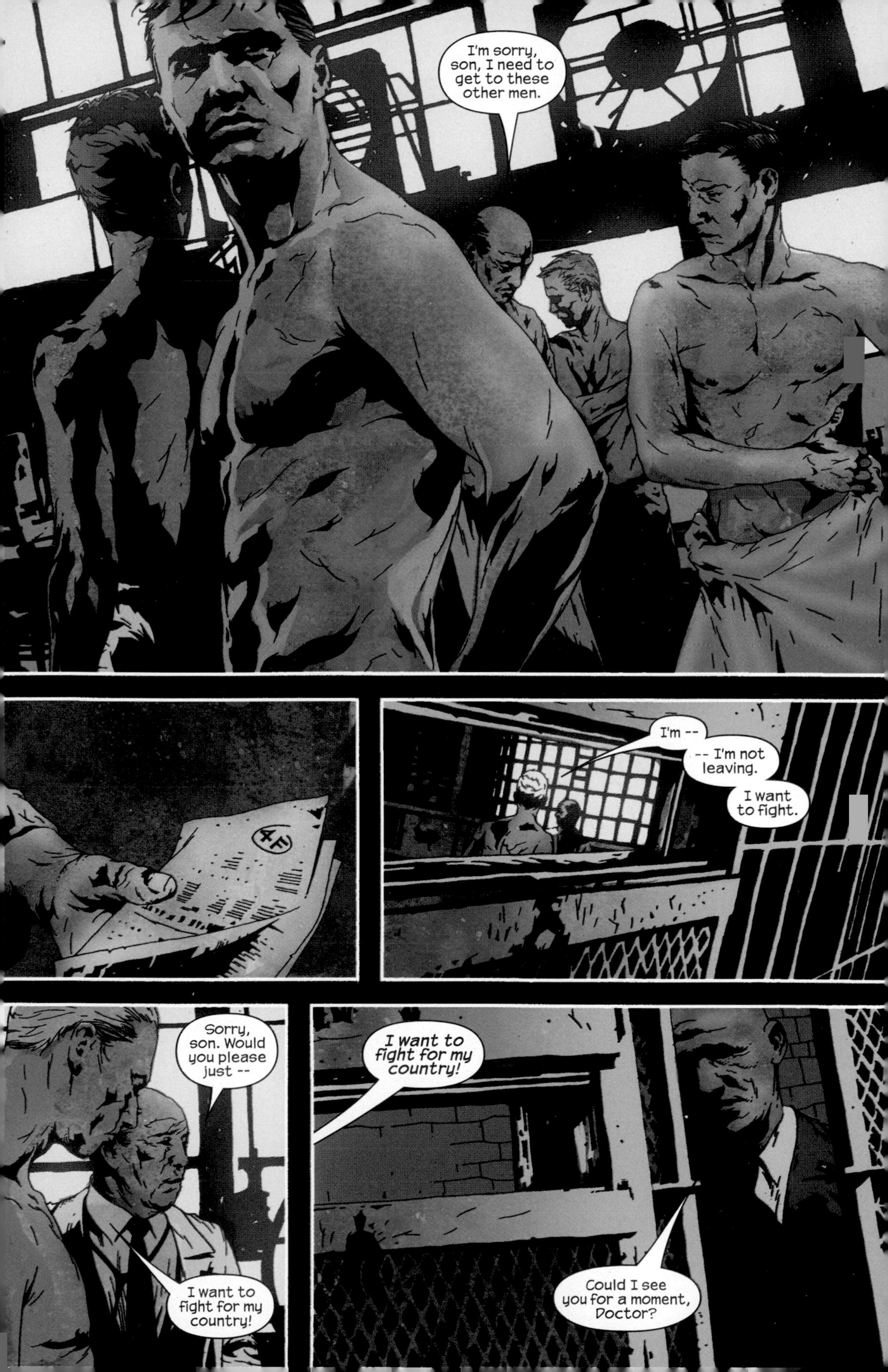
I'm sorry, son, I need to get to these other men.
4F
I'm --
-- I'm not leaving.
I want to fight.
Sorry, son. Would you please just --
I want to fight for my country!
I want to fight for my country!
Could I see you for a moment, Doctor?

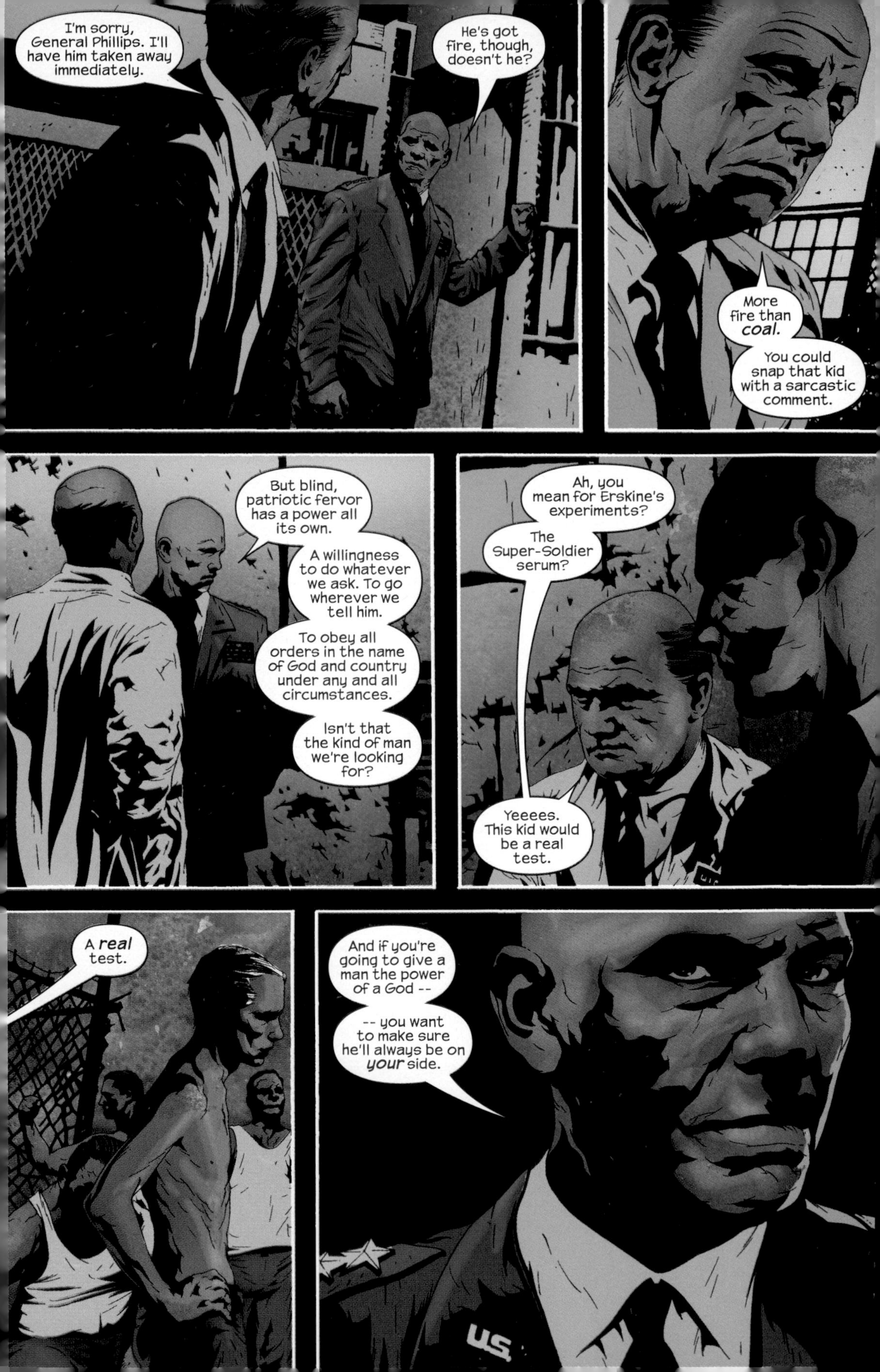
I'm sorry, General Phillips. I'll have him taken away immediately.
He's got fire, though, doesn't he?
More fire than *coal.*
You could snap that kid with a sarcastic comment.
But blind, patriotic fervor has a power all its own.
A willingness to do whatever we ask. To go wherever we tell him.
To obey all orders in the name of God and country under any and all circumstances.
Isn't that the kind of man we're looking for?
Ah, you mean for Erskine's experiments?
The Super-Soldier serum?
Yeeees. This kid would be a real test.
A *real* test.
And if you're going to give a man the power of a God --
-- you want to make sure he'll always be on *your* side.
U.S.

No, Mister President, I *cannot* assure you that they will not intervene.

Captain America's moral stance has *altered* since we gave him the serum and the powers, for reasons we *cannot* understand.

He will now no longer kill under *any* circumstances, and has begun to see himself as a protector of the world --

-- and *NOT* just our United States.

"It might have something to do with seeing Erskine murdered before his eyes.

"You remember Erskine.

"It was his project in the first place -- the Super-Soldier serum.

"But whatever Rogers' reasons for becoming such a "humanist," they run counter to our impending plans.

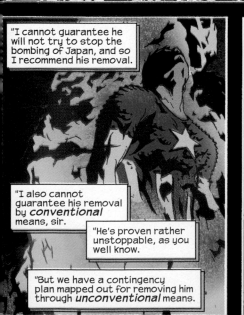

"I cannot guarantee he will not try to stop the bombing of Japan, and so I recommend his removal.

"I also cannot guarantee his removal by *conventional* means, sir.

"He's proven rather unstoppable, as you well know.

"But we have a contingency plan mapped out for removing him through *unconventional* means.

"A plan that leaves an element of deniability, should his removal be less than permanent.

"We only require your approval, Mister President --

" -- and we'll likely never see Captain America, ever again."

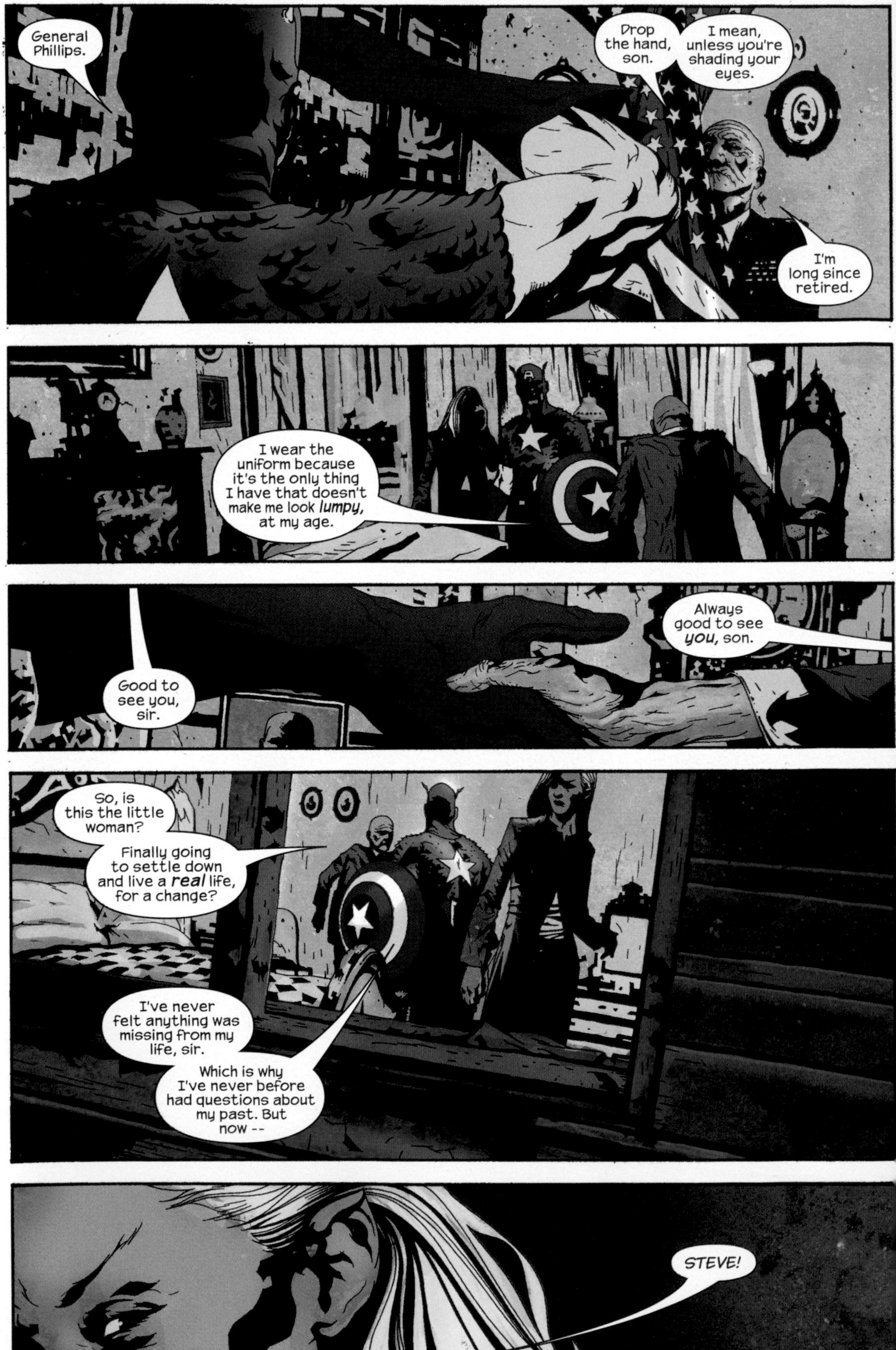
General Phillips.
Drop the hand, son.
I mean, unless you're shading your eyes.
I'm long since retired.
I wear the uniform because it's the only thing I have that doesn't make me look *lumpy,* at my age.
Good to see you, sir.
Always good to see *you,* son.
So, is this the little woman?
Finally going to settle down and live a *real* life, for a change?
I've never felt anything was missing from my life, sir.
Which is why I've never before had questions about my past. But now --
STEVE!

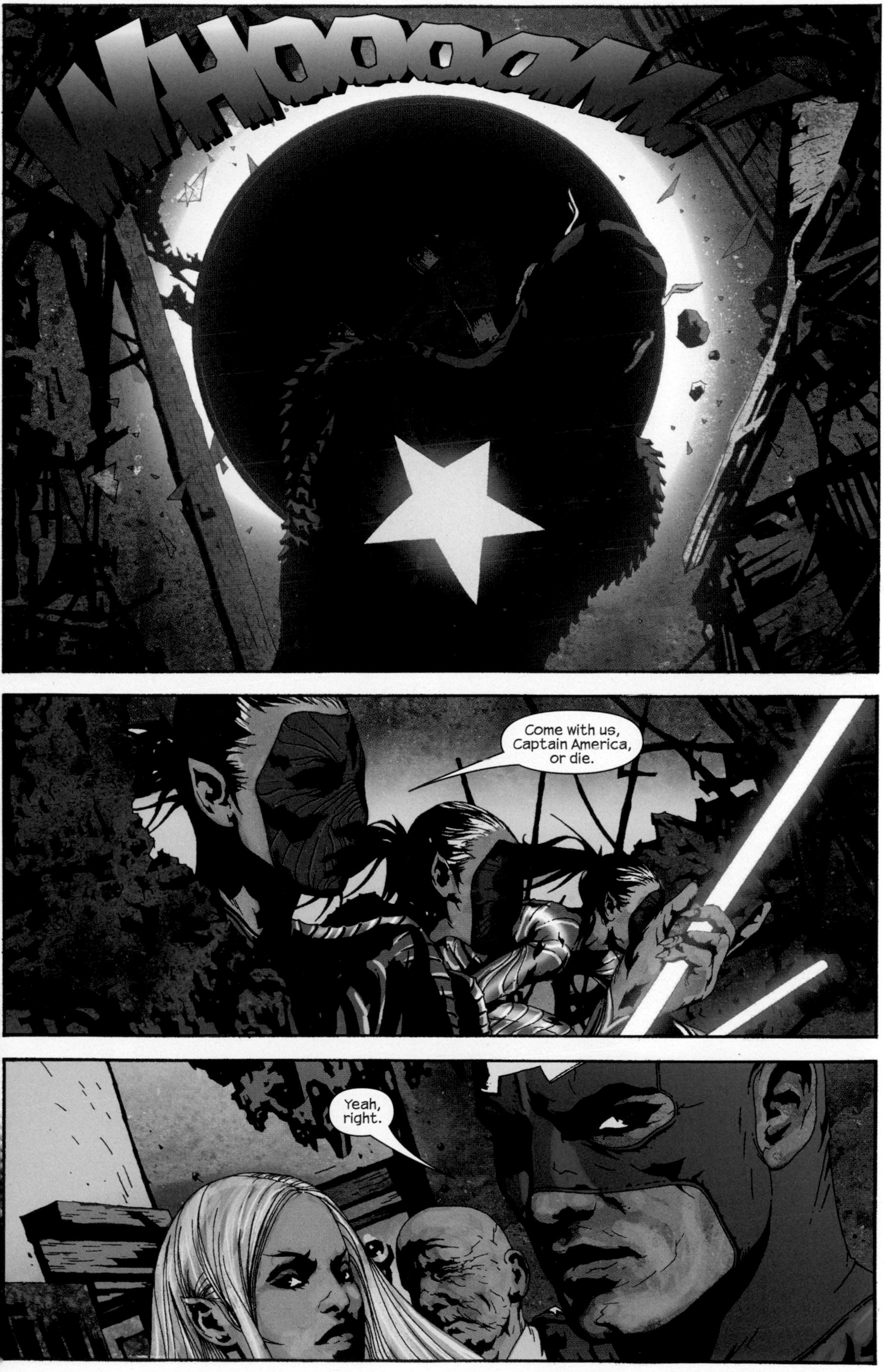
WHOOOOOM
Come with us, Captain America, or die.
Yeah, right.

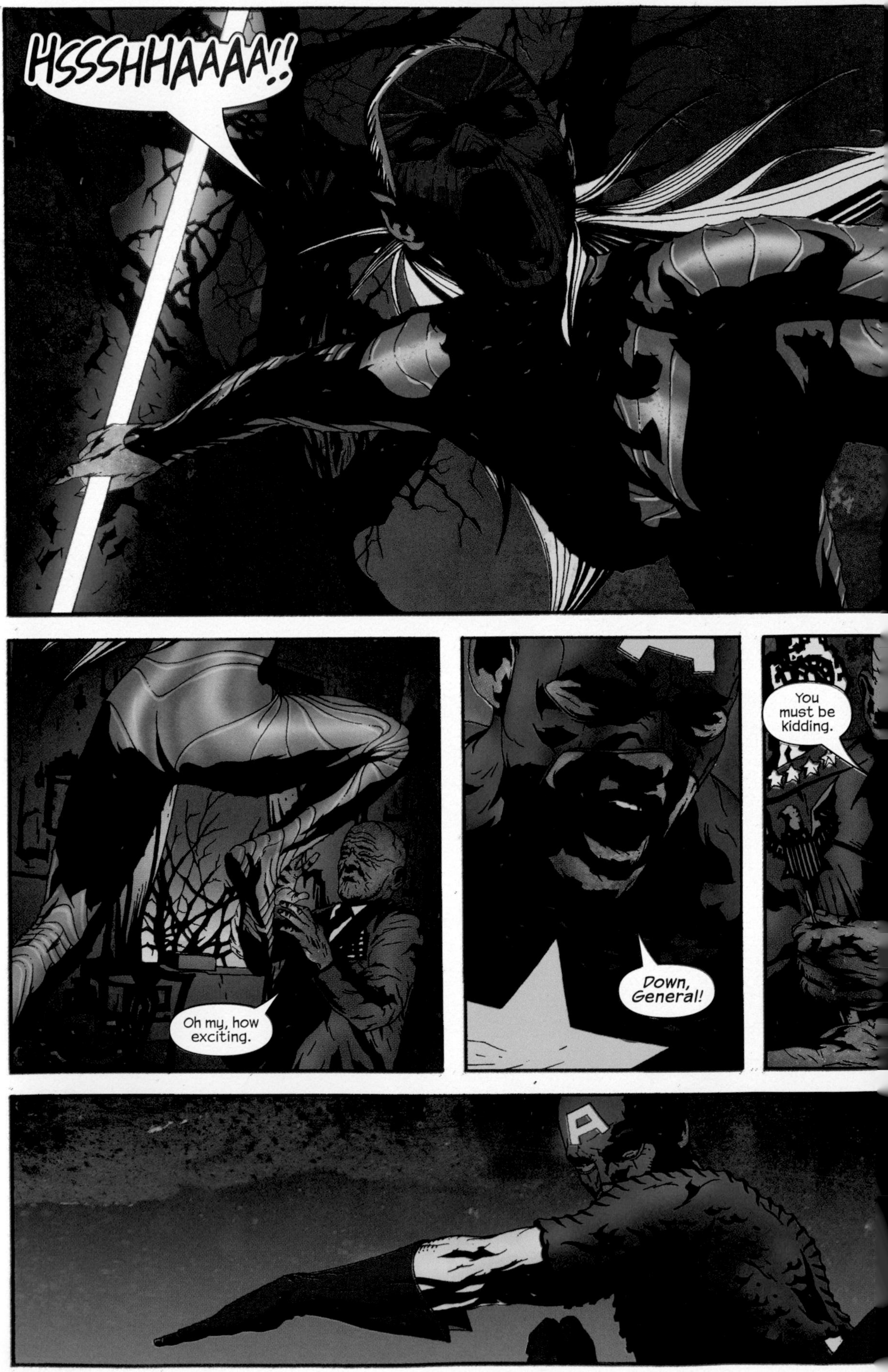
HSSSHHAAAA!!
Oh my, how exciting.
Down, General!
You must be kidding.

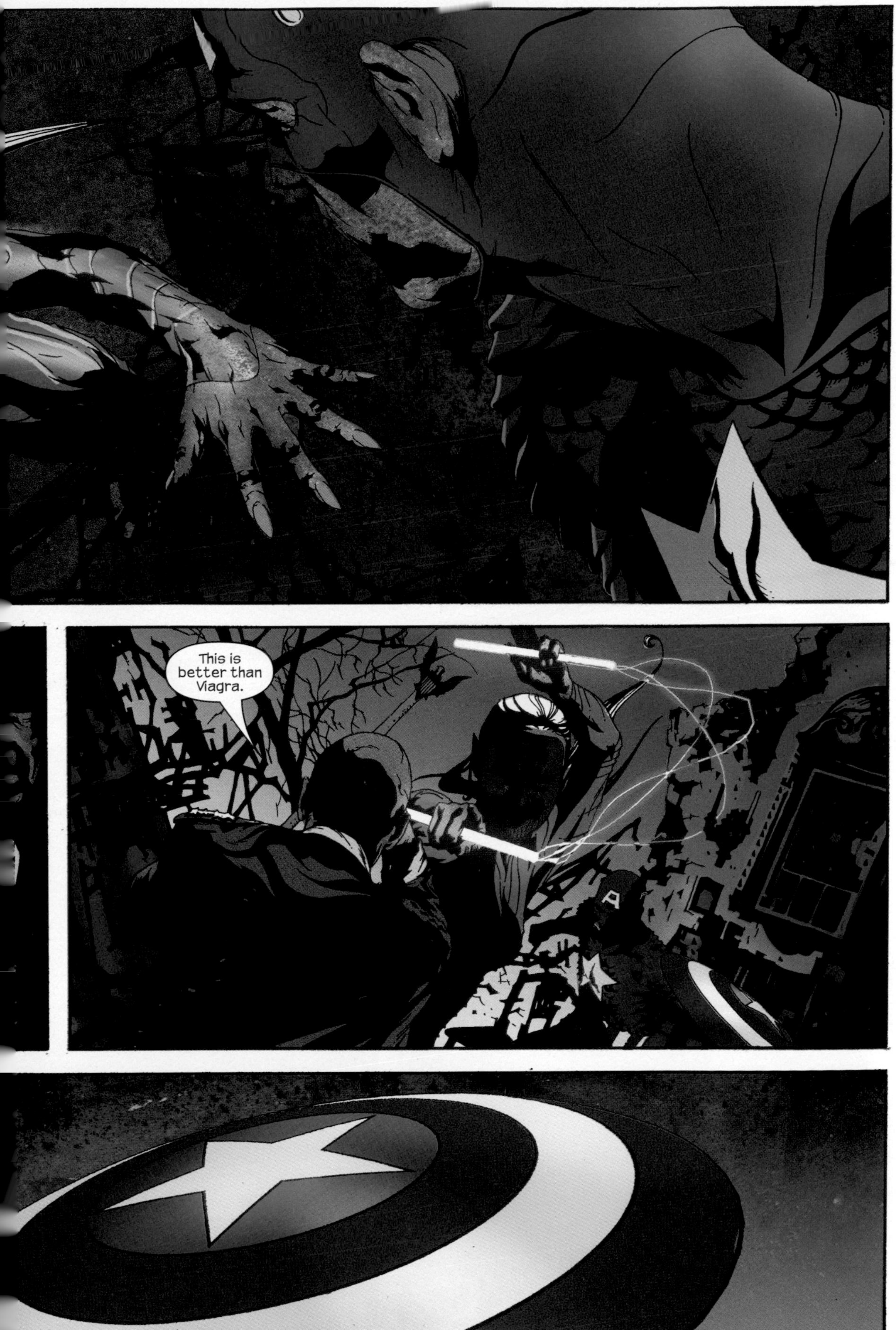
This is better than Viagra.

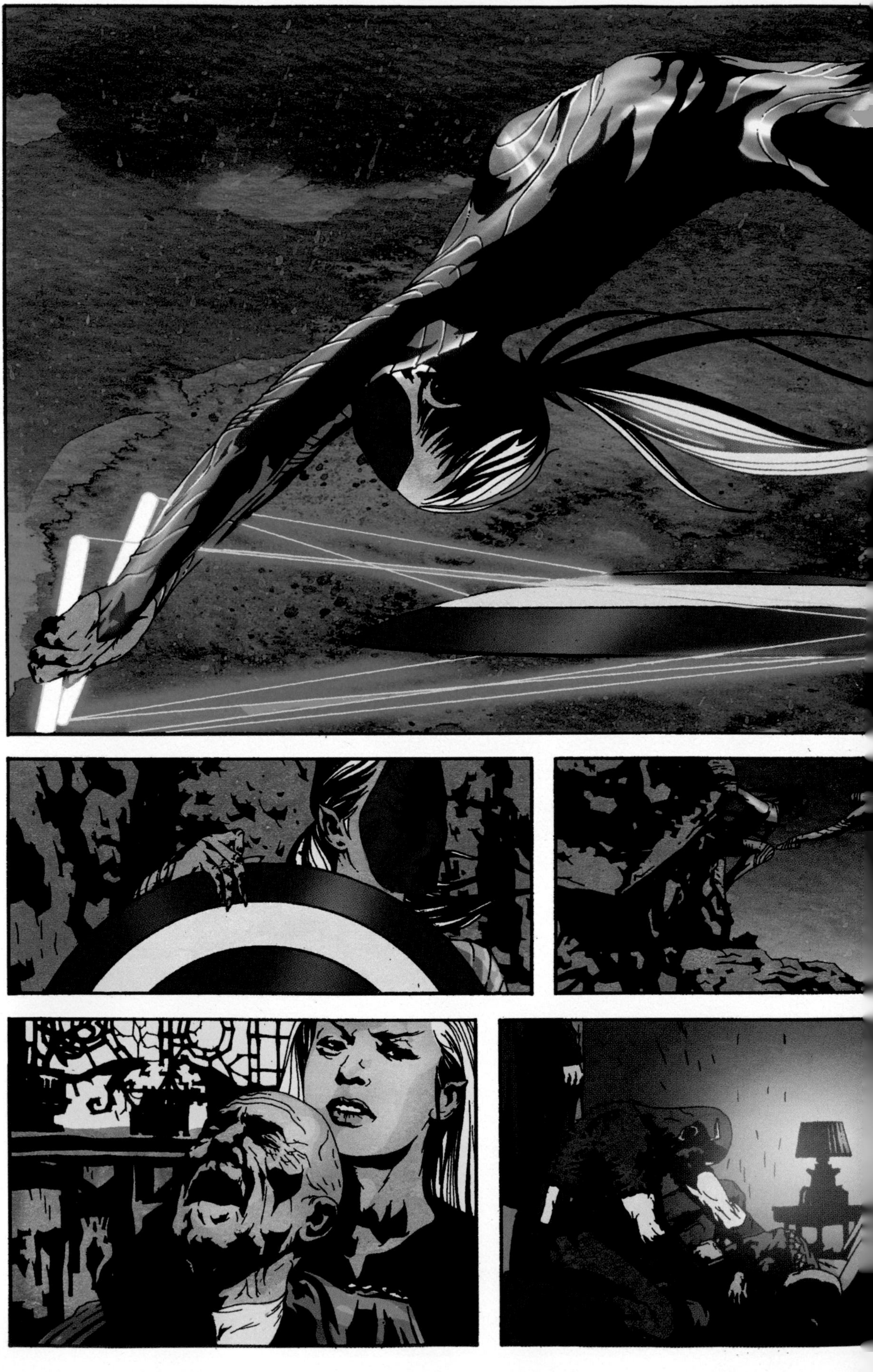

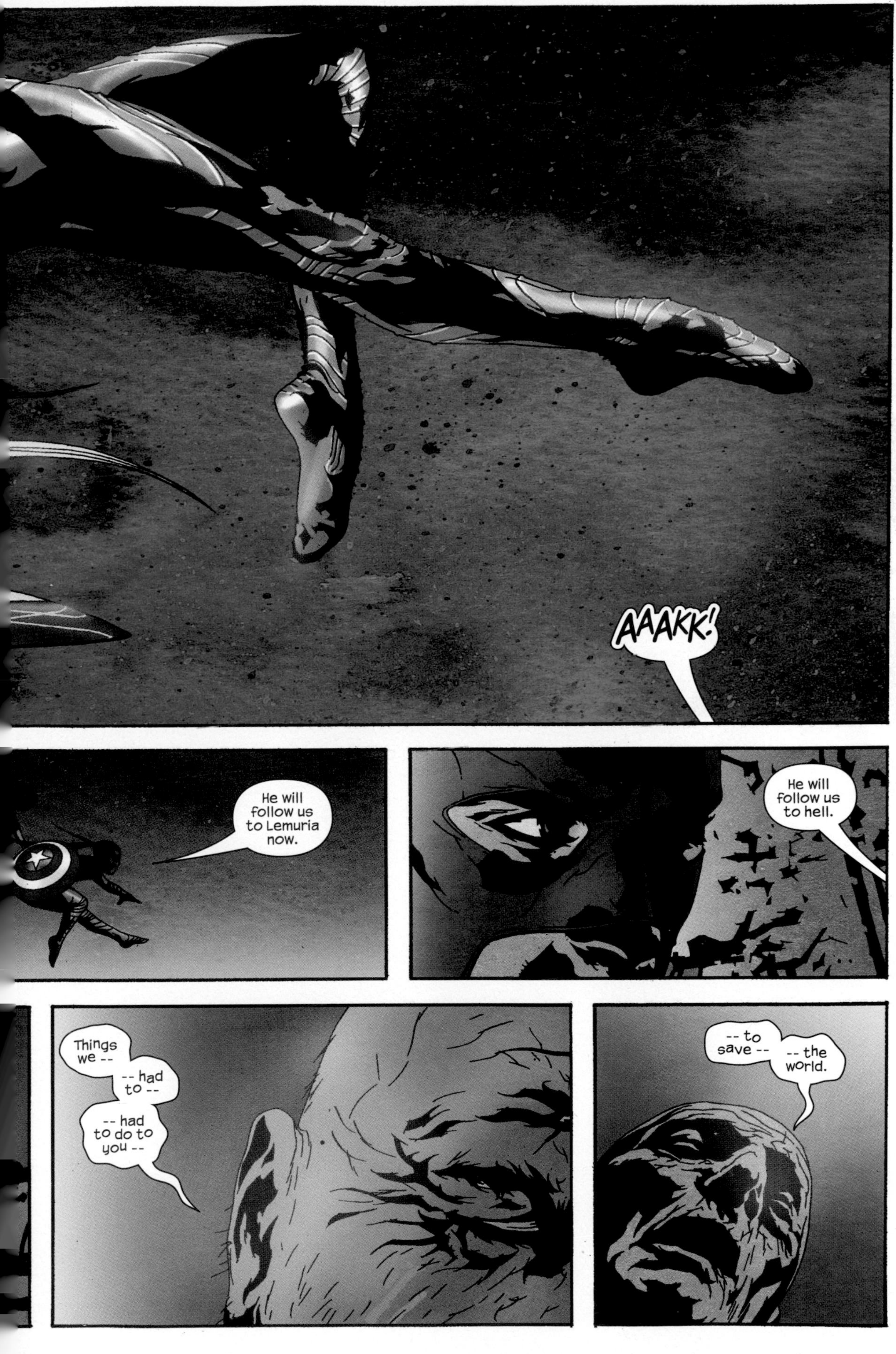
AAAKK!
He will follow us to Lemuria now.
He will follow us to hell.
Things we --
-- had to --
-- had to do to you --
-- to save --
-- the world.

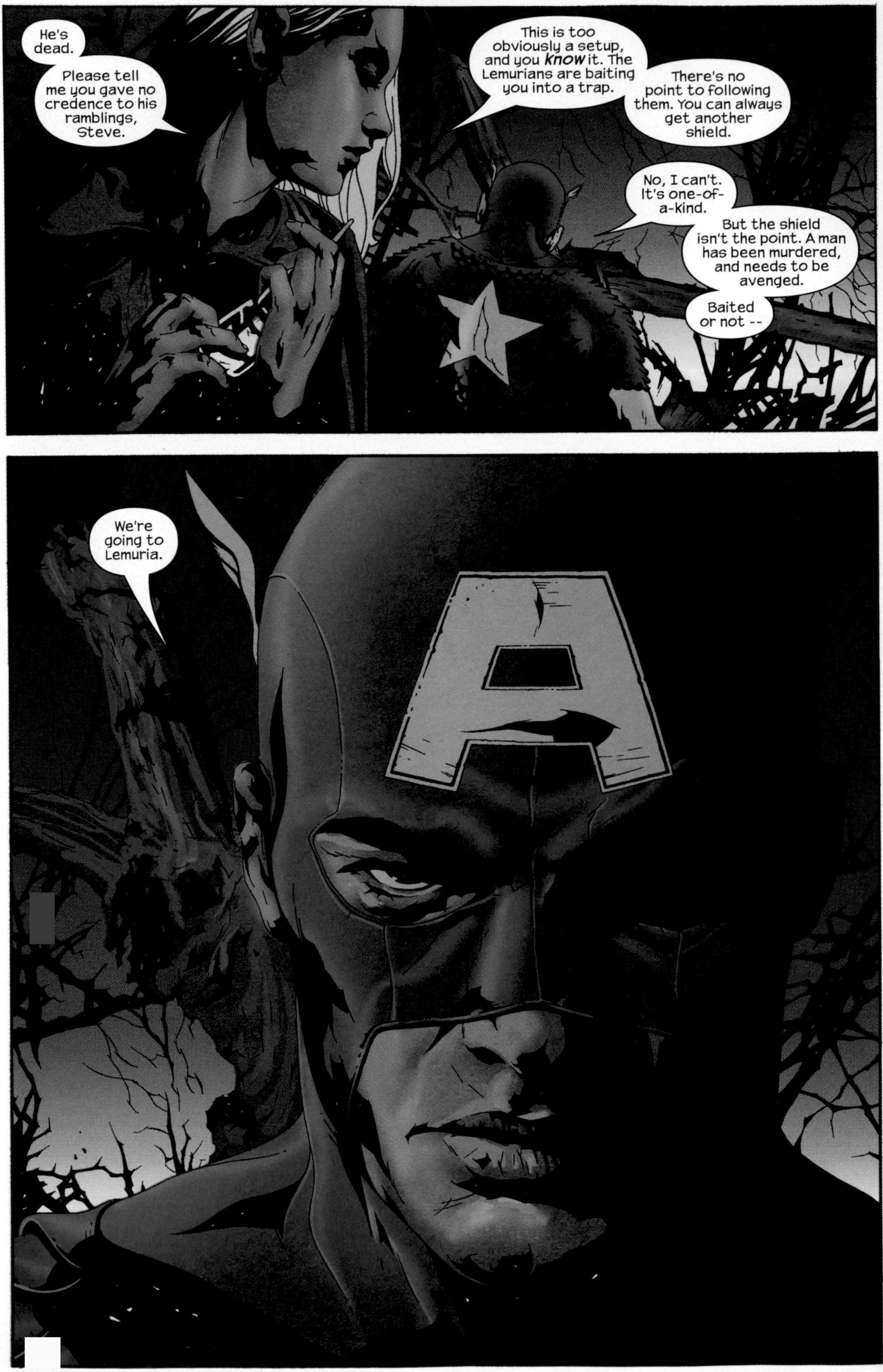
He's dead.
Please tell me you gave no credence to his ramblings, Steve.
This is too obviously a setup, and you *KNOW* it. The Lemurians are baiting you into a trap.
There's no point to following them. You can always get another shield.
No, I can't. It's one-of-a-kind.
But the shield isn't the point. A man has been murdered, and needs to be avenged.
Baited or not --
We're going to Lemuria.

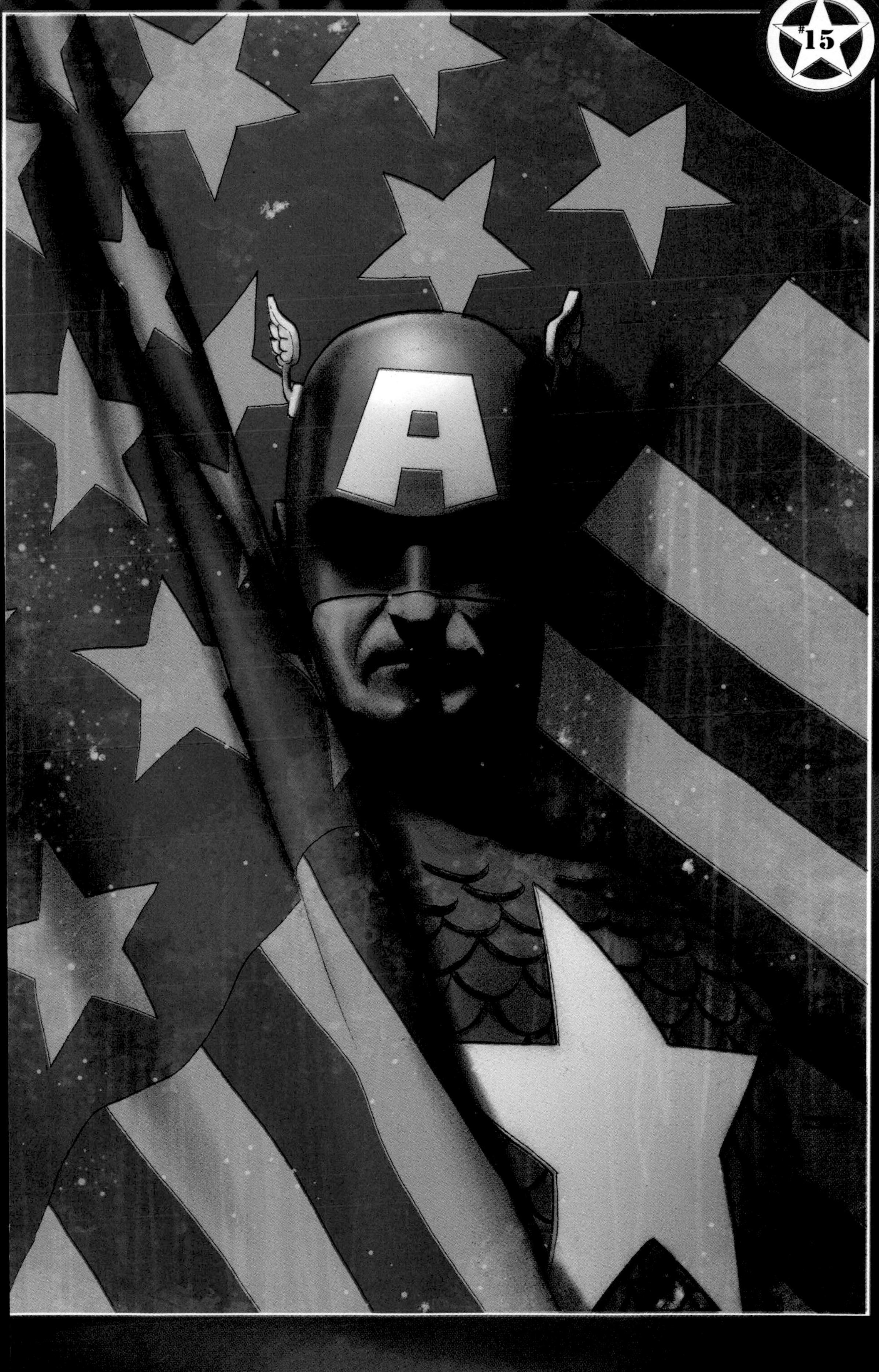
#15

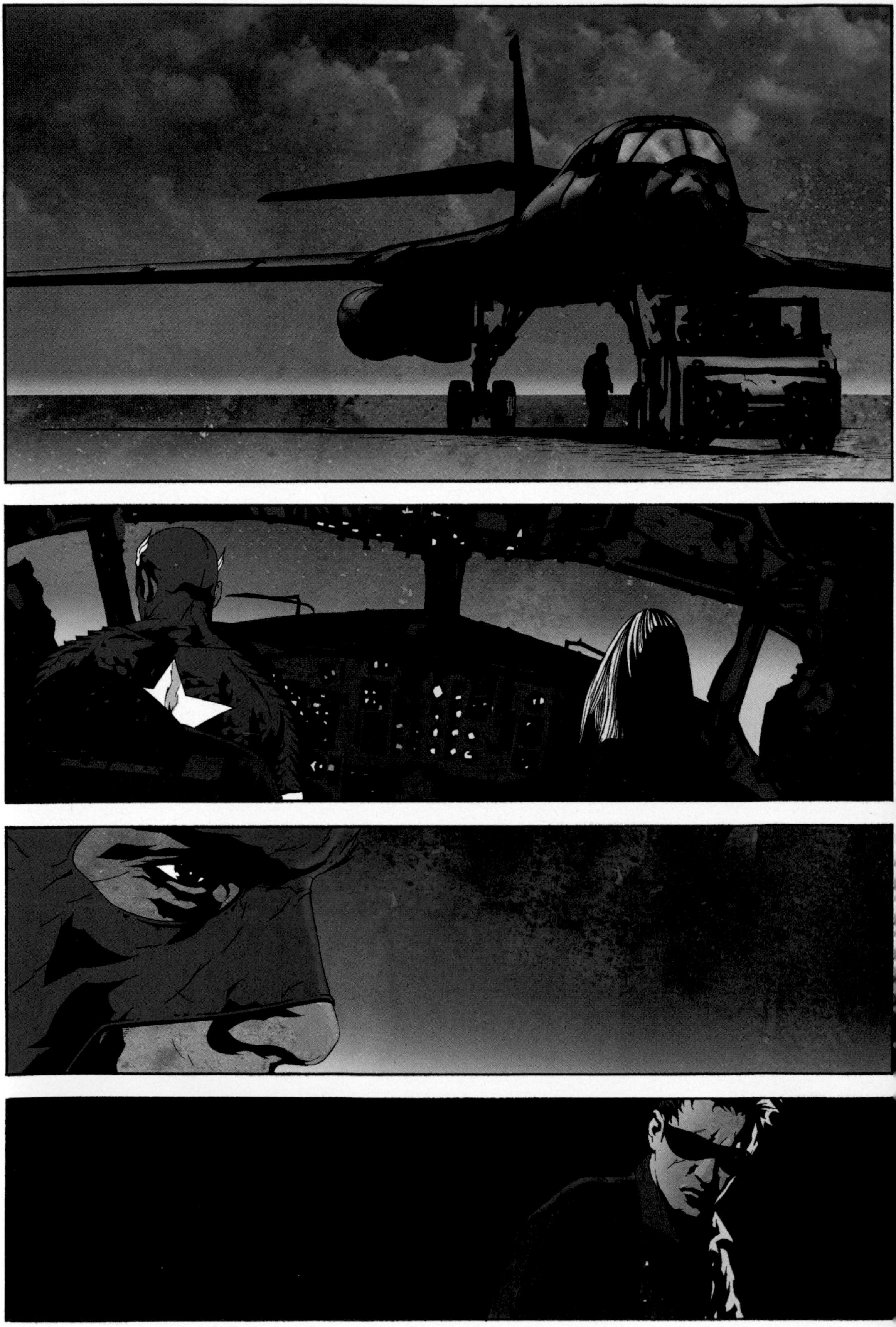

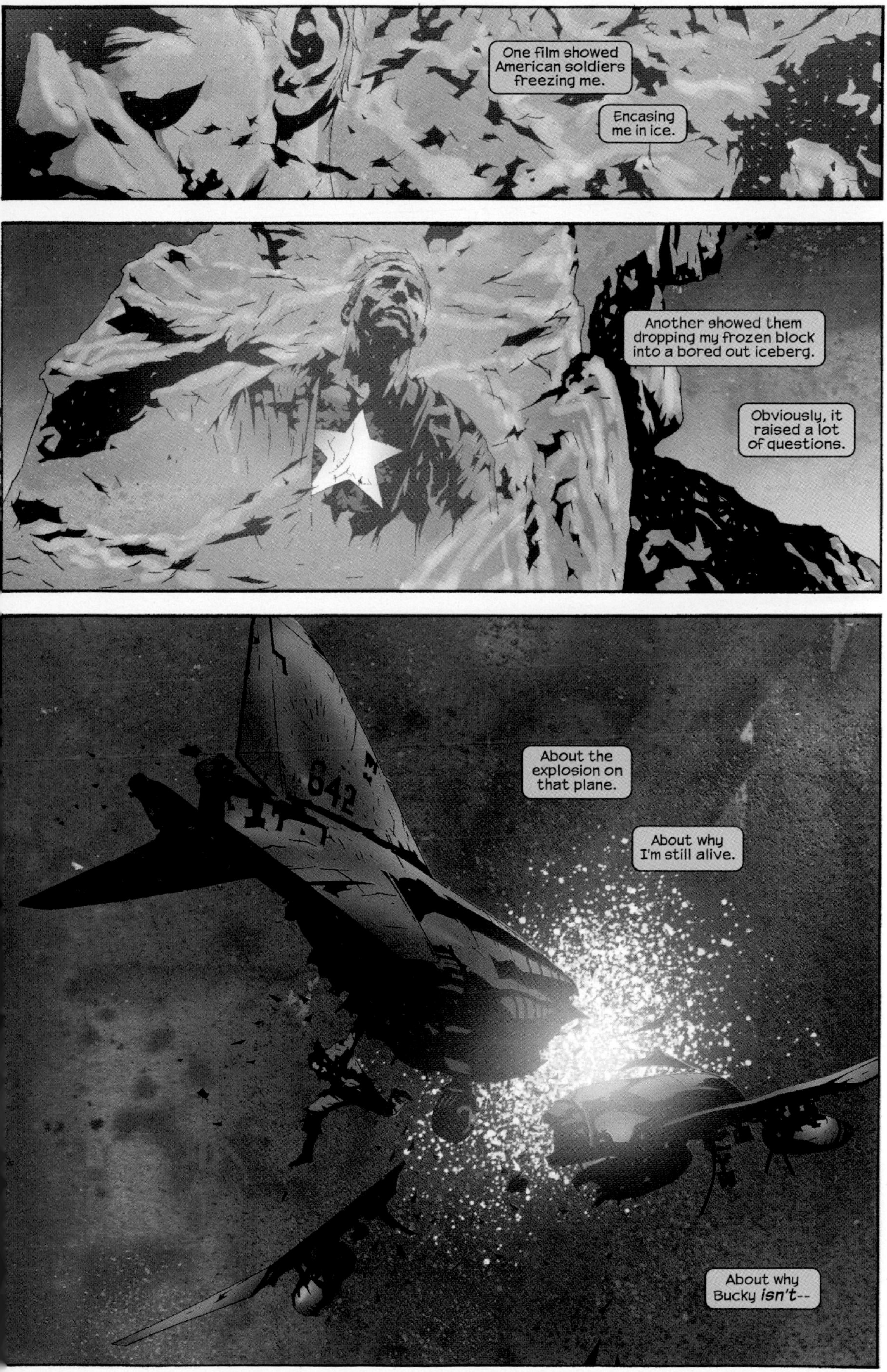
One film showed American soldiers freezing me.
Encasing me in ice.
Another showed them dropping my frozen block into a bored out iceberg.
Obviously, it raised a lot of questions.
About the explosion on that plane.
About why I'm still alive.
642
About why Bucky *isn't*--

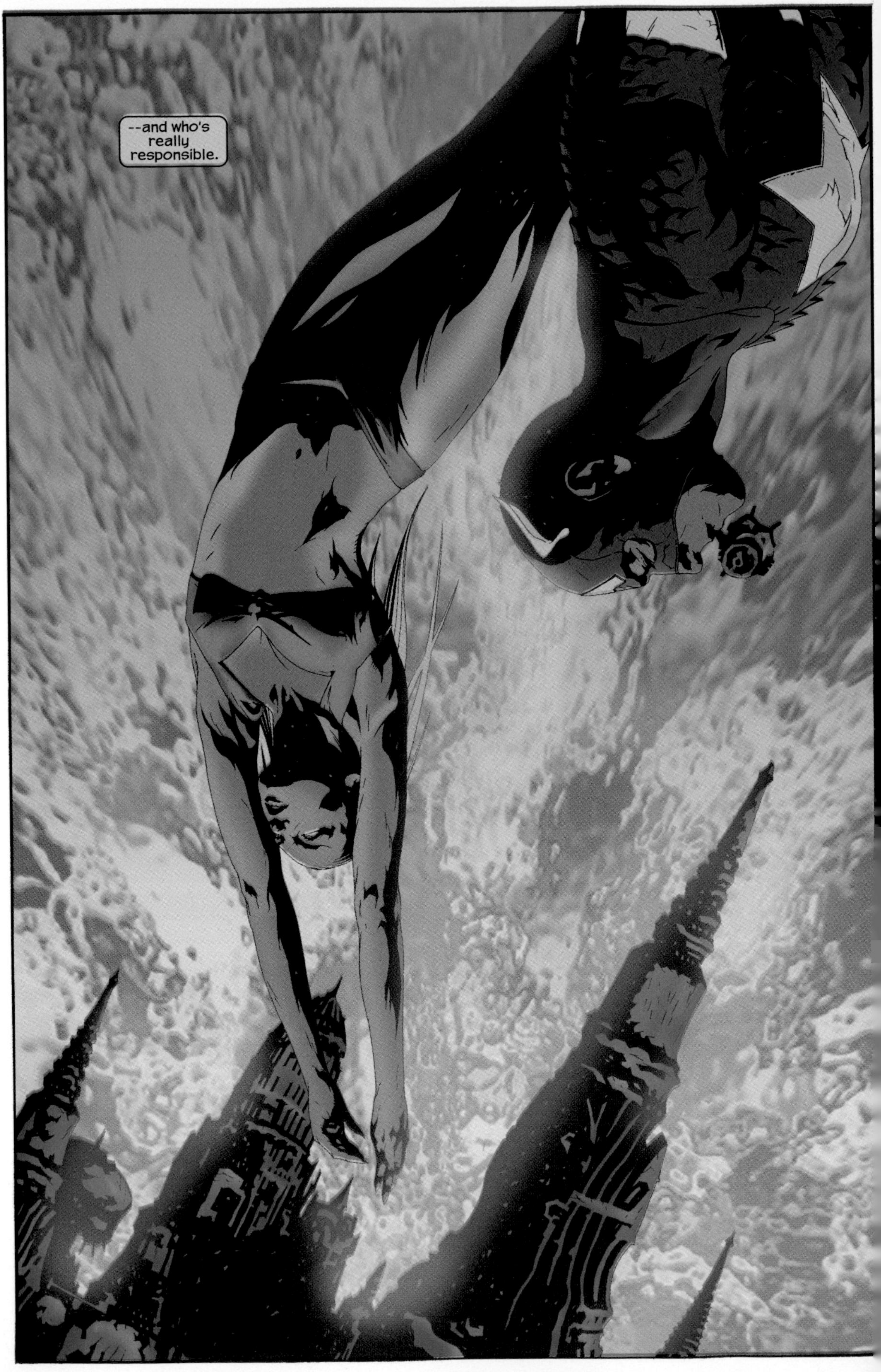
--and who's really responsible.

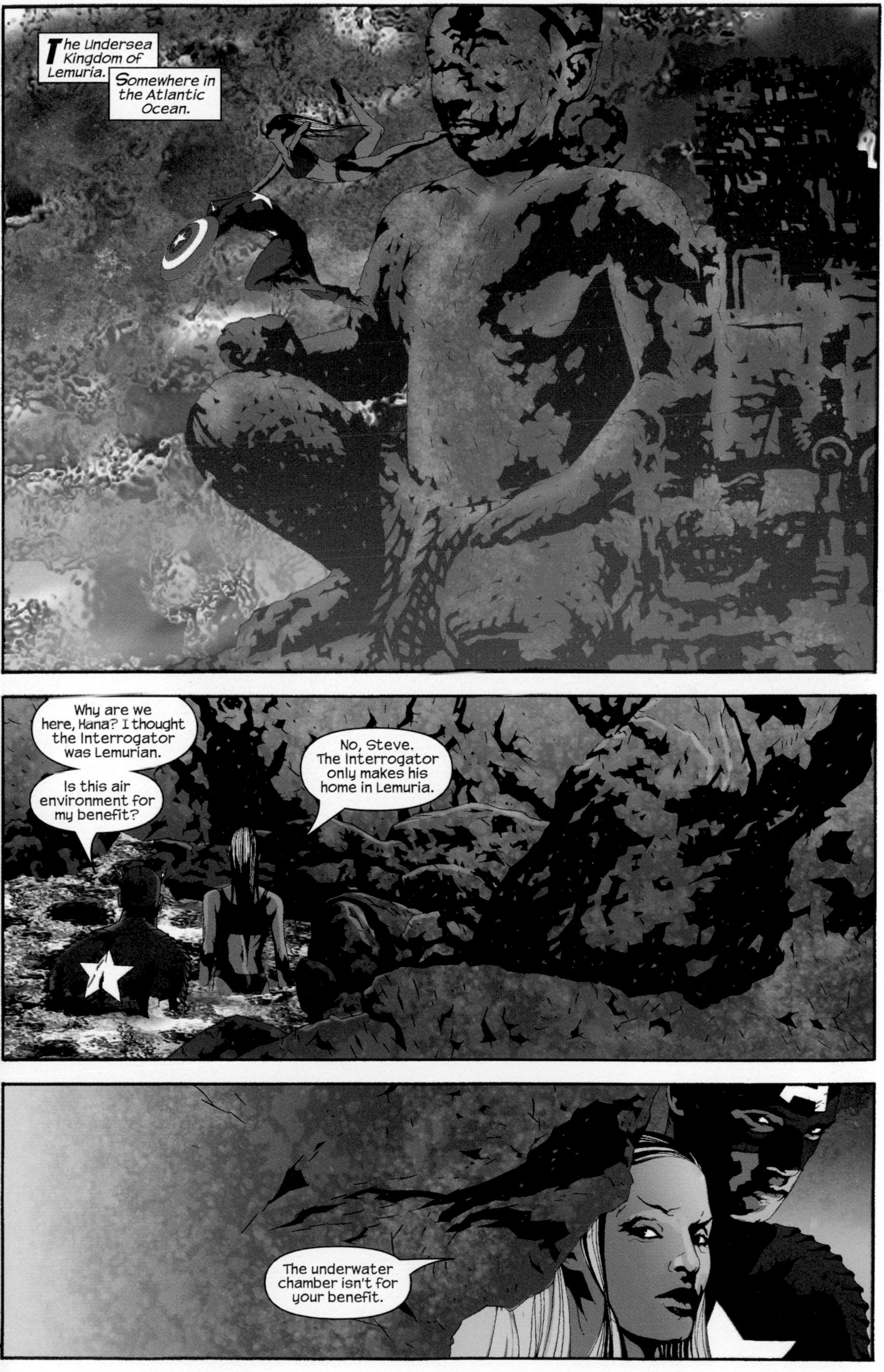
The Undersea Kingdom of Lemuria.
Somewhere in the Atlantic Ocean.
Why are we here, Hana? I thought the Interrogator was Lemurian.
Is this air environment for my benefit?
No, Steve. The Interrogator only makes his home in Lemuria.
The underwater chamber isn't for your benefit.

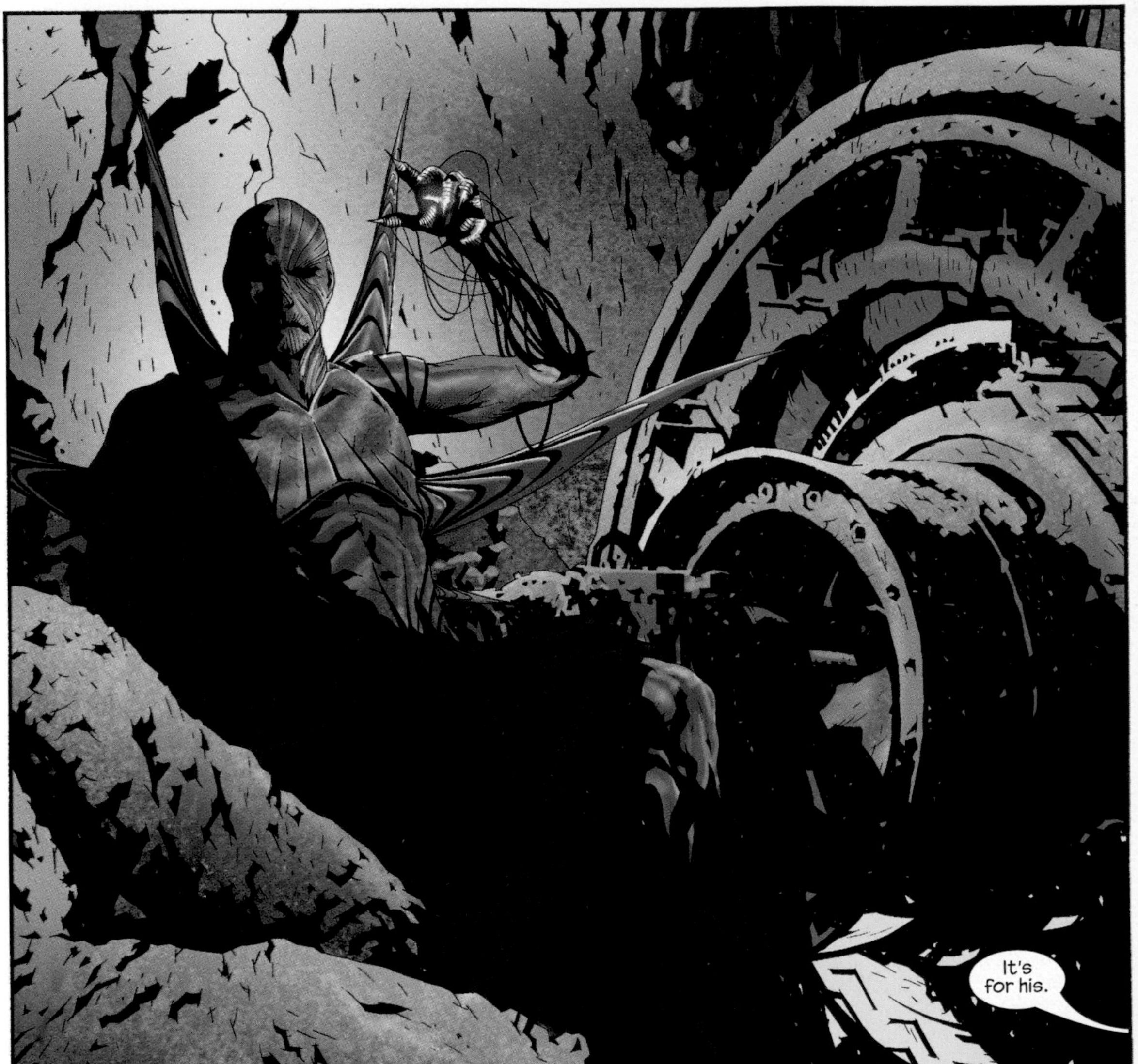
It's for his.

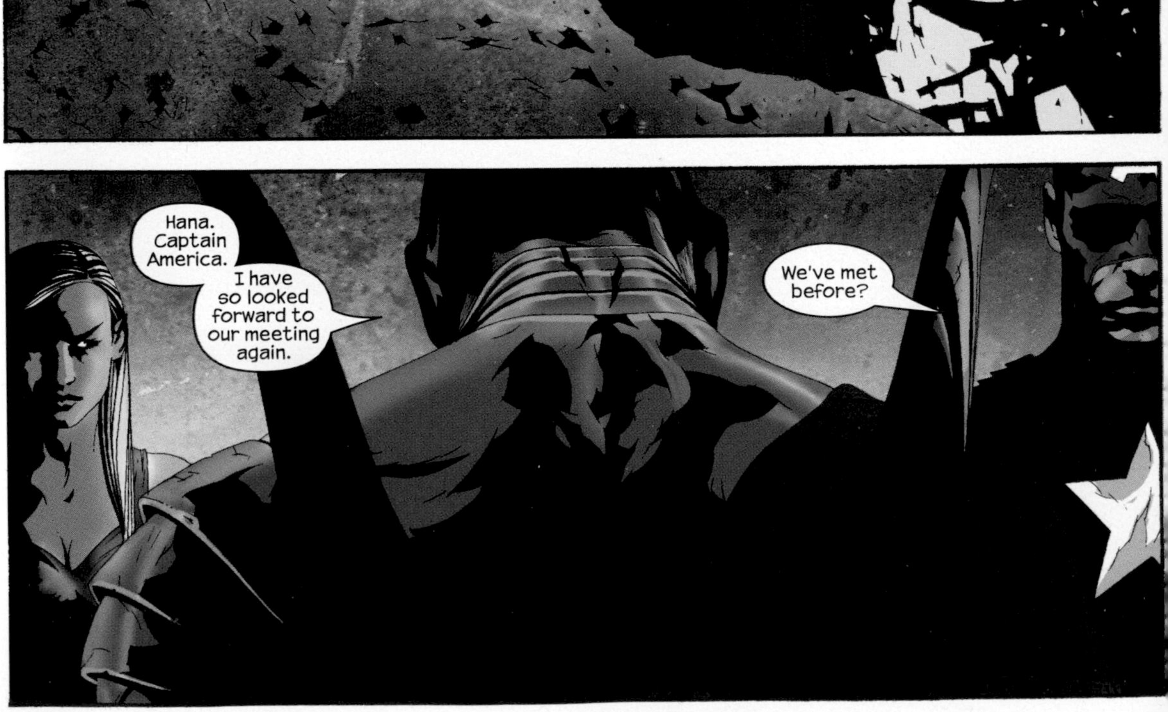
Hana. Captain America.
I have so looked forward to our meeting again.
We've met before?

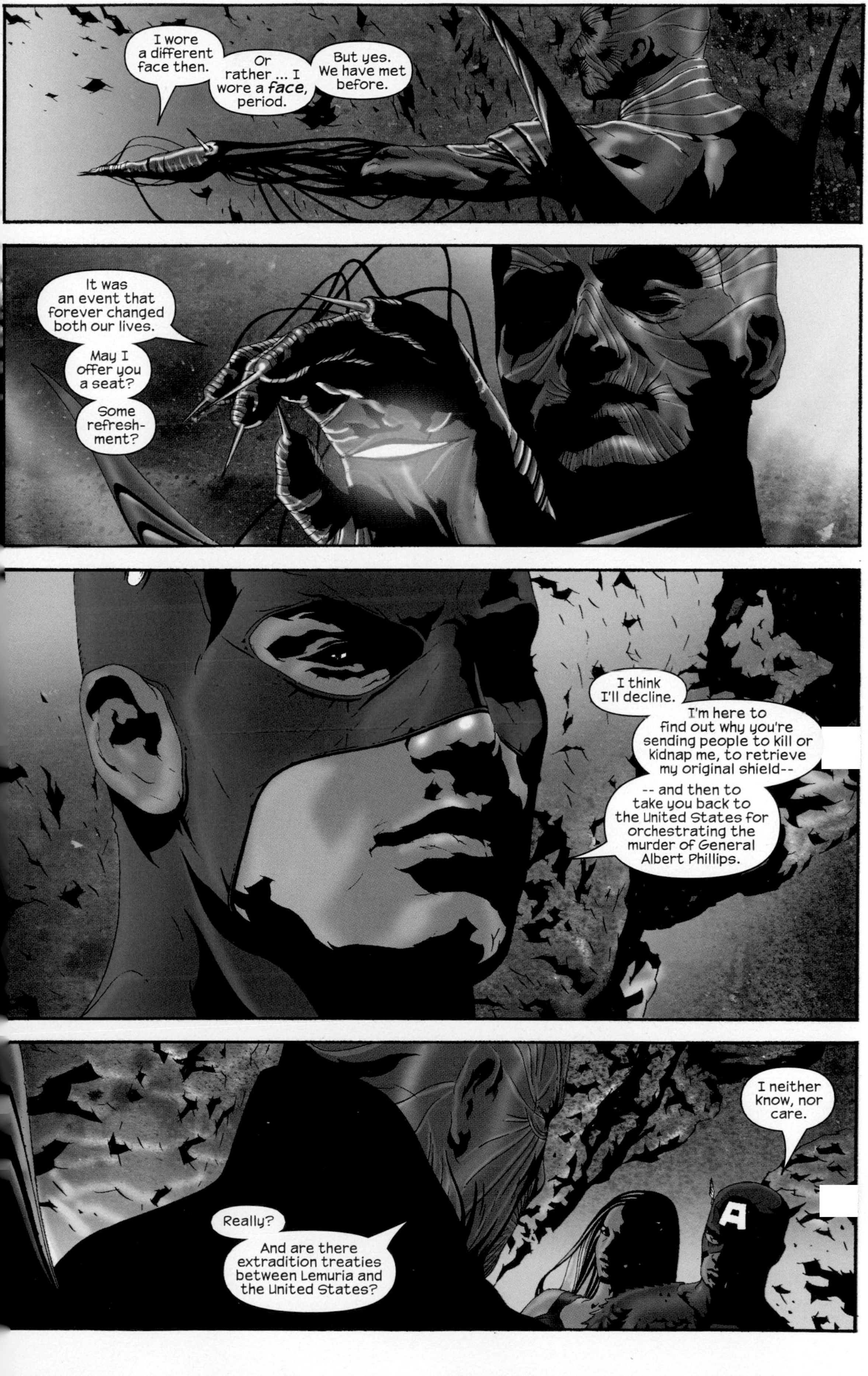
I wore a different face then.
Or rather ... I wore a *face*, period.
But yes. We have met before.
It was an event that forever changed both our lives.
May I offer you a seat?
Some refresh-ment?
I think I'll decline.
I'm here to find out why you're sending people to kill or kidnap me, to retrieve my original shield--
-- and then to take you back to the United States for orchestrating the murder of General Albert Phillips.
I neither know, nor care.
Really?
And are there extradition treaties between Lemuria and the United States?

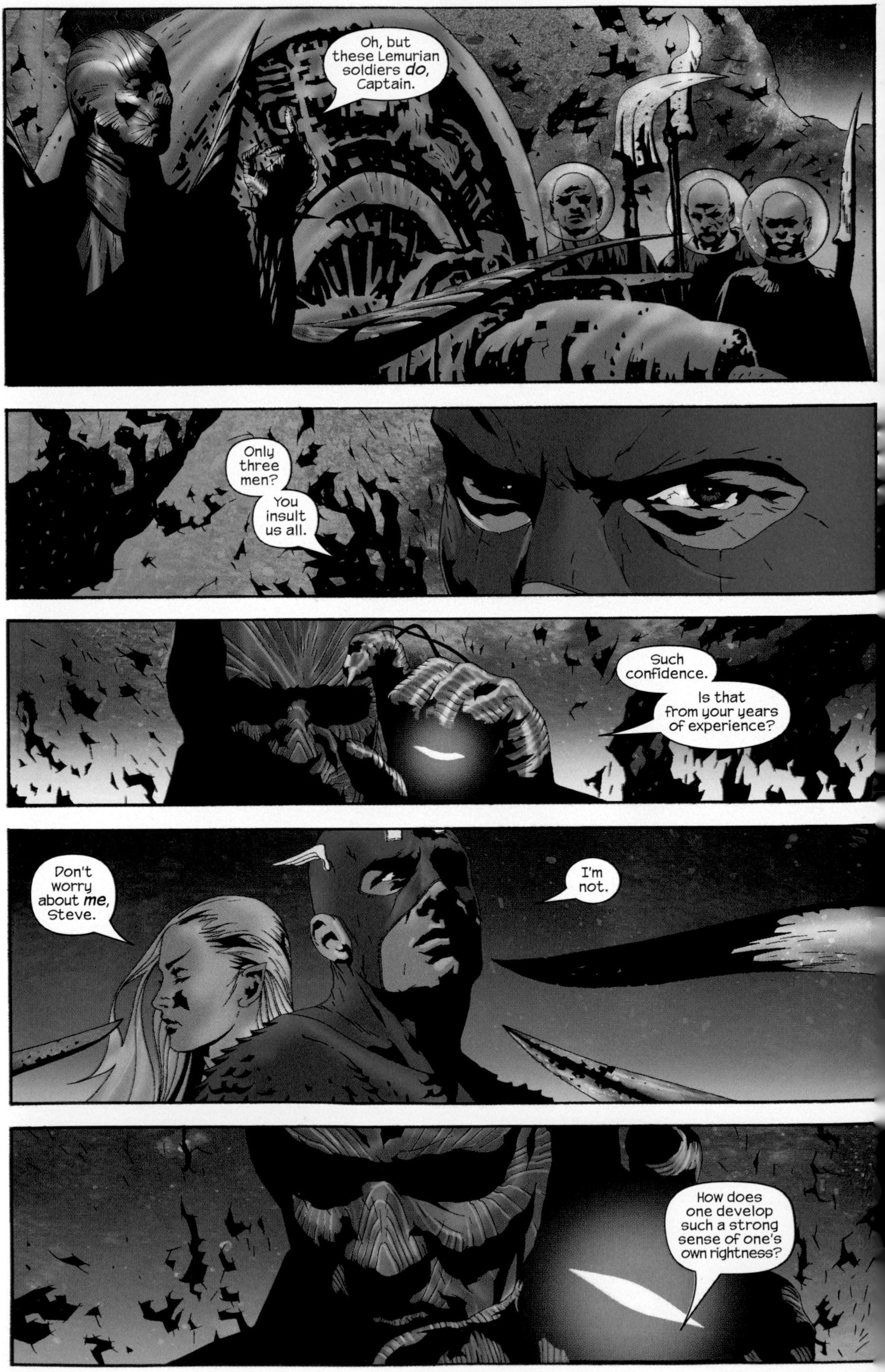
Oh, but these Lemurian soldiers *do*, Captain.
Only three men?
You insult us all.
Such confidence.
Is that from your years of experience?
Don't worry about *me*, Steve.
I'm not.
How does one develop such a strong sense of one's own rightness?

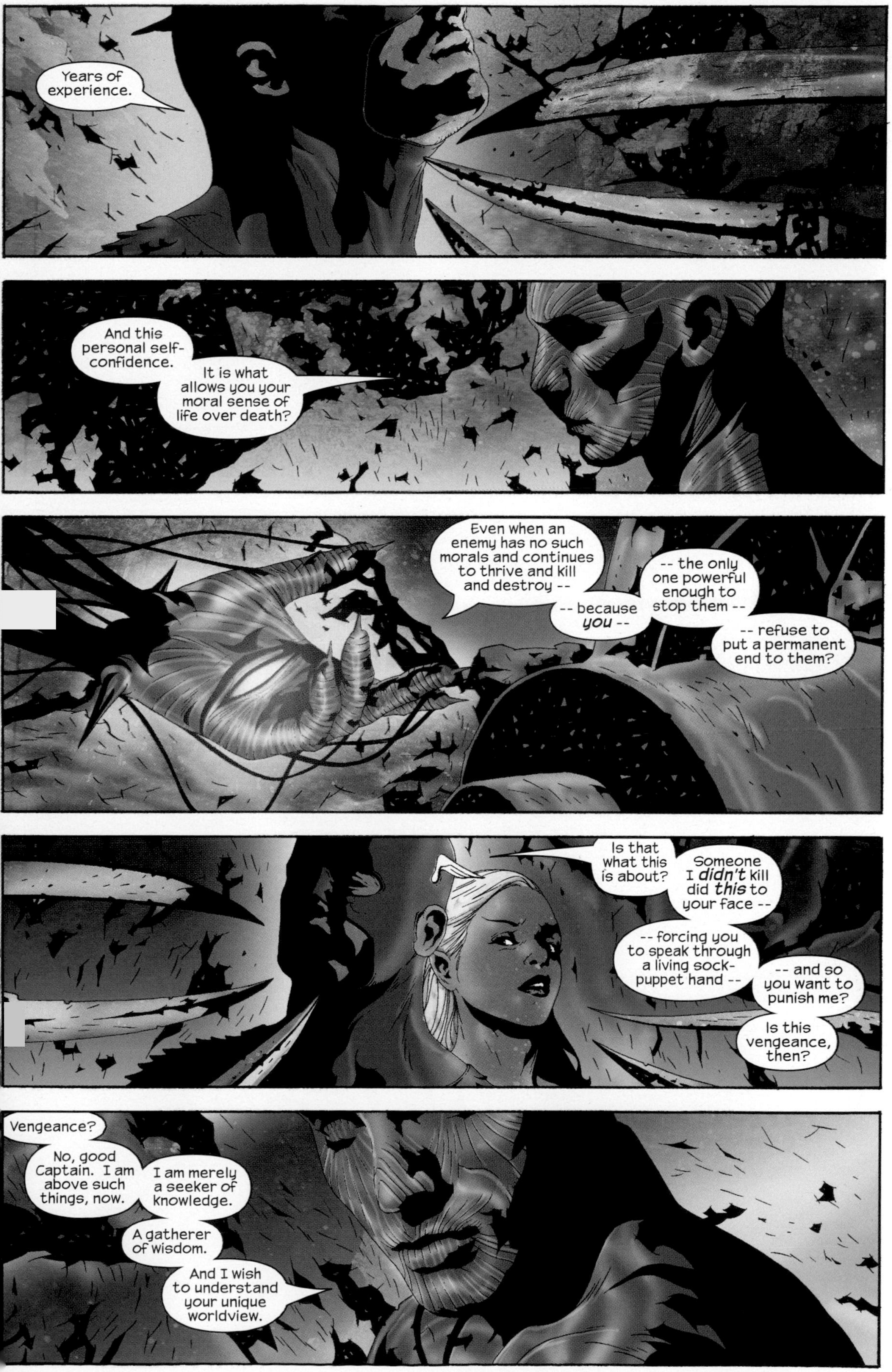
Years of experience.
And this personal self-confidence.
It is what allows you your moral sense of life over death?
Even when an enemy has no such morals and continues to thrive and kill and destroy --
-- because you --
-- the only one powerful enough to stop them --
-- refuse to put a permanent end to them?
Is that what this is about?
Someone I didn't kill did this to your face --
-- forcing you to speak through a living sock-puppet hand --
-- and so you want to punish me?
Is this vengeance, then?
Vengeance?
No, good Captain. I am above such things, now.
I am merely a seeker of knowledge.
A gatherer of wisdom.
And I wish to understand your unique worldview.

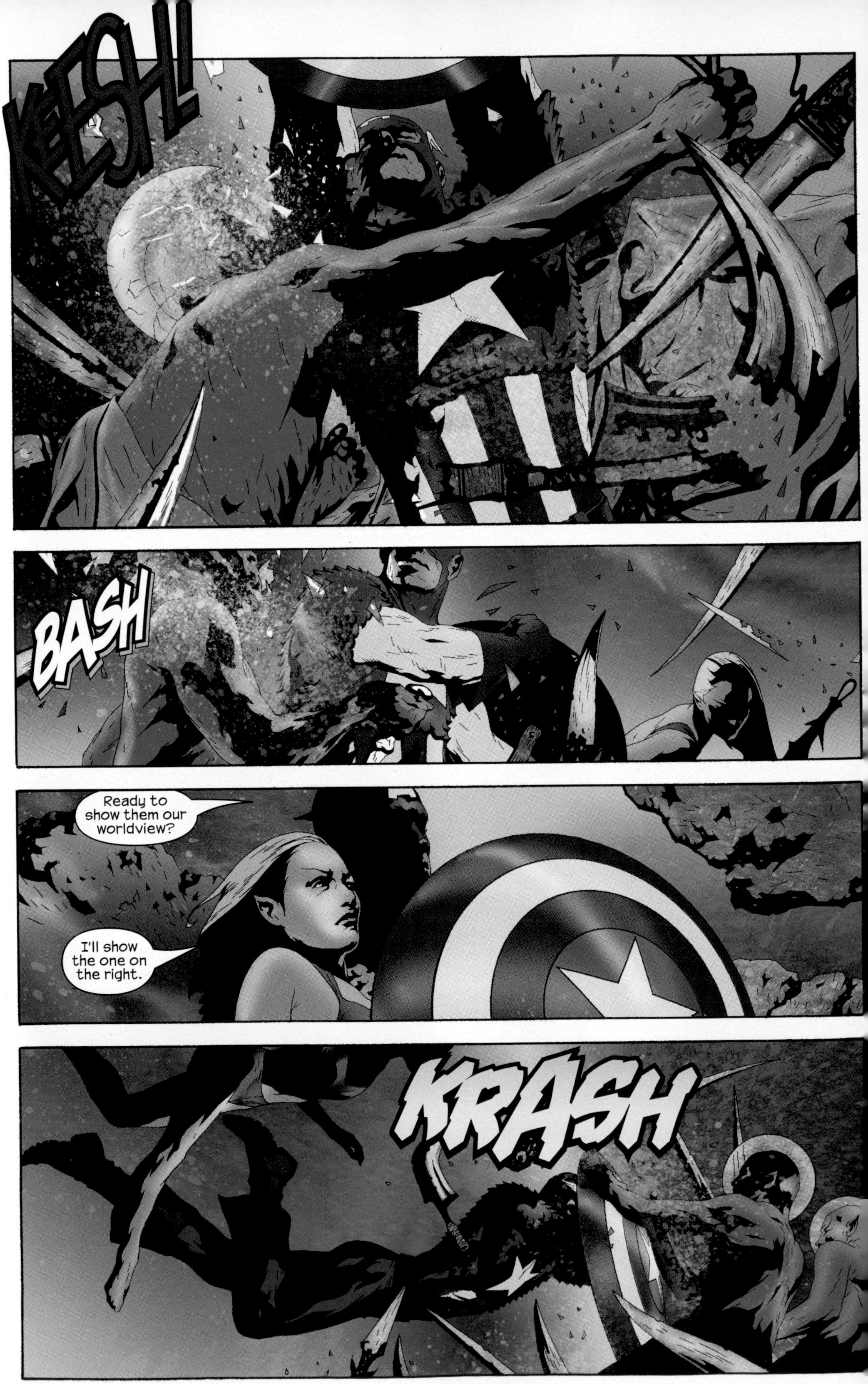
KEESH!
BASH
Ready to show them our worldview?
I'll show the one on the right.
KRASH

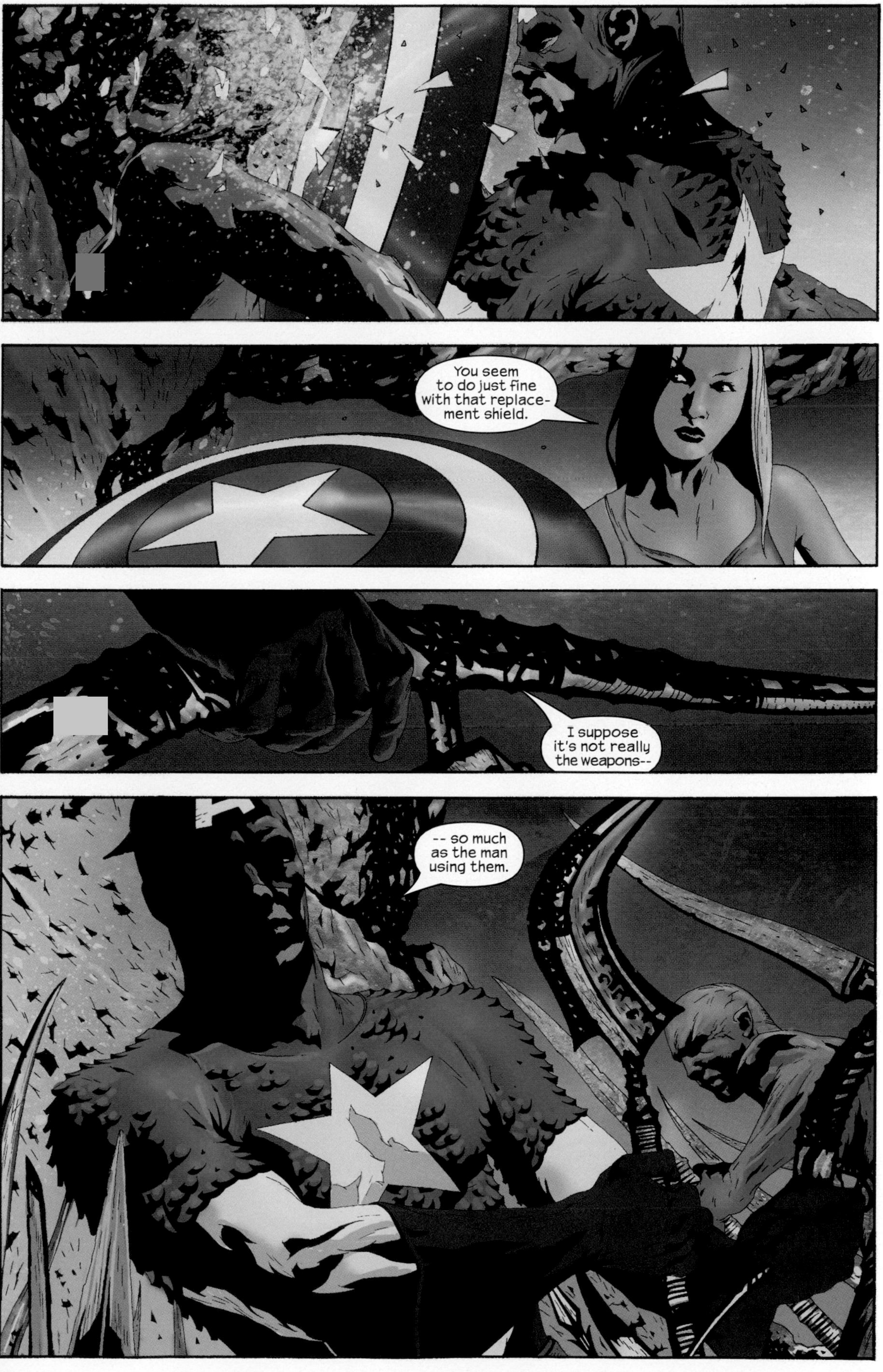
You seem to do just fine with that replacement shield.
I suppose it's not really the weapons--
-- so much as the man using them.

HOOOOO--
AAAAAAHHHH!!!

SKEEGH

INTERROGATOR!

Yes, Captain?

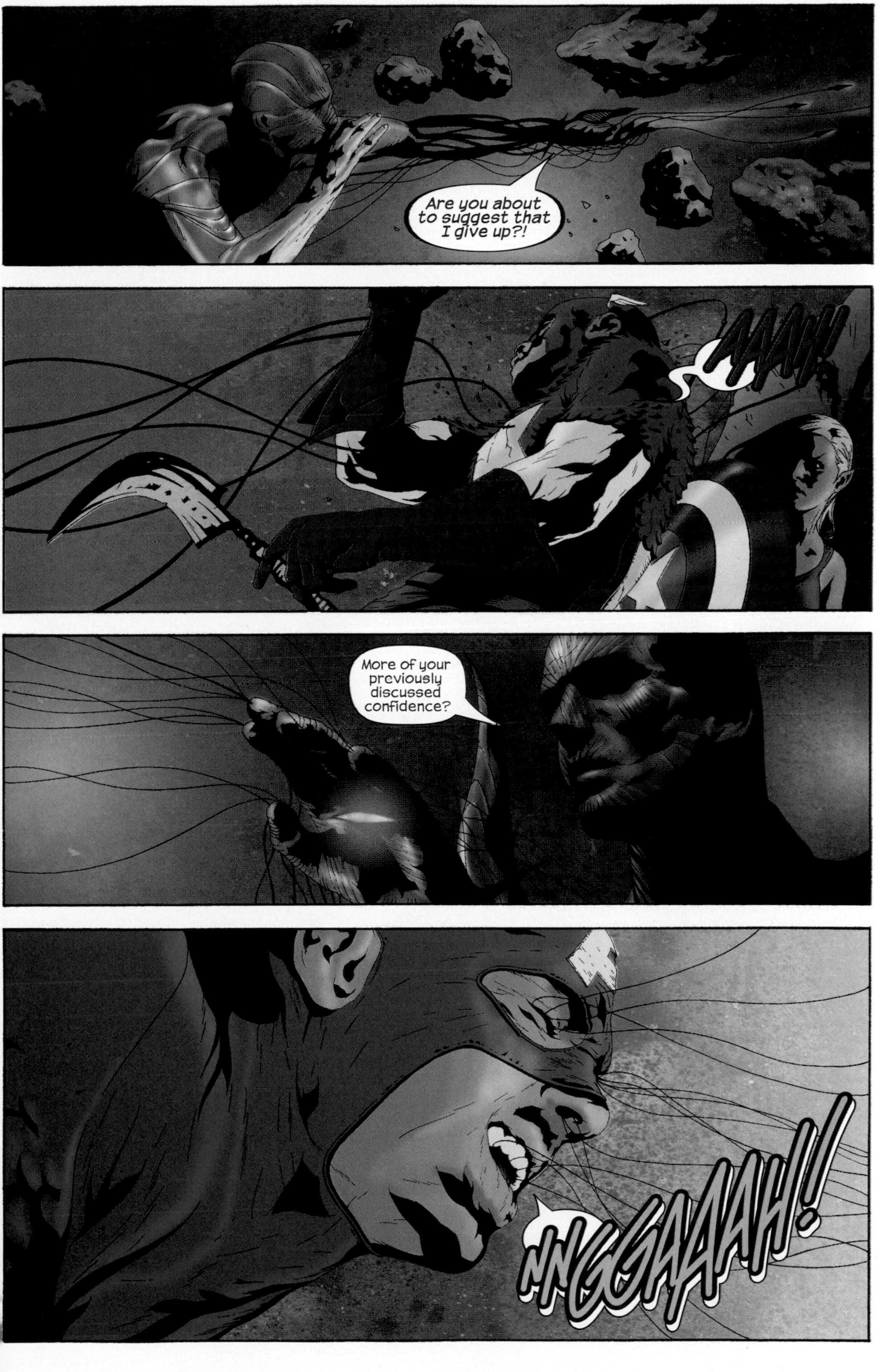
Are you about to suggest that I give up?!
AAAAH!
More of your previously discussed confidence?
NNGGAAAAH!

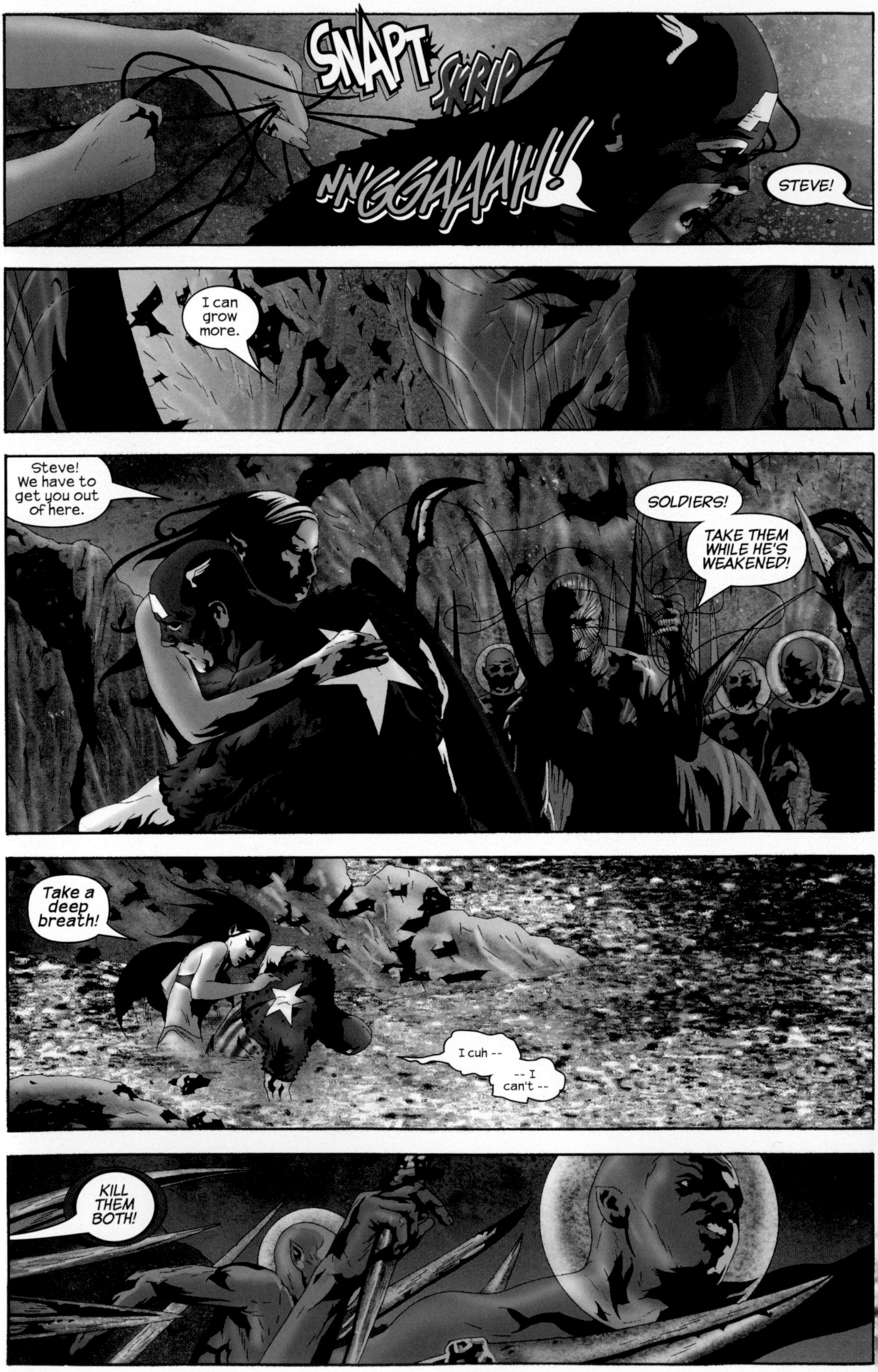
SNAPT
SKRIP
NNGGAAAH!
STEVE!
I can grow more.
Steve! We have to get you out of here.
SOLDIERS!
TAKE THEM WHILE HE'S WEAKENED!
Take a deep breath!
I cuh --
-- I can't --
KILL THEM BOTH!

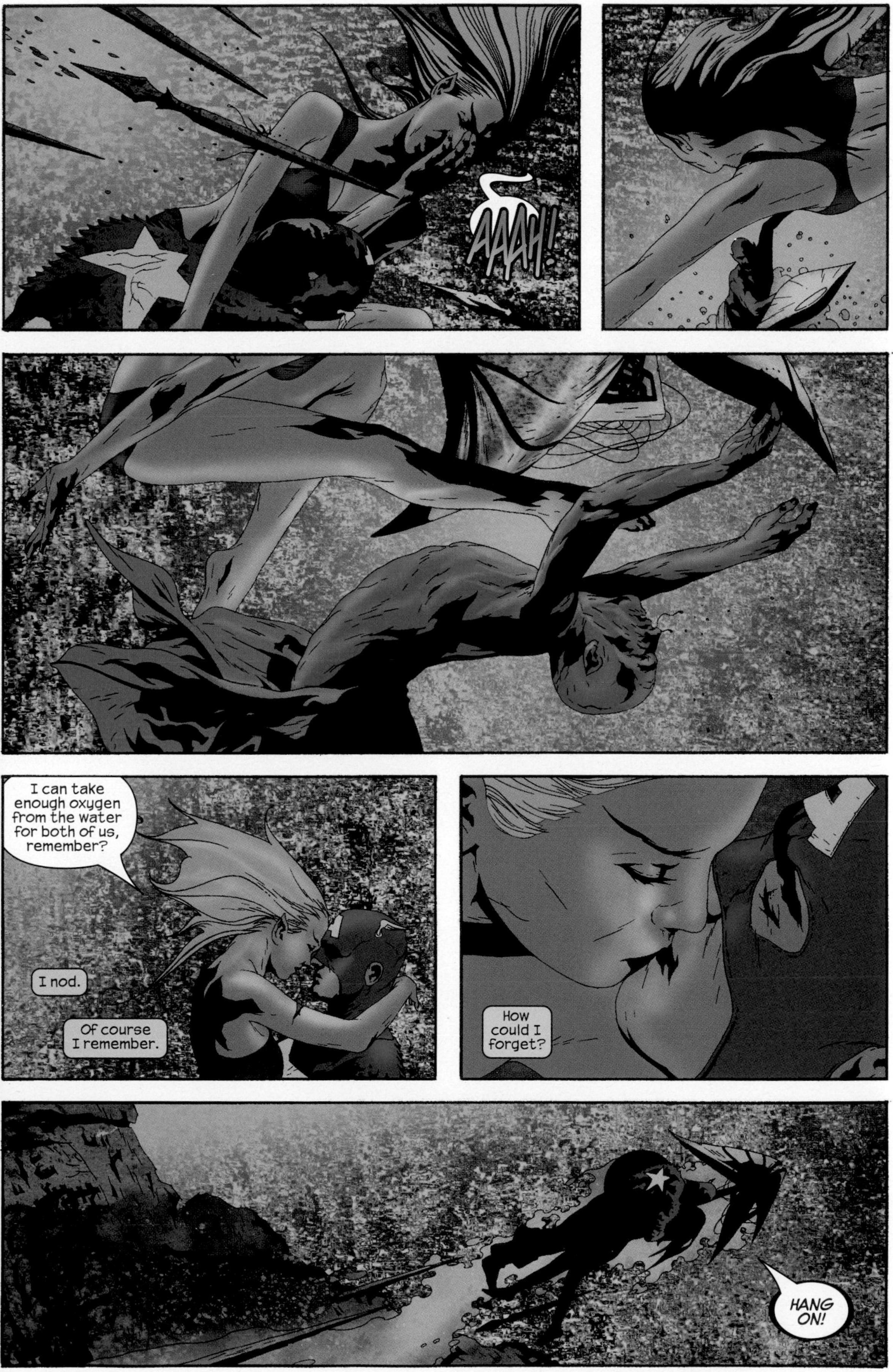
AAAH!
I can take enough oxygen from the water for both of us, remember?
I nod.
Of course I remember.
How could I forget?
HANG ON!

Stopping for me to breathe will slow us down.

Make us vulnerable.

So I fight the need for air.

Worse.

I fight the sudden need for *more* than air.

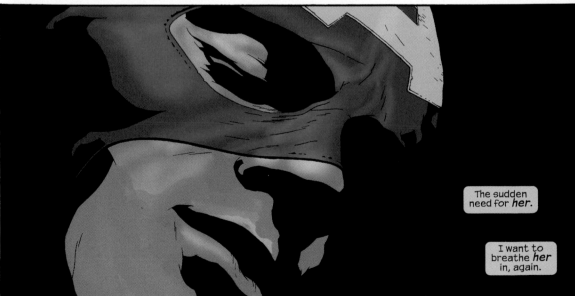

The sudden need for *her.*

I want to breathe *her* in, again.

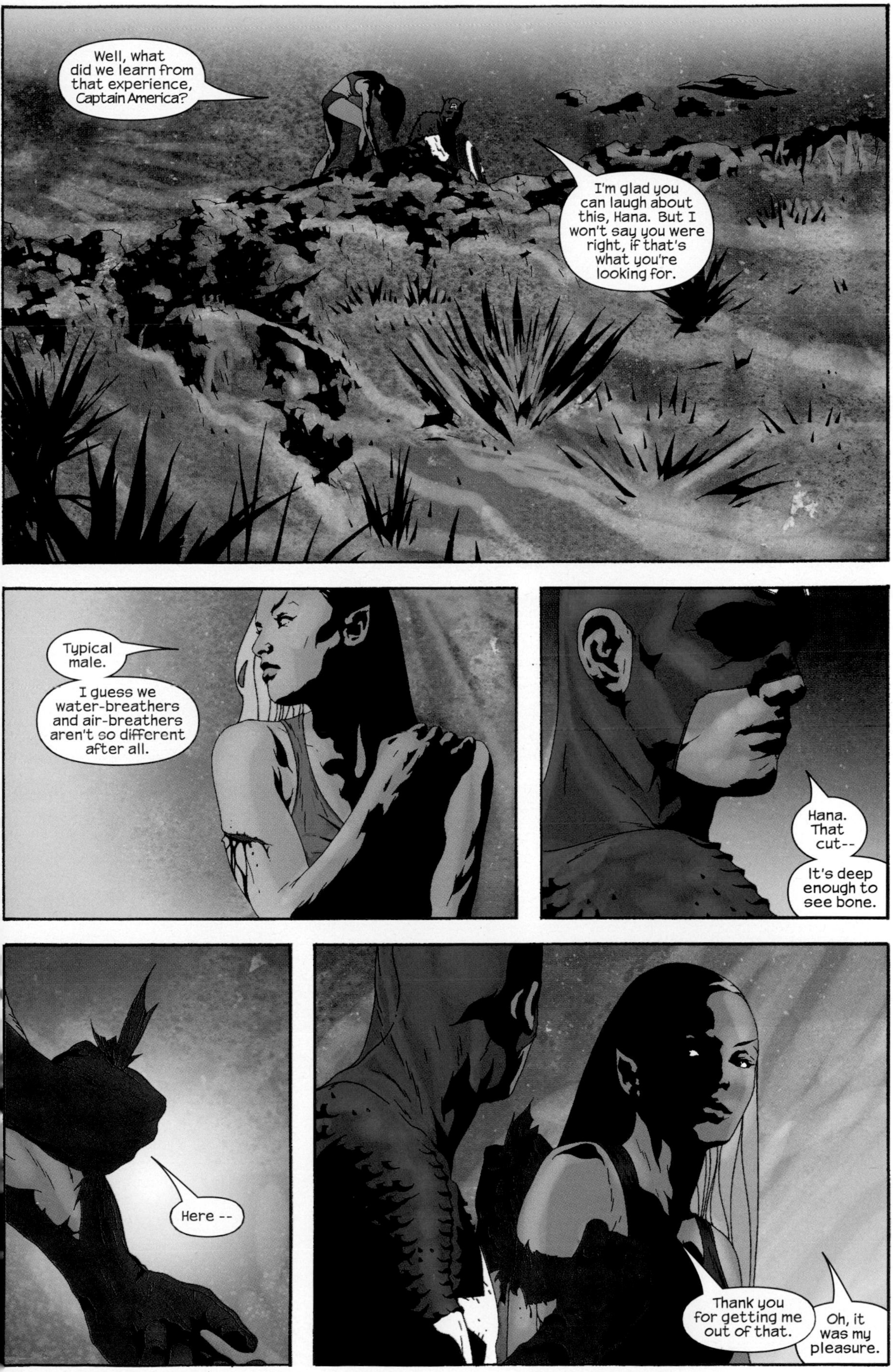
Well, what did we learn from that experience, Captain America?
I'm glad you can laugh about this, Hana. But I won't say you were right, if that's what you're looking for.
Typical male.
I guess we water-breathers and air-breathers aren't so different after all.
Hana. That cut--
It's deep enough to see bone.
Here --
Thank you for getting me out of that.
Oh, it was my pleasure.

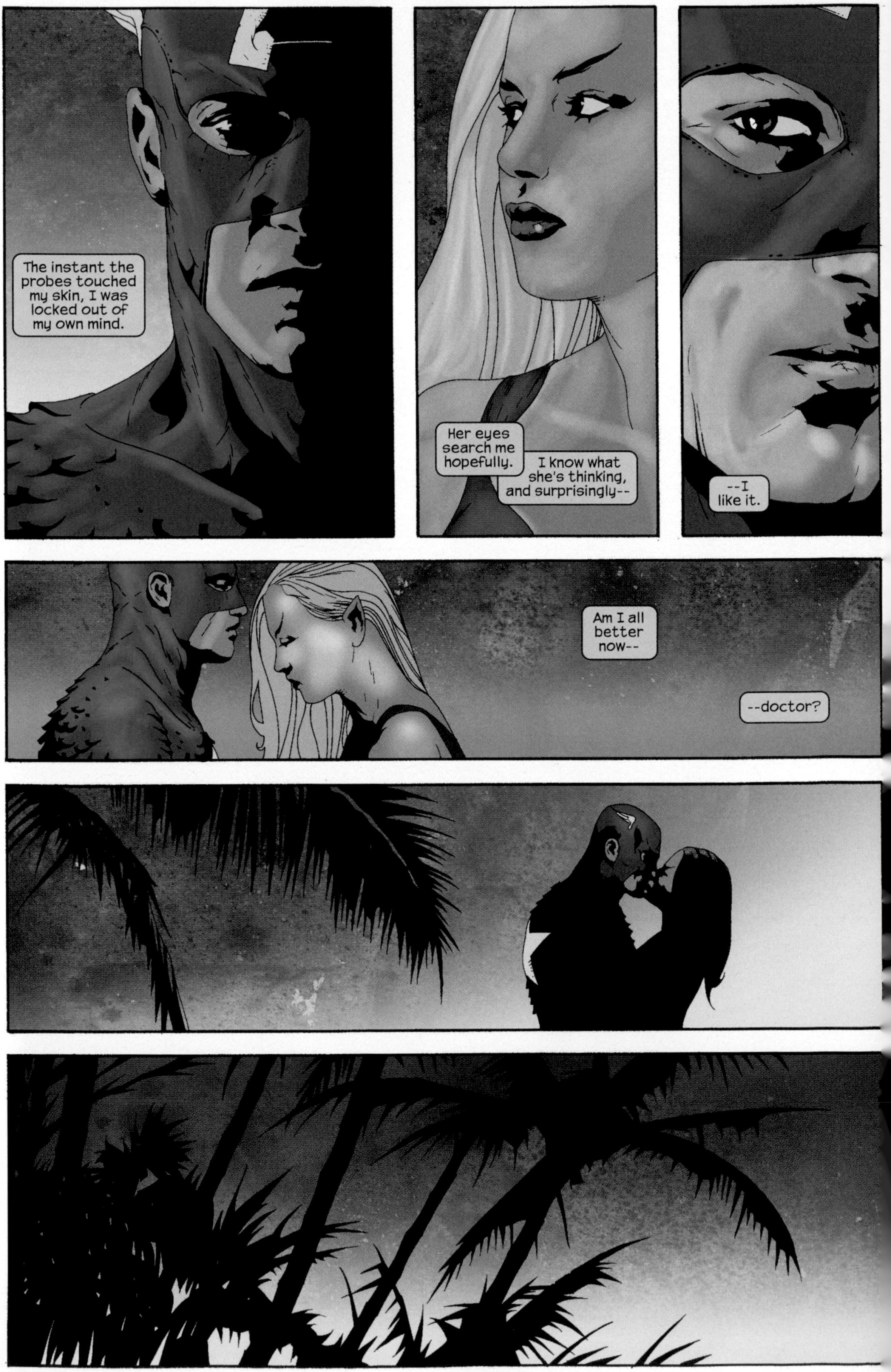
The instant the probes touched my skin, I was locked out of my own mind.
Her eyes search me hopefully.
I know what she's thinking, and surprisingly--
--I like it.
Am I all better now--
--doctor?

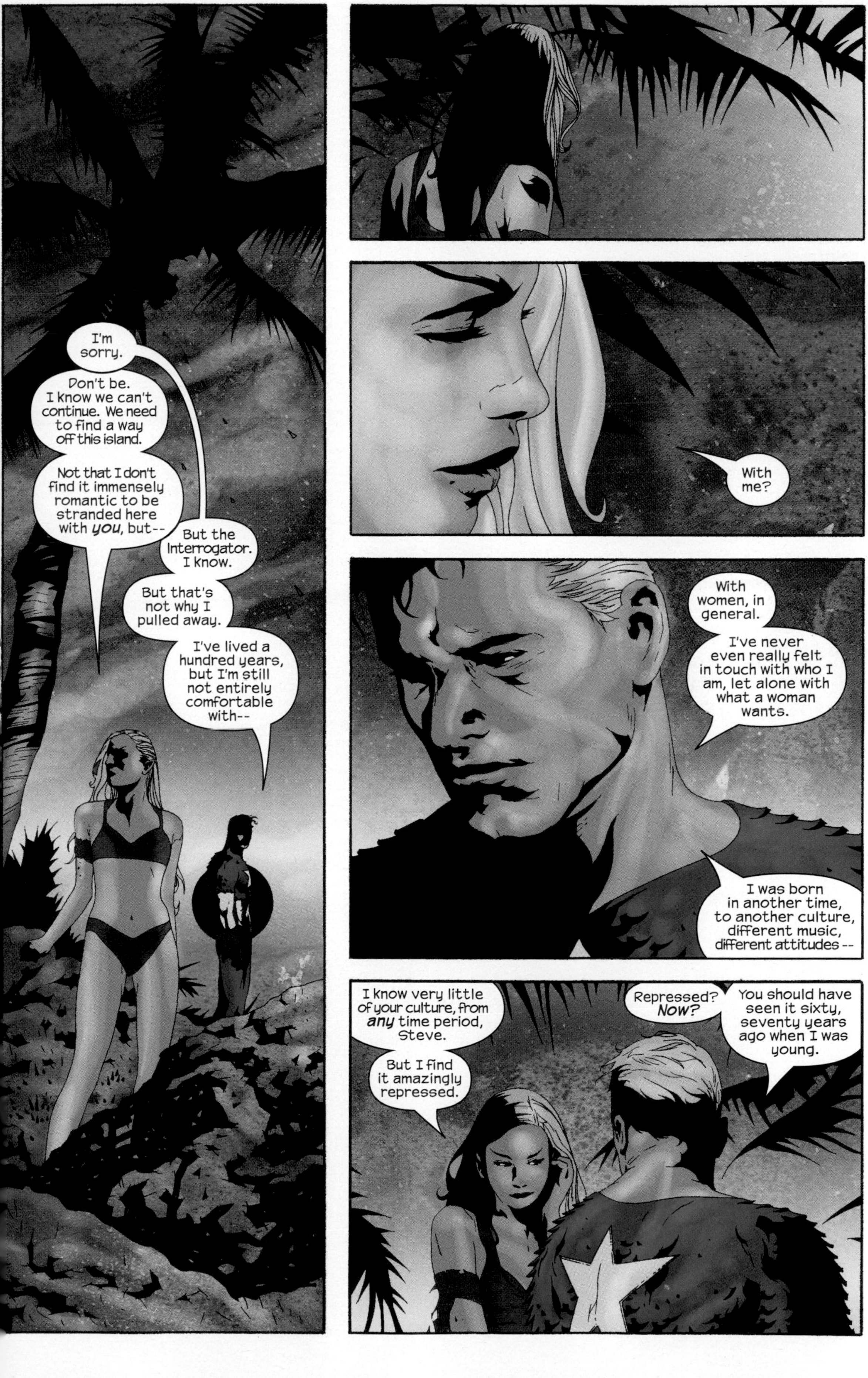
I'm sorry.
Don't be. I know we can't continue. We need to find a way off this island.
Not that I don't find it immensely romantic to be stranded here with *you*, but--
But the Interrogator. I know.
But that's not why I pulled away.
I've lived a hundred years, but I'm still not entirely comfortable with--
With me?
With women, in general.
I've never even really felt in touch with who I am, let alone with what a woman wants.
I was born in another time, to another culture, different music, different attitudes--
I know very little of your culture, from *any* time period, Steve.
But I find it amazingly repressed.
Repressed? *Now?*
You should have seen it sixty, seventy years ago when I was young.

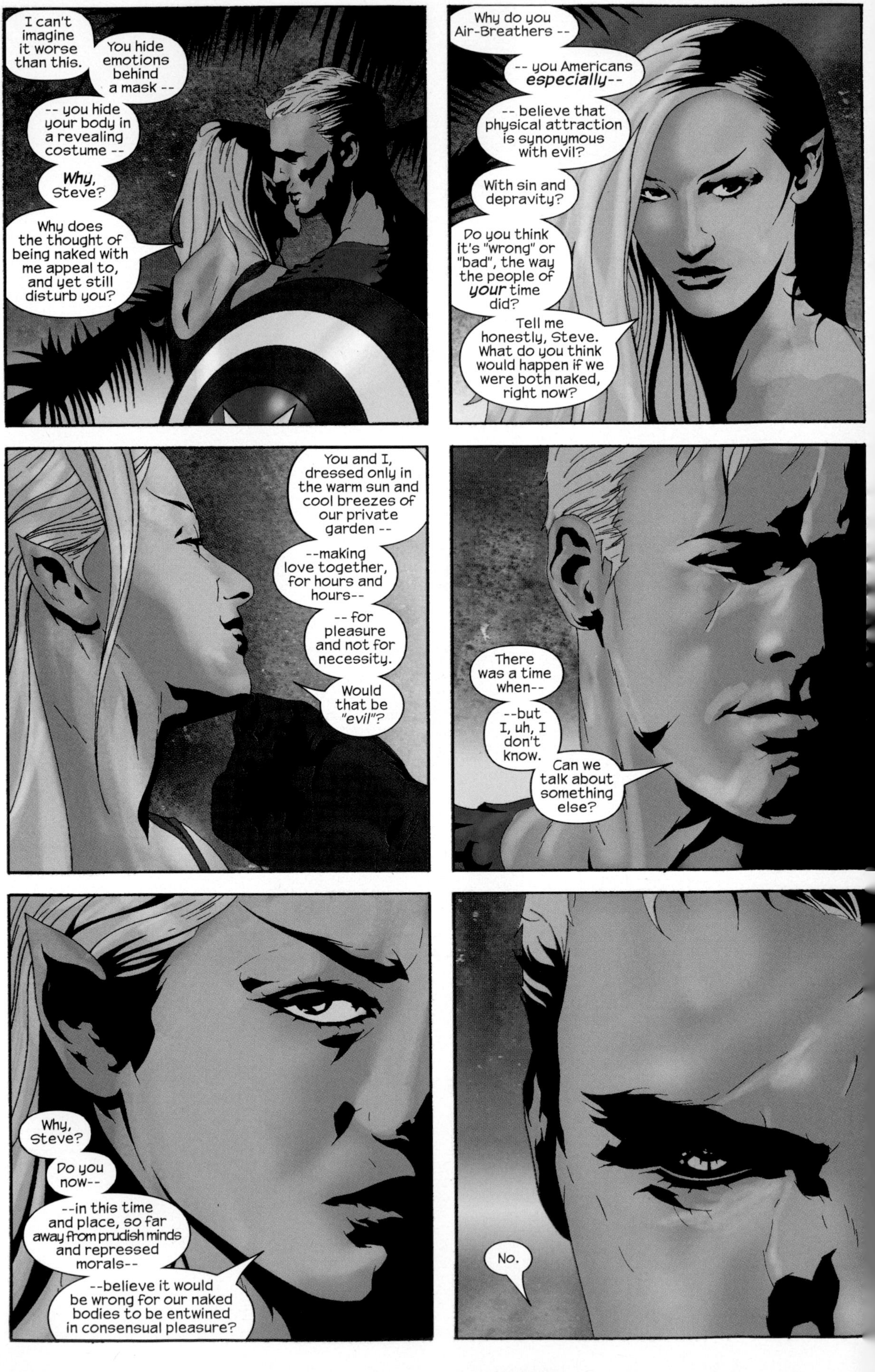
I can't imagine it worse than this.
You hide emotions behind a mask --
-- you hide your body in a revealing costume --
Why, Steve?
Why does the thought of being naked with me appeal to, and yet still disturb you?
Why do you Air-Breathers --
-- you Americans especially--
-- believe that physical attraction is synonymous with evil?
With sin and depravity?
Do you think it's "wrong" or "bad", the way the people of your time did?
Tell me honestly, Steve. What do you think would happen if we were both naked, right now?
You and I, dressed only in the warm sun and cool breezes of our private garden --
--making love together, for hours and hours--
-- for pleasure and not for necessity.
Would that be "evil"?
There was a time when--
--but I, uh, I don't know.
Can we talk about something else?
Why, Steve?
Do you now--
--in this time and place, so far away from prudish minds and repressed morals--
--believe it would be wrong for our naked bodies to be entwined in consensual pleasure?
No.

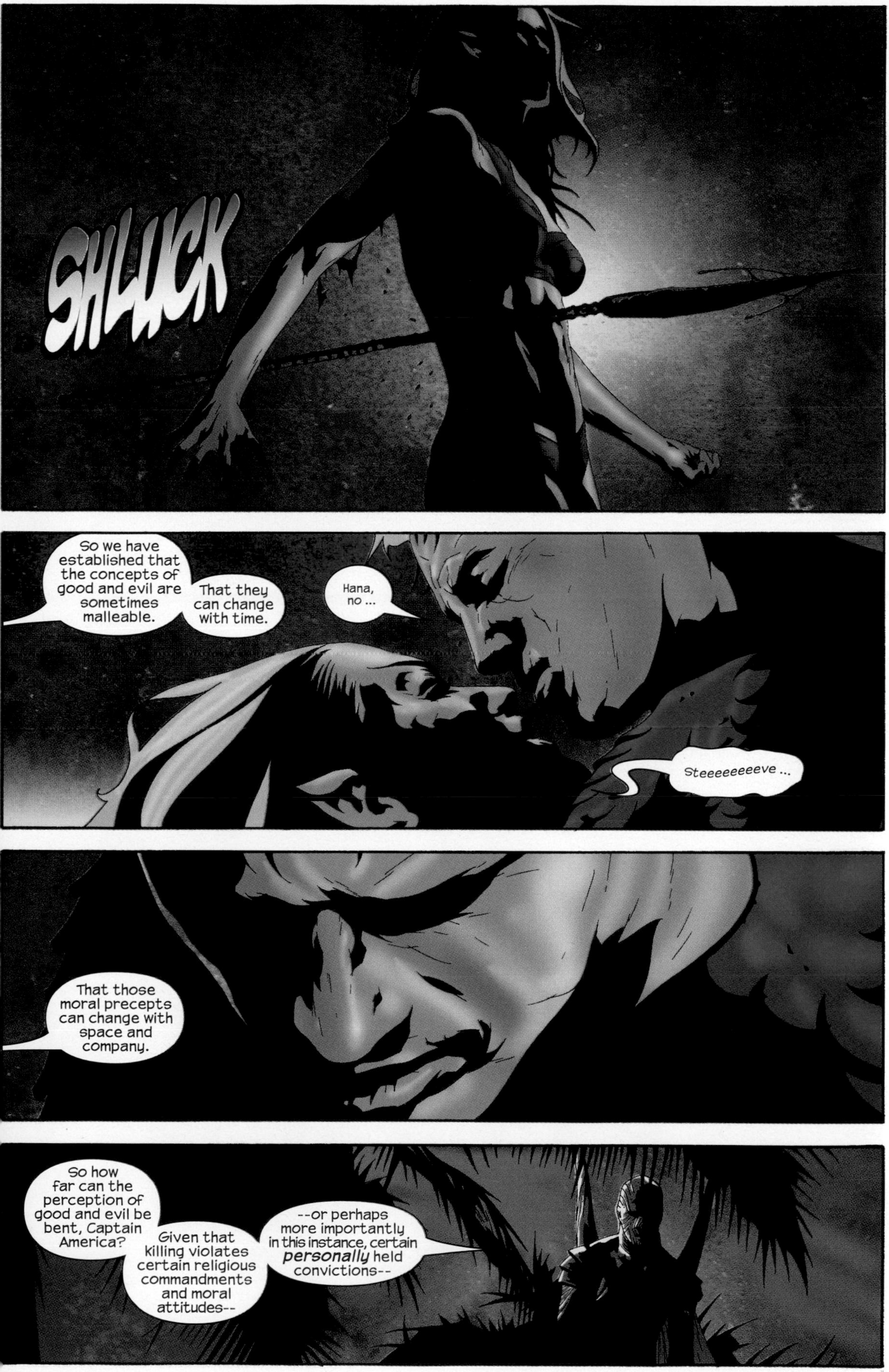
SHLUCK
So we have established that the concepts of good and evil are sometimes malleable.
That they can change with time.
Hana, no ...
Steeeeeeeeve ...
That those moral precepts can change with space and company.
So how far can the perception of good and evil be bent, Captain America?
Given that killing violates certain religious commandments and moral attitudes--
--or perhaps more importantly in this instance, certain *personally* held convictions--

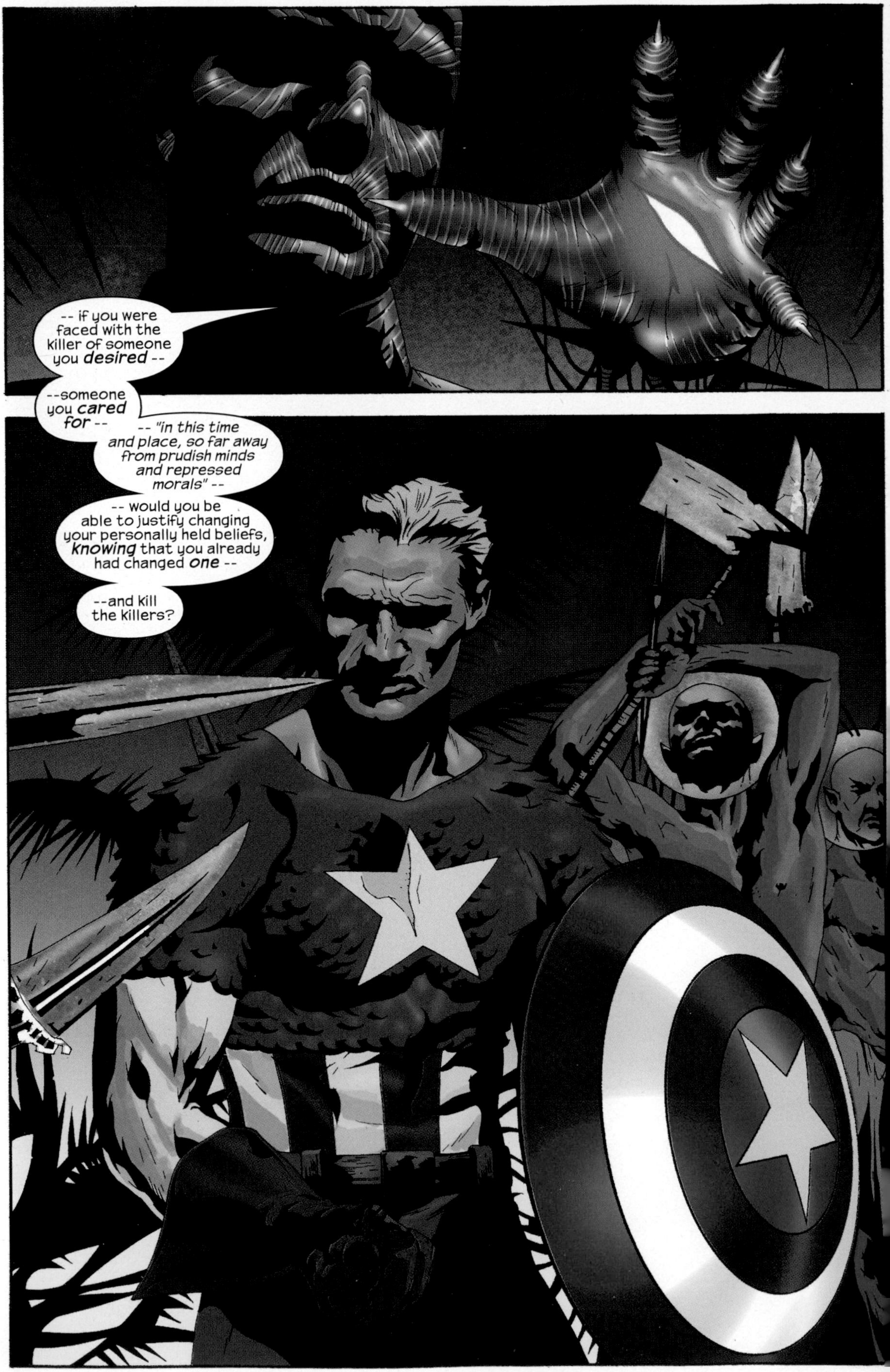
-- if you were faced with the killer of someone you *desired* --
--someone you *cared for* --
-- *"in this time and place, so far away from prudish minds and repressed morals"* --
-- would you be able to justify changing your personally held beliefs, *knowing* that you already had changed *one* --
--and kill the killers?

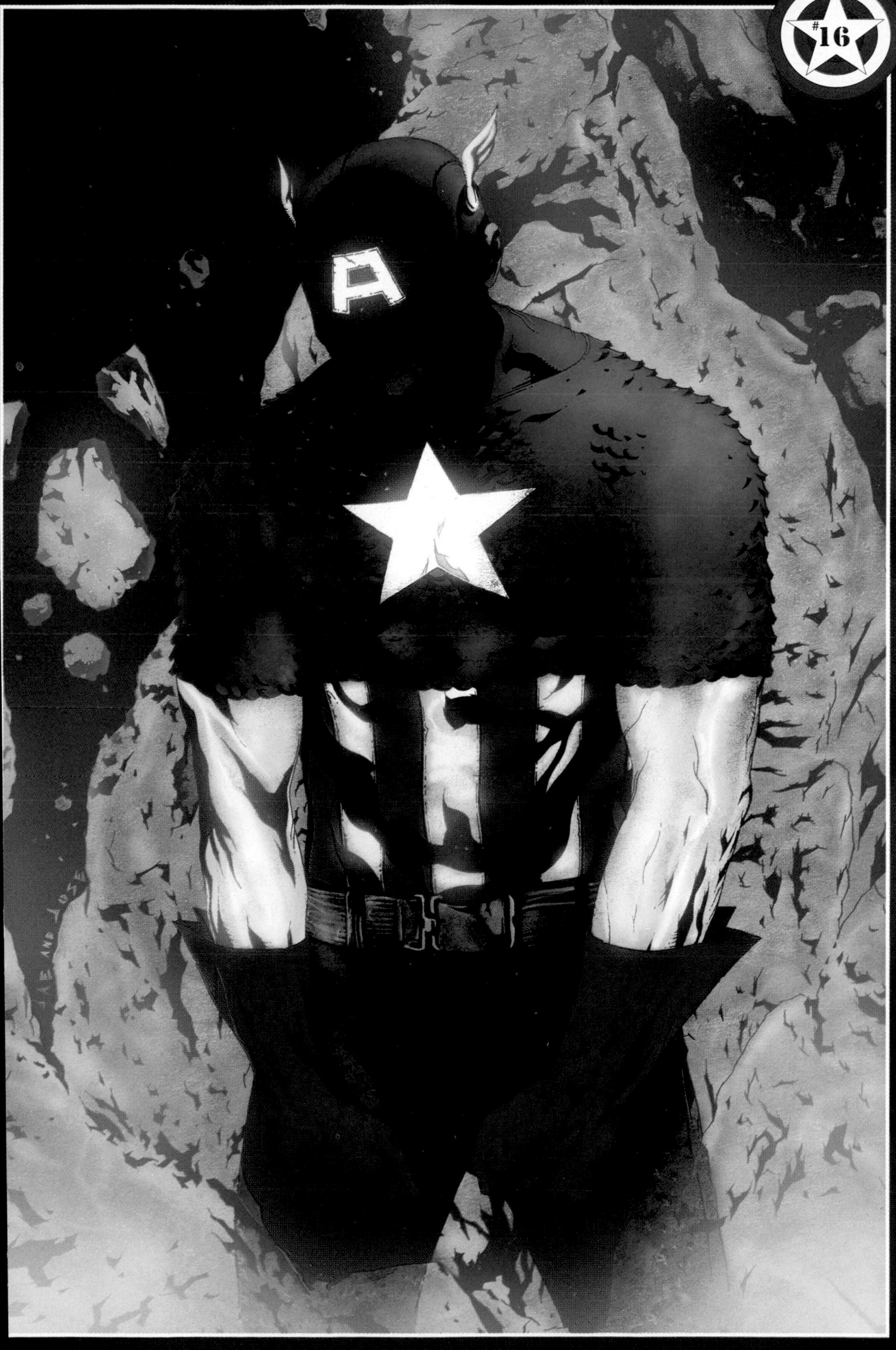
#16

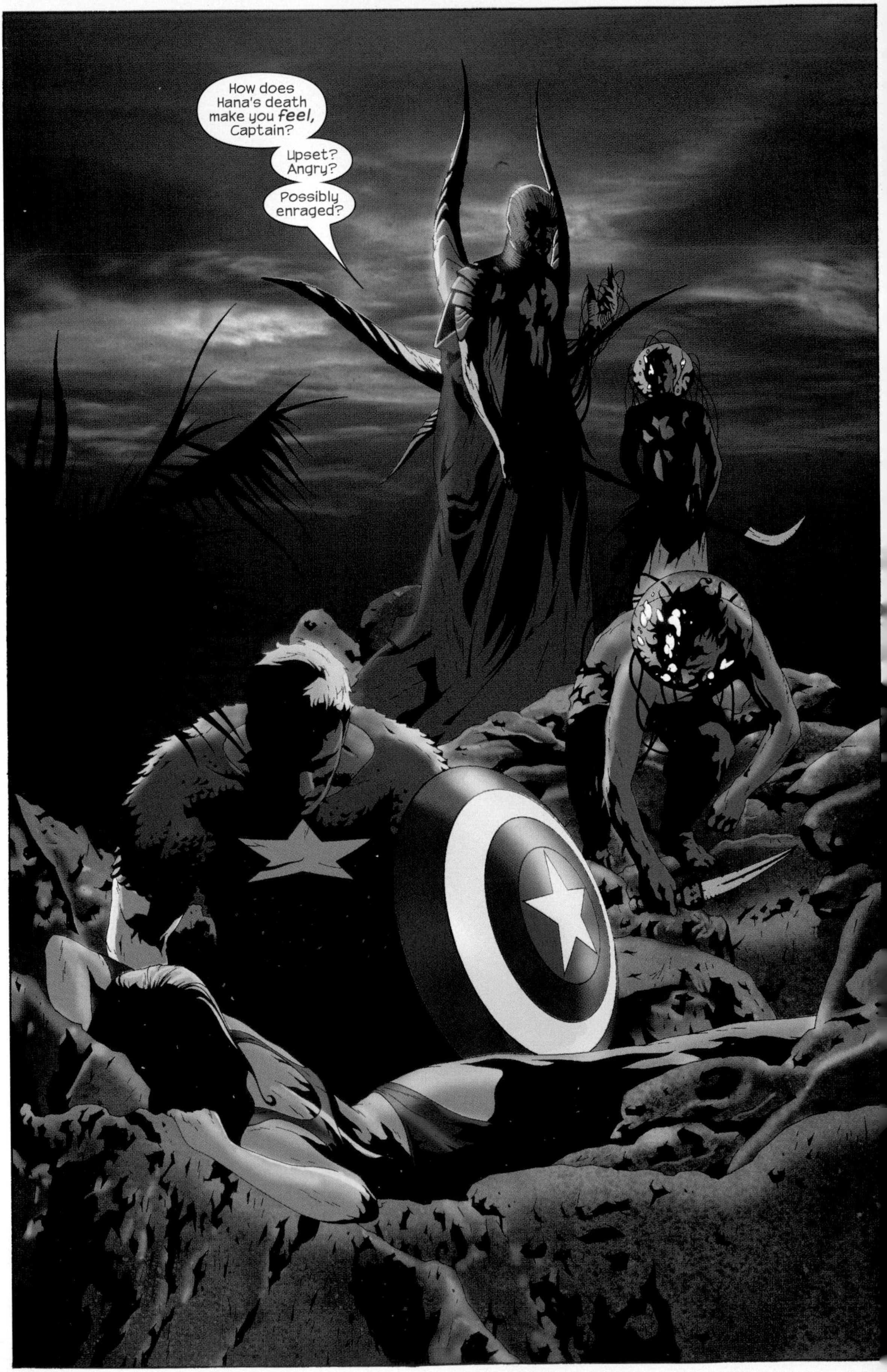
How does Hana's death make you *feel,* Captain?
Upset? Angry?
Possibly enraged?

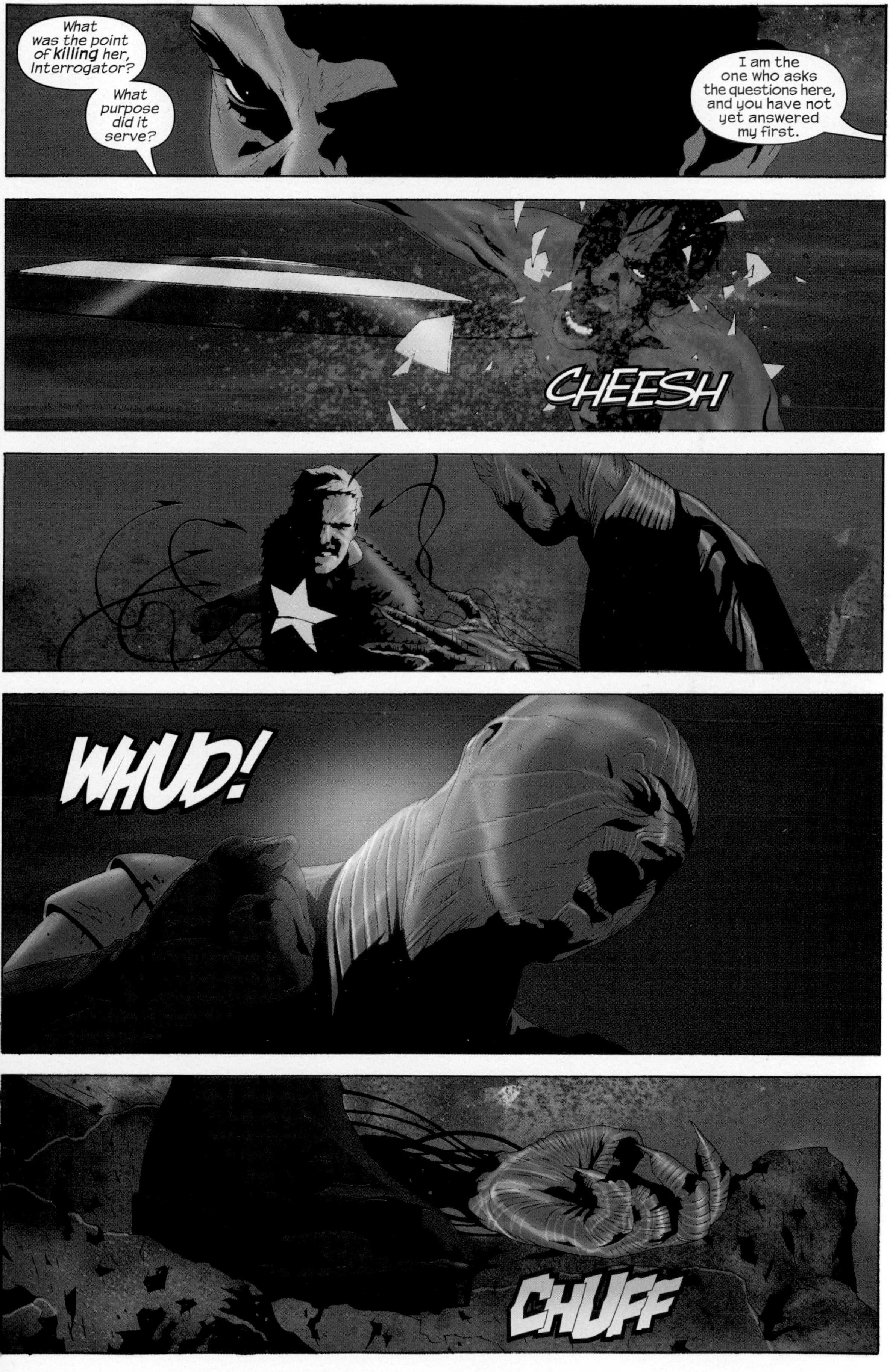
What was the point of killing her, Interrogator?
What purpose did it serve?
I am the one who asks the questions here, and you have not yet answered my first.
CHEESH
WHUD!
CHUFF

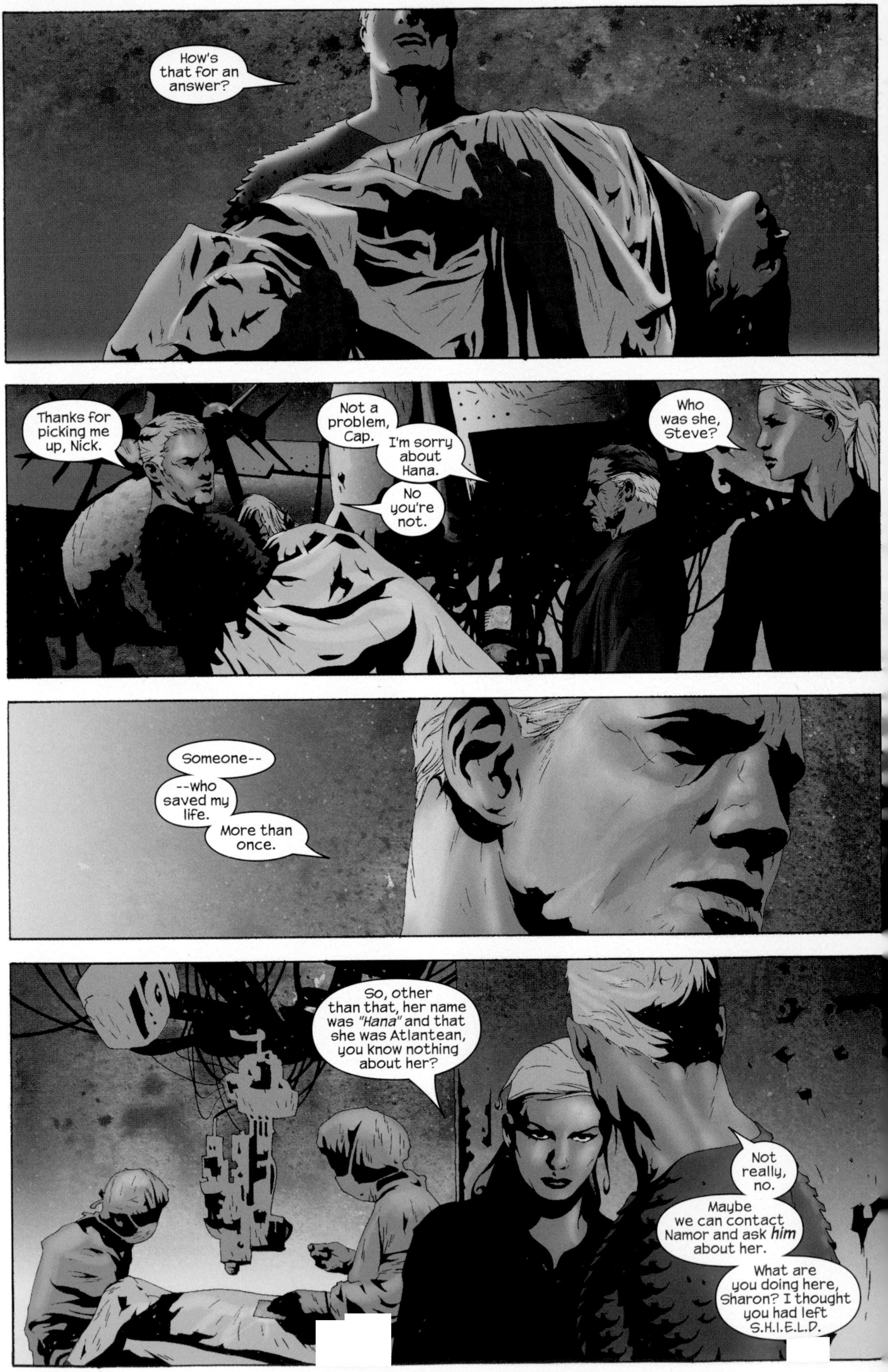
How's that for an answer?
Thanks for picking me up, Nick.
Not a problem, Cap.
I'm sorry about Hana.
No you're not.
Who was she, Steve?
Someone--
--who saved my life.
More than once.
So, other than that, her name was "Hana" and that she was Atlantean, you know nothing about her?
Not really, no.
Maybe we can contact Namor and ask *him* about her.
What are you doing here, Sharon? I thought you had left S.H.I.E.L.D.

No one ever *really* leaves S.H.I.E.L.D., do they, Steve?

Don't you know that by now?

This Hana.

She got to you, didn't she?

I've never seen you so affected by someone's death.

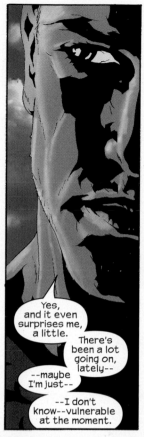

Yes, and it even surprises me, a little.

There's been a lot going on, lately--

--maybe I'm just--

--I don't know--vulnerable at the moment.

Why don't we have dinner and you can tell me about it.

I'd like that.

-- so you think these memories of you and Bucky being frozen by the American government--

--you actually think they might be real?

That's the thing, I can't say for sure.

I'm feeling a little off-kilter about a lot of things right now, not the least of which is Hana being killed.

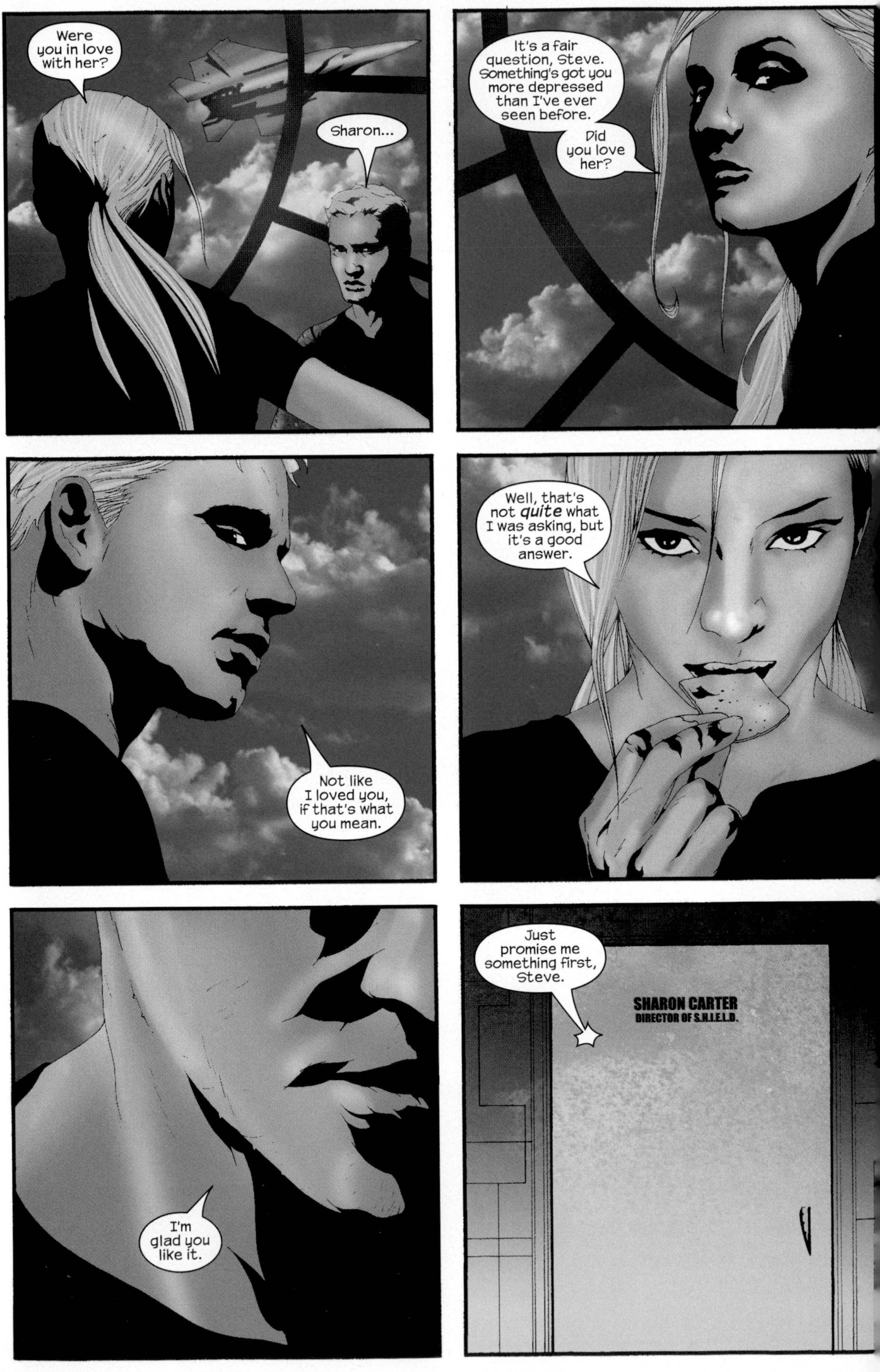
Were you in love with her?
Sharon...
It's a fair question, Steve. Something's got you more depressed than I've ever seen before.
Did you love her?
Not like I loved you, if that's what you mean.
Well, that's not *quite* what I was asking, but it's a good answer.
I'm glad you like it.
Just promise me something first, Steve.
SHARON CARTER
DIRECTOR OF S.H.I.E.L.D.

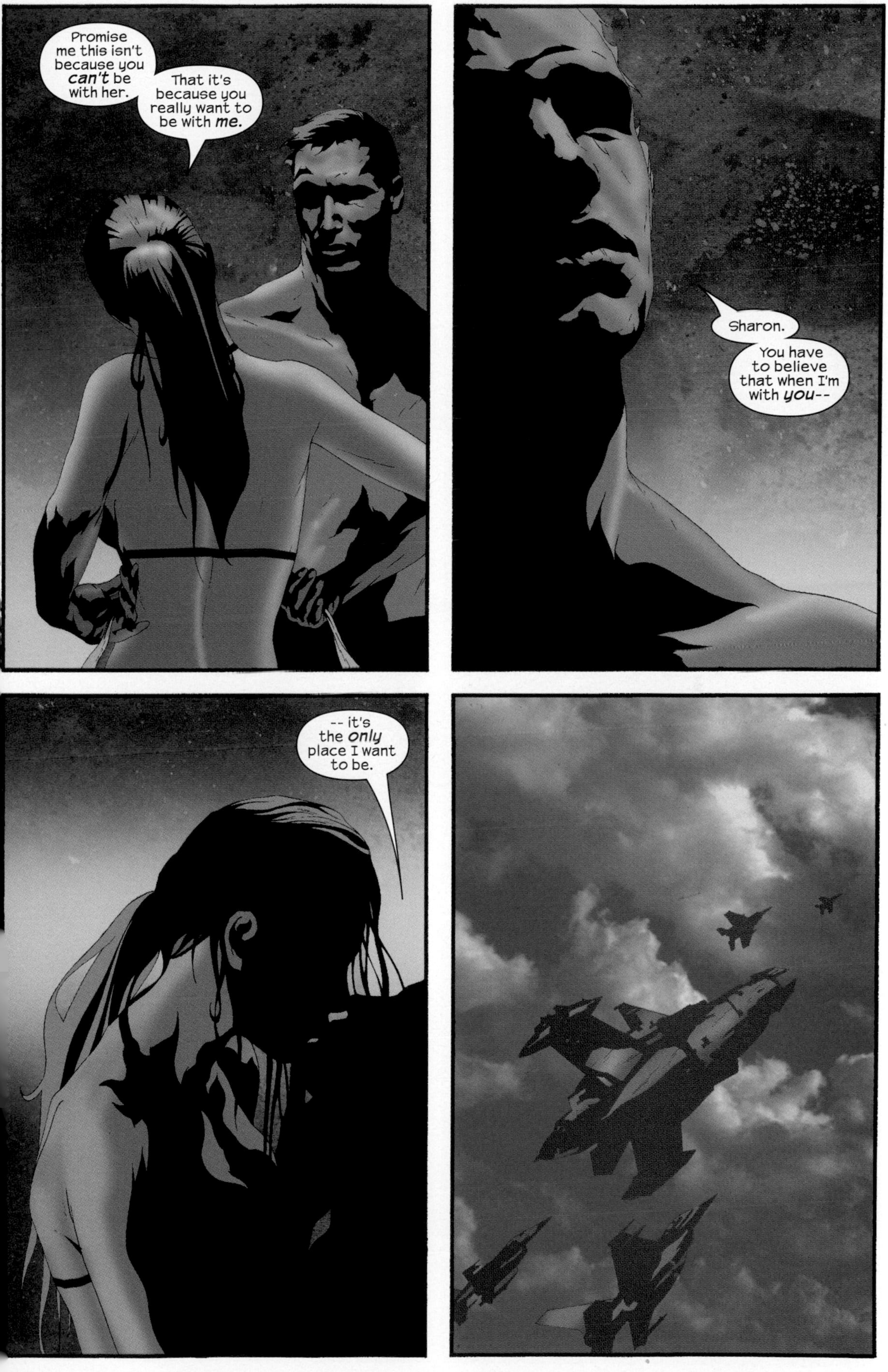
Promise me this isn't because you *can't* be with her.
That it's because you really want to be with *me.*
Sharon.
You have to believe that when I'm with *you*--
-- it's the *only* place I want to be.

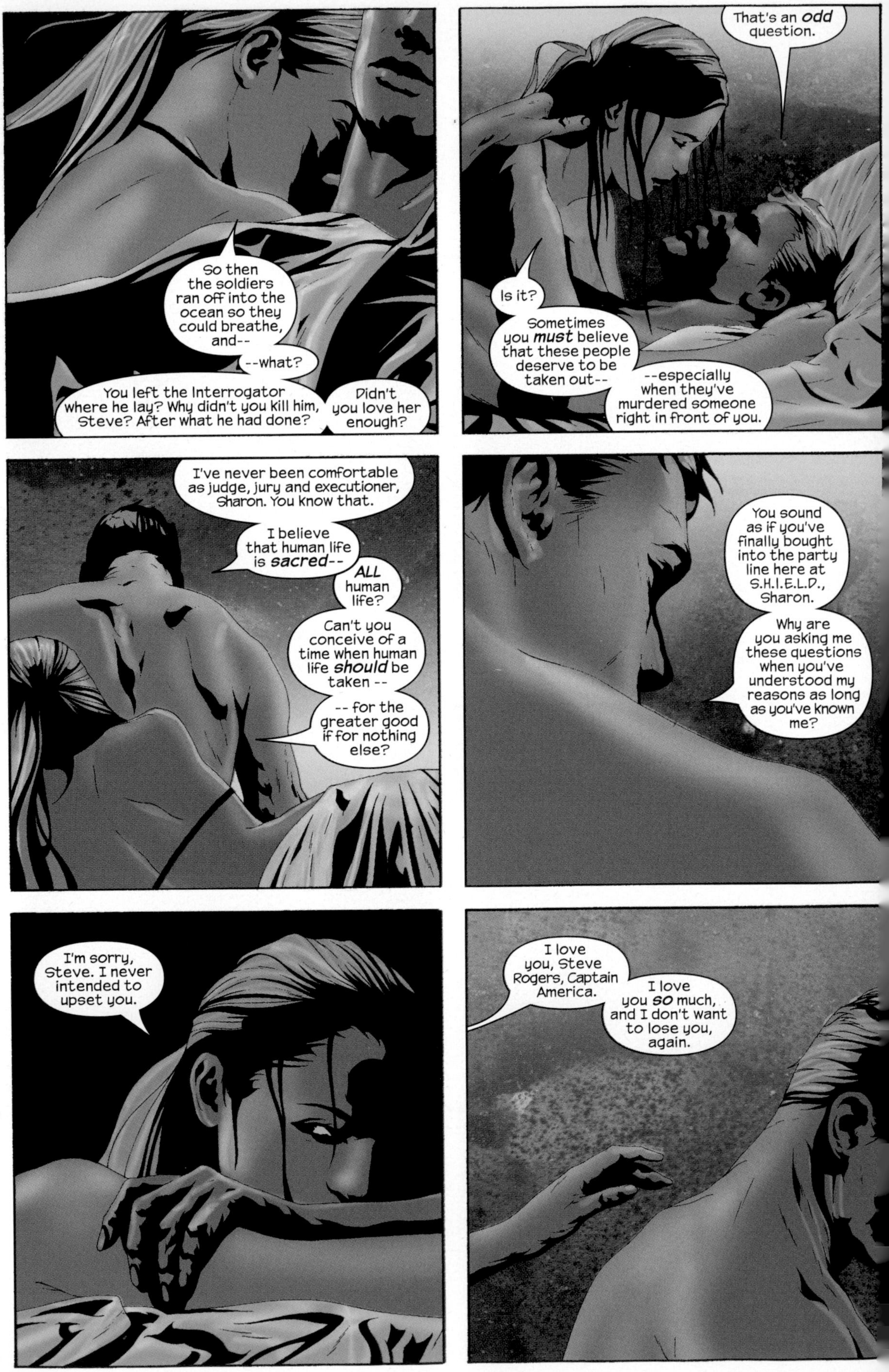
So then the soldiers ran off into the ocean so they could breathe, and--
--what?
You left the Interrogator where he lay? Why didn't you kill him, Steve? After what he had done?
Didn't you love her enough?
That's an odd question.
Is it?
Sometimes you must believe that these people deserve to be taken out--
--especially when they've murdered someone right in front of you.
I've never been comfortable as judge, jury and executioner, Sharon. You know that.
I believe that human life is sacred--
ALL human life?
Can't you conceive of a time when human life should be taken --
-- for the greater good if for nothing else?
You sound as if you've finally bought into the party line here at S.H.I.E.L.D., Sharon.
Why are you asking me these questions when you've understood my reasons as long as you've known me?
I'm sorry, Steve. I never intended to upset you.
I love you, Steve Rogers, Captain America.
I love you so much, and I don't want to lose you, again.

Welcome, Captain. How lovely to see you again.

Baron? Baron Blood?

Indeed, Captain. Care to join me for some dinner?

She's fresh.

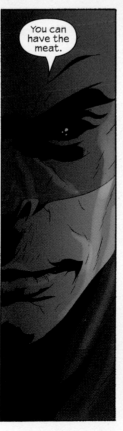

You can have the meat.

I only want the blood.

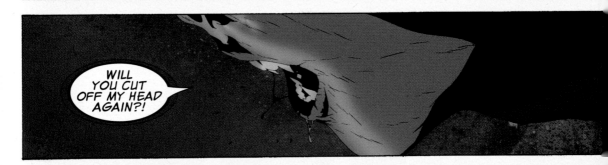

Will you kill me, Captain?

CHUNK-CRKKL

WILL YOU CUT OFF MY HEAD AGAIN?!

IS MY LIFE NOT SANCTIFIED?!

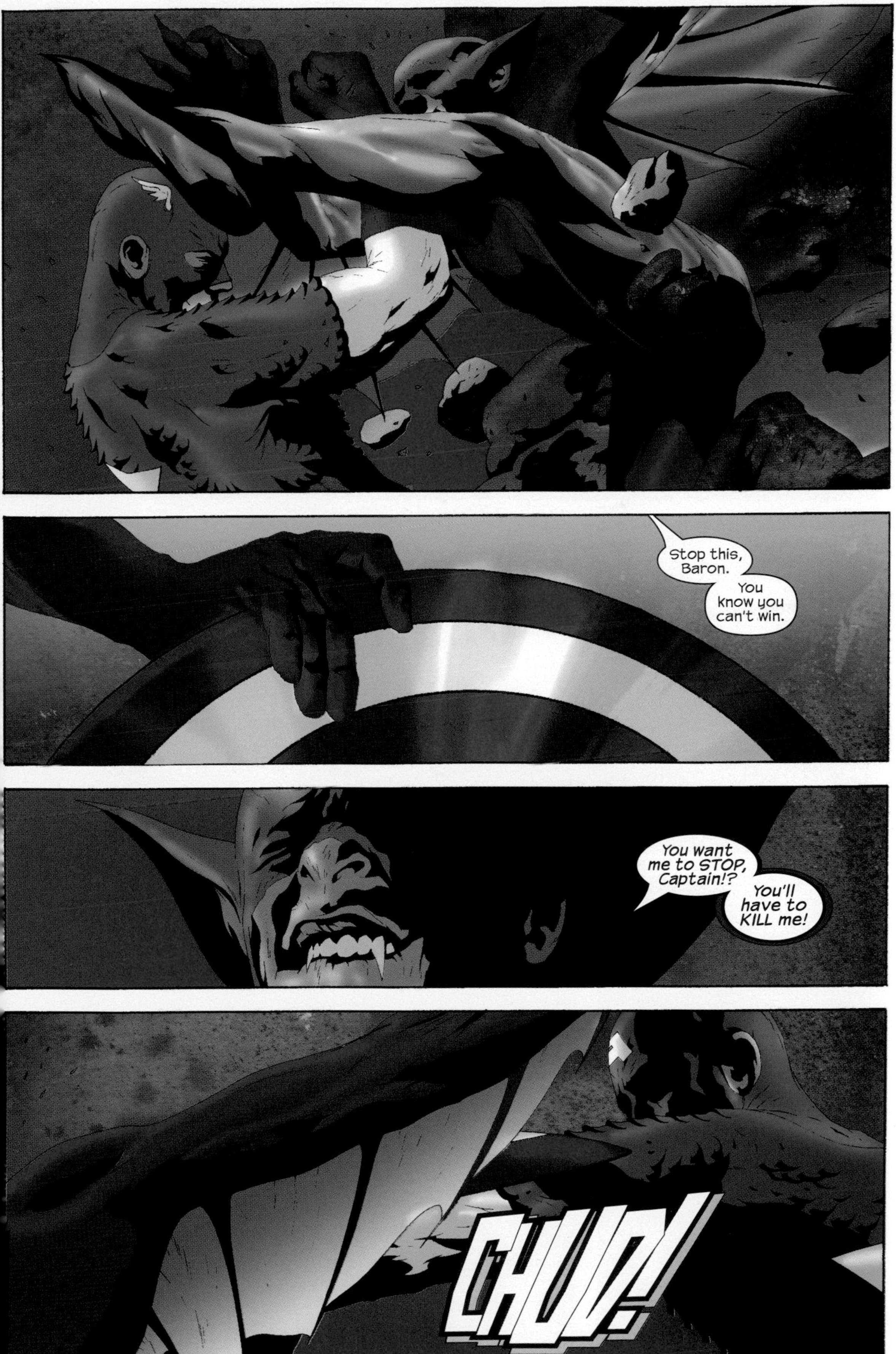
Stop this, Baron.
You know you can't win.
You want me to STOP, Captain!?
You'll have to KILL me!
CHUD!

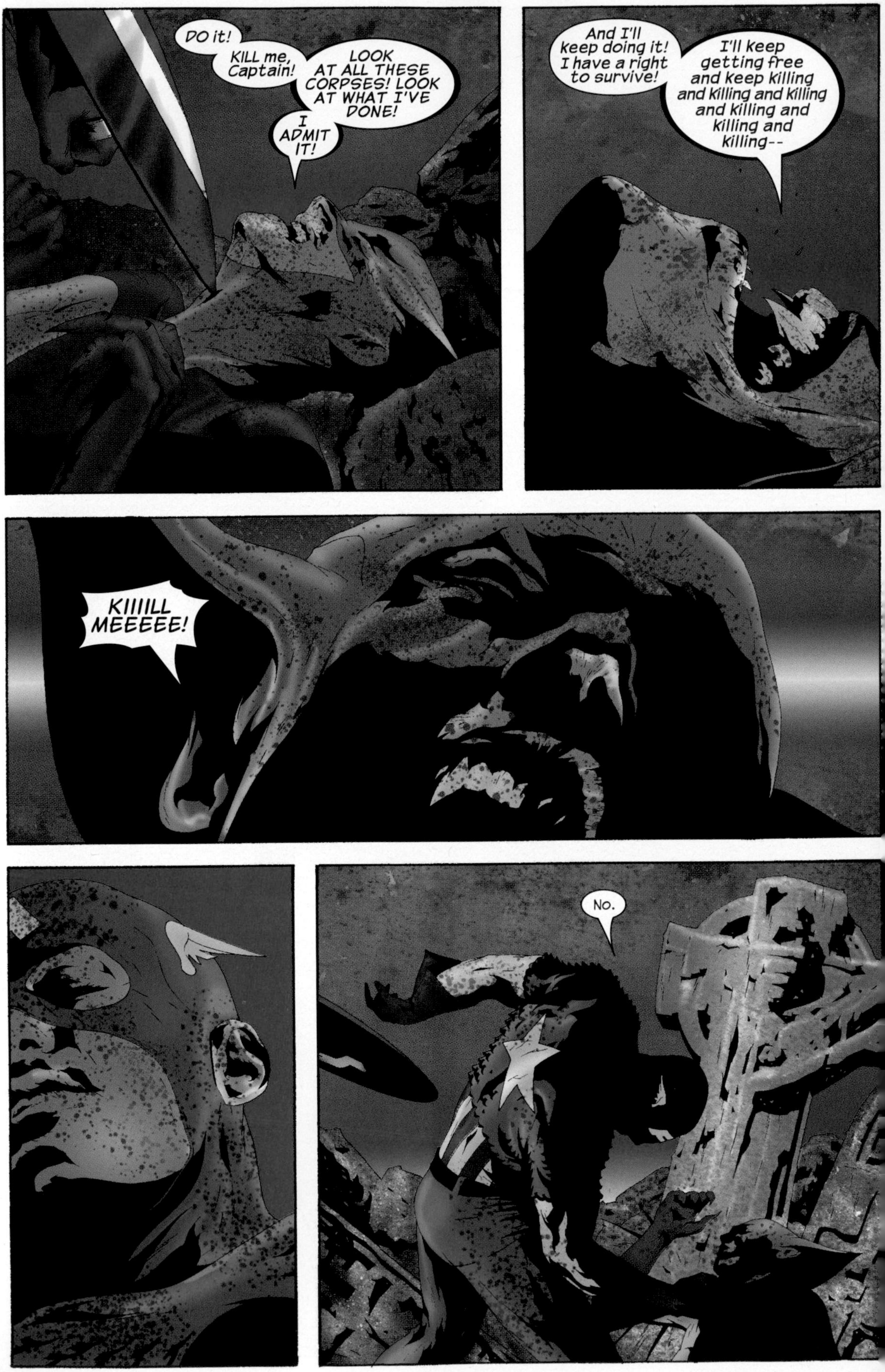
DO it!
KILL me, Captain!
LOOK AT ALL THESE CORPSES! LOOK AT WHAT I'VE DONE!
I ADMIT IT!
And I'll keep doing it! I have a right to survive!
I'll keep getting free and keep killing and killing and killing and killing and killing and killing--
KIIIILL MEEEEEE!
No.

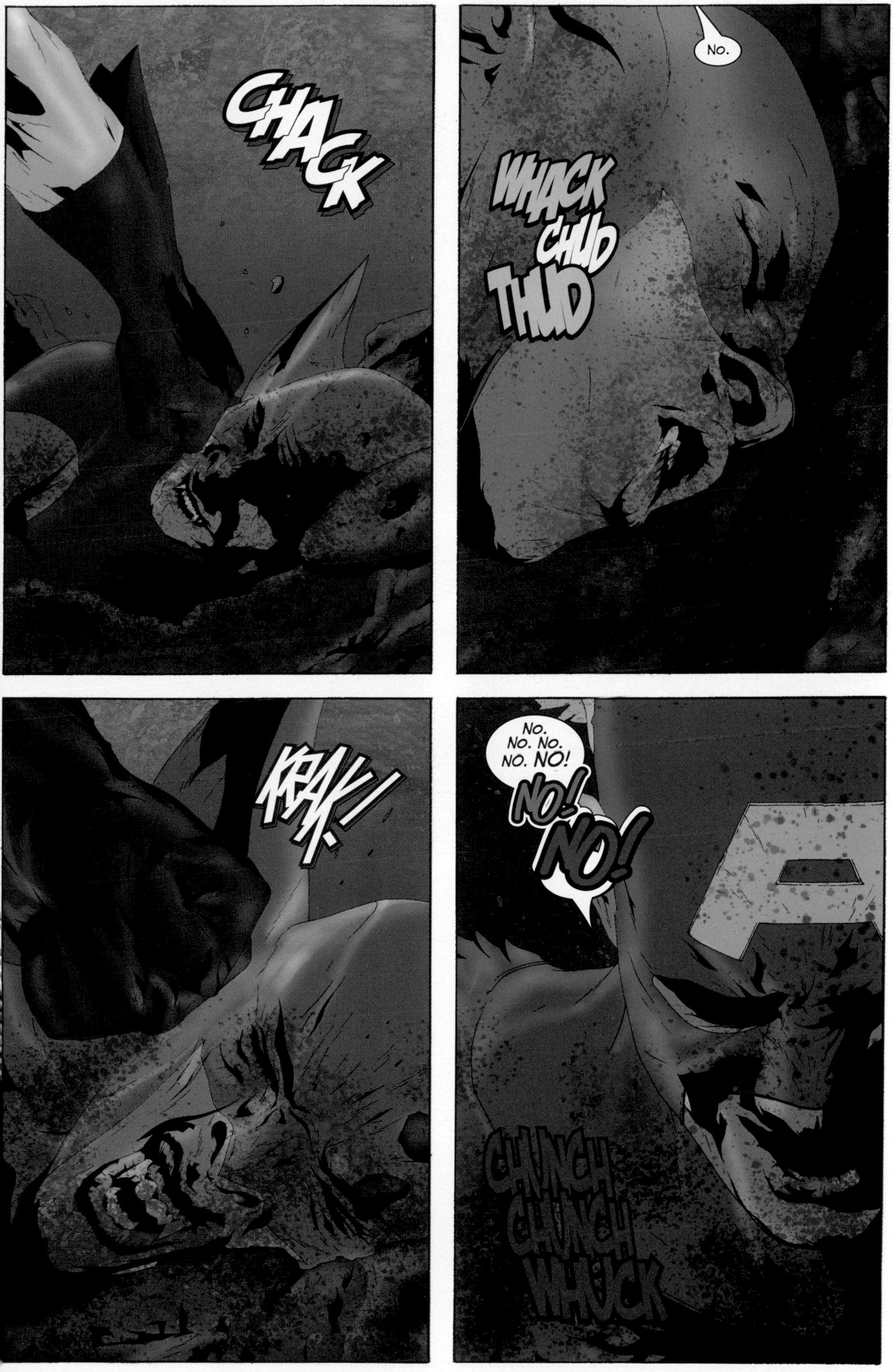
CHACK
No.
WHACK
CHUD
THUD
KRAK!
No.
No. No.
No. NO!
NO!
NO!
CHUNCH
CHUNCH
WHUCK

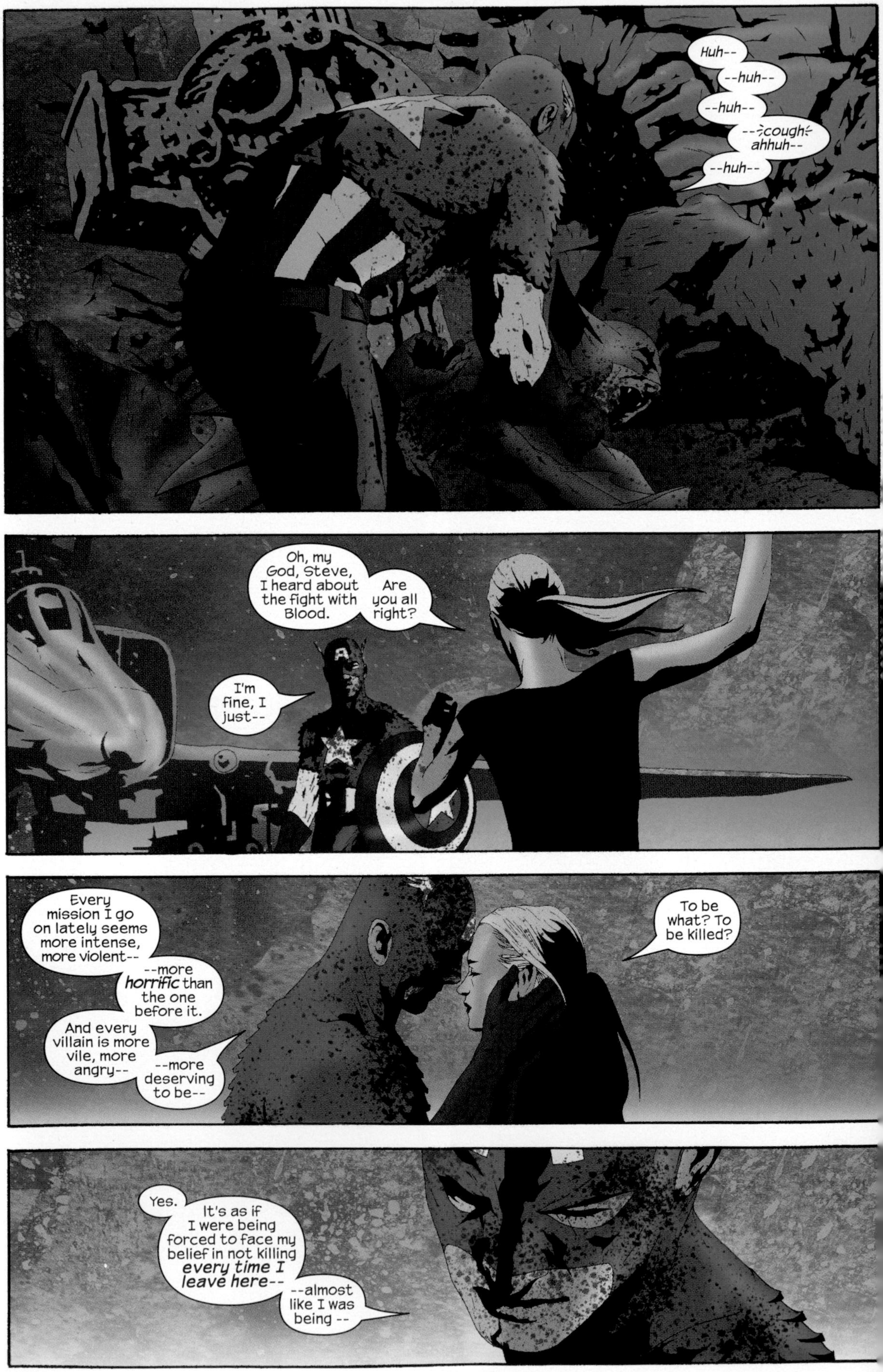
Huh--
--huh--
--huh--
--cough-- ahhuh--
--huh--
Oh, my God, Steve, I heard about the fight with Blood.
Are you all right?
I'm fine, I just--
Every mission I go on lately seems more intense, more violent--
--more *horrific* than the one before it.
And every villain is more vile, more angry--
--more deserving to be--
To be what? To be killed?
Yes.
It's as if I were being forced to face my belief in not killing *every time I leave here*--
--almost like I was being --

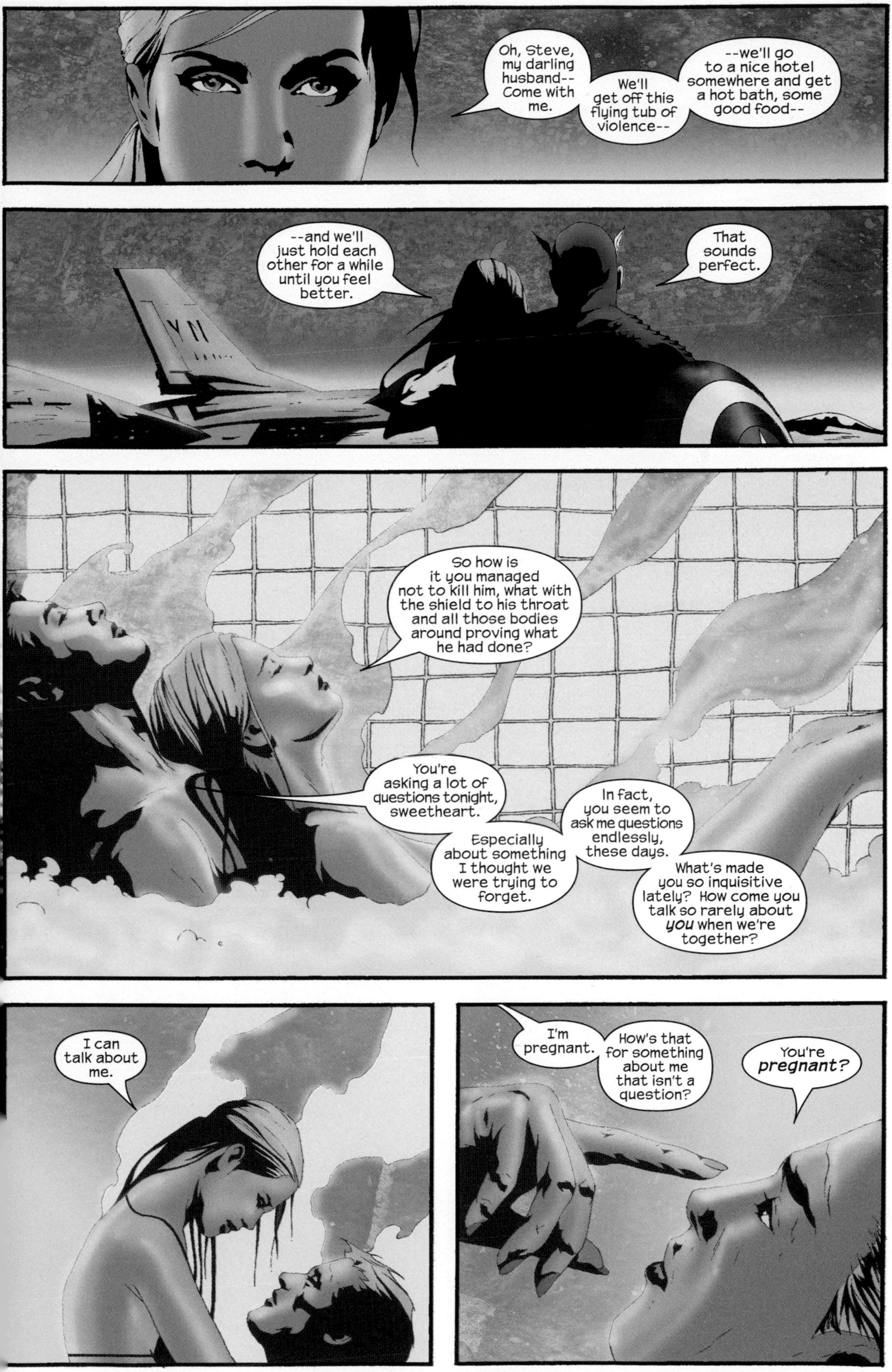
Oh, Steve, my darling husband-- Come with me.
We'll get off this flying tub of violence--
--we'll go to a nice hotel somewhere and get a hot bath, some good food--
--and we'll just hold each other for a while until you feel better.
That sounds perfect.
So how is it you managed not to kill him, what with the shield to his throat and all those bodies around proving what he had done?
You're asking a lot of questions tonight, sweetheart.
Especially about something I thought we were trying to forget.
In fact, you seem to ask me questions endlessly, these days.
What's made you so inquisitive lately? How come you talk so rarely about *you* when we're together?
I can talk about me.
I'm pregnant.
How's that for something about me that isn't a question?
You're ***pregnant?***

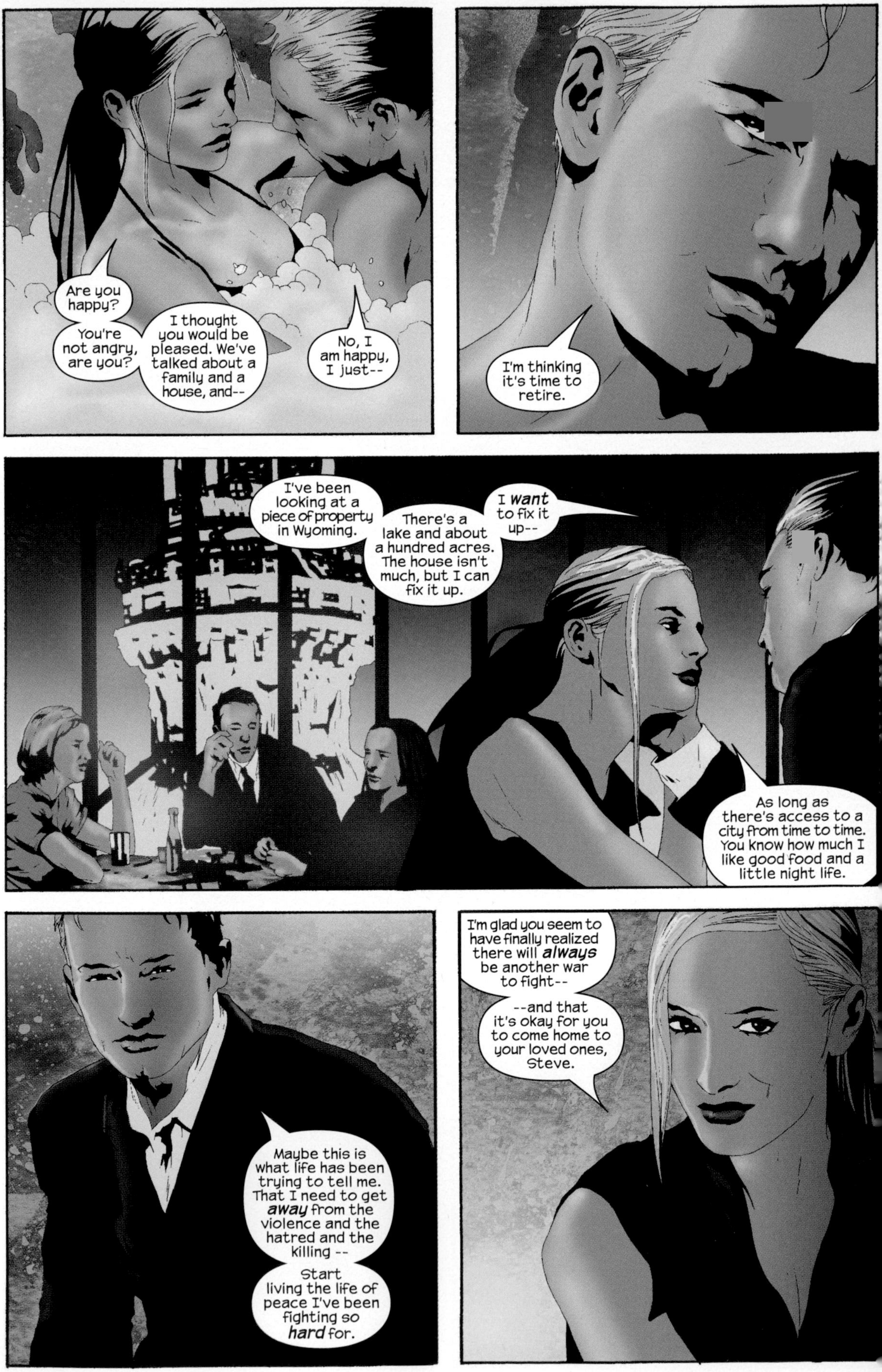

Are you happy?
You're not angry, are you?
I thought you would be pleased. We've talked about a family and a house, and--
No, I am happy, I just--
I'm thinking it's time to retire.
I've been looking at a piece of property in Wyoming.
There's a lake and about a hundred acres. The house isn't much, but I can fix it up.
I *want* to fix it up--
As long as there's access to a city from time to time. You know how much I like good food and a little night life.
Maybe this is what life has been trying to tell me. That I need to get *away* from the violence and the hatred and the killing --
Start living the life of peace I've been fighting so *hard* for.
I'm glad you seem to have finally realized there will *always* be another war to fight--
--and that it's okay for you to come home to your loved ones, Steve.

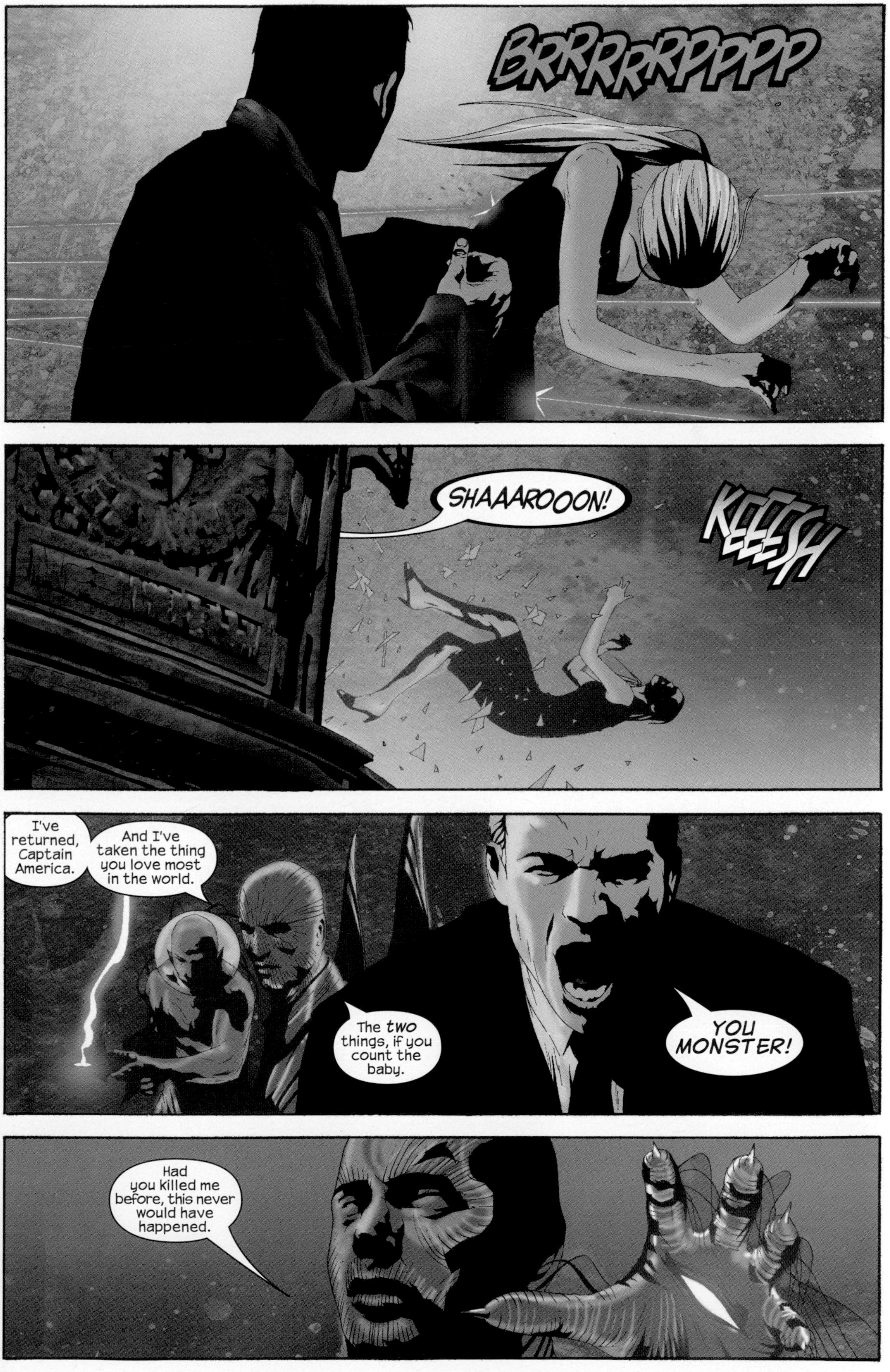
BRRRRRPPPPP
SHAAAROOON!
KEEESH
I've returned, Captain America.
And I've taken the thing you love most in the world.
The two things, if you count the baby.
YOU MONSTER!
Had you killed me before, this never would have happened.

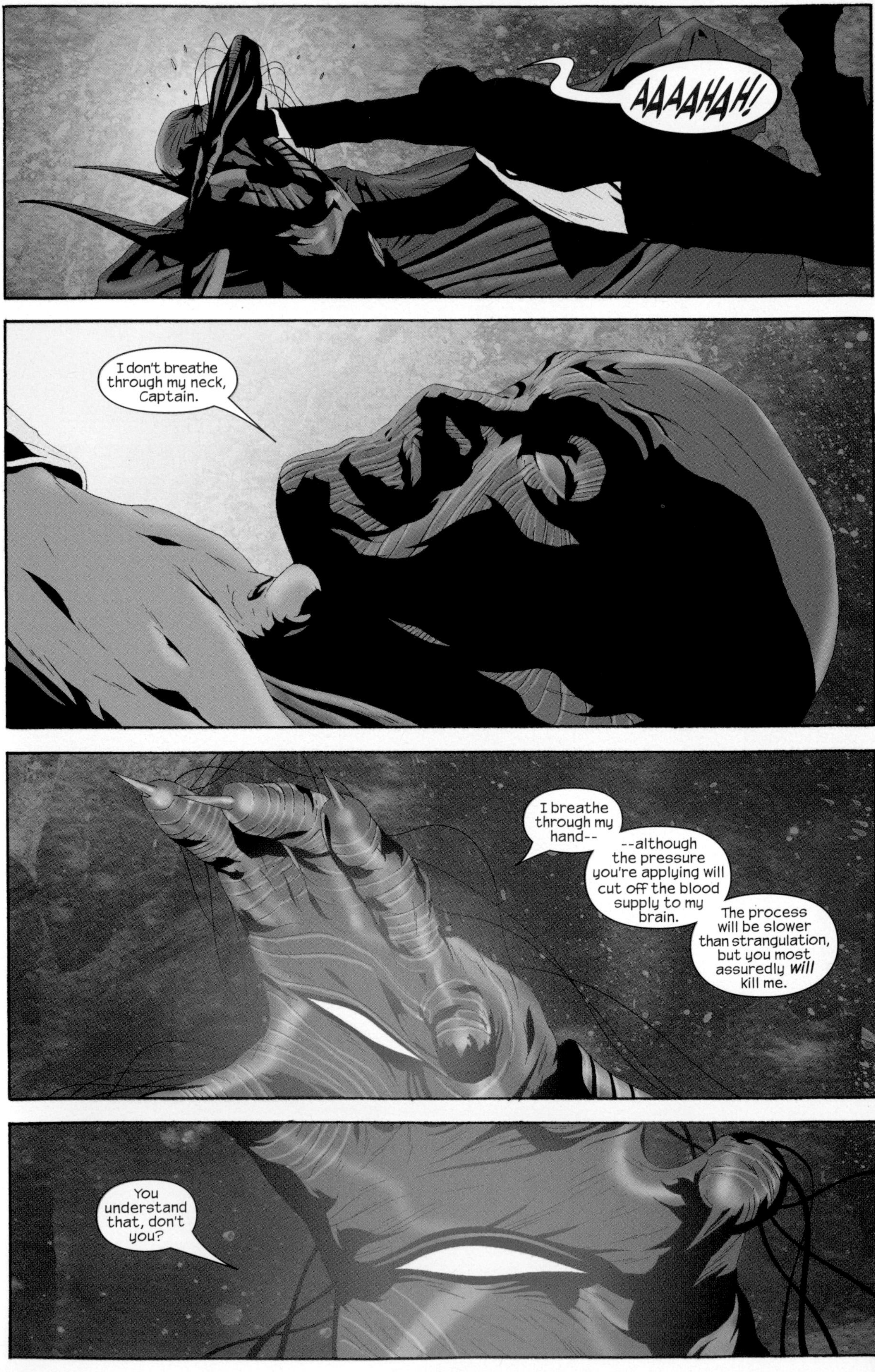
AAAAHAH!
I don't breathe through my neck, Captain.
I breathe through my hand--
--although the pressure you're applying will cut off the blood supply to my brain.
The process will be slower than strangulation, but you most assuredly *will* kill me.
You understand that, don't you?

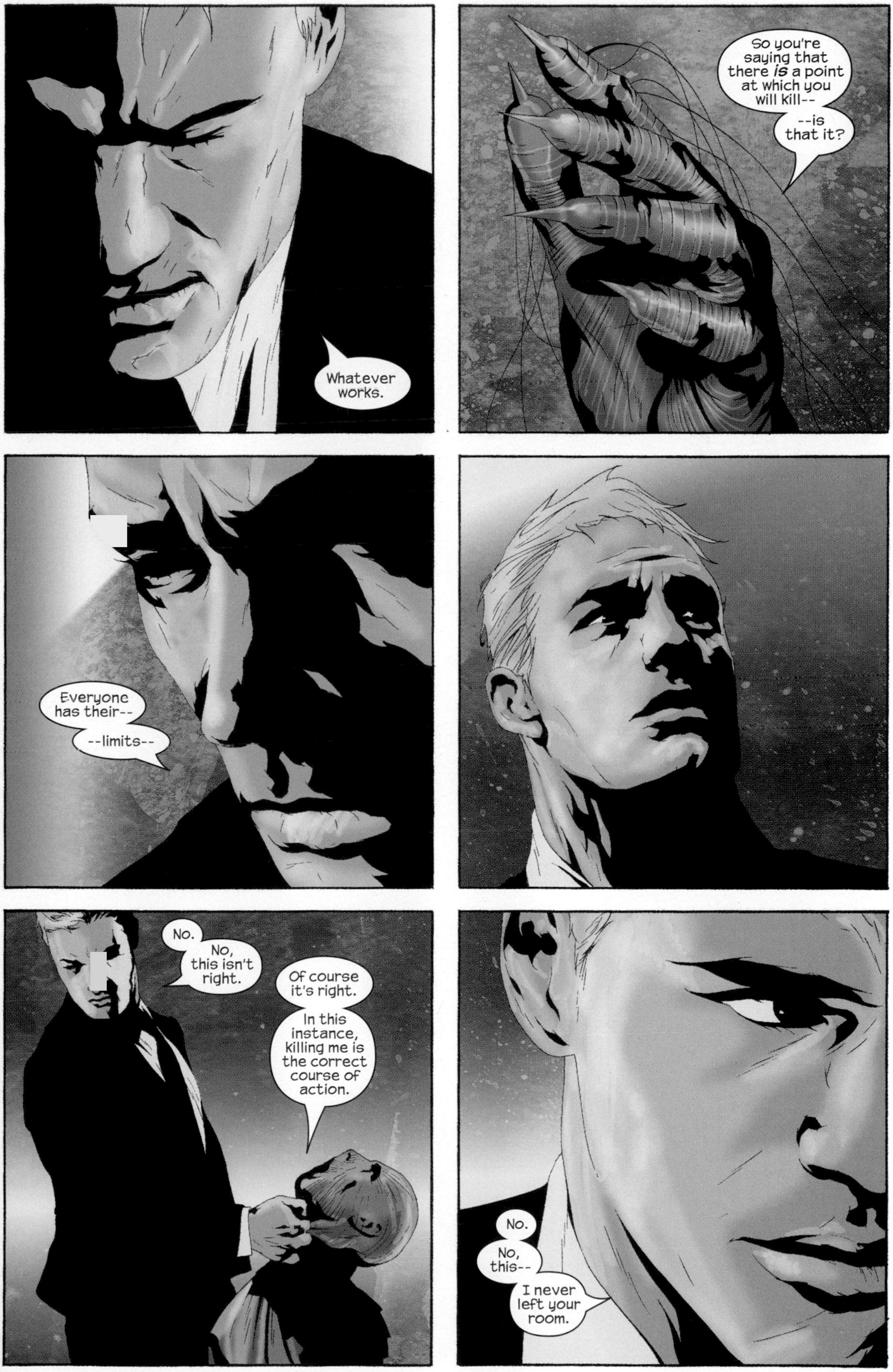
Whatever works.
So you're saying that there *is* a point at which you will kill--
--is that it?
Everyone has their--
--limits--
No.
No, this isn't right.
Of course it's right.
In this instance, killing me is the correct course of action.
No.
No, this--
I never left your room.

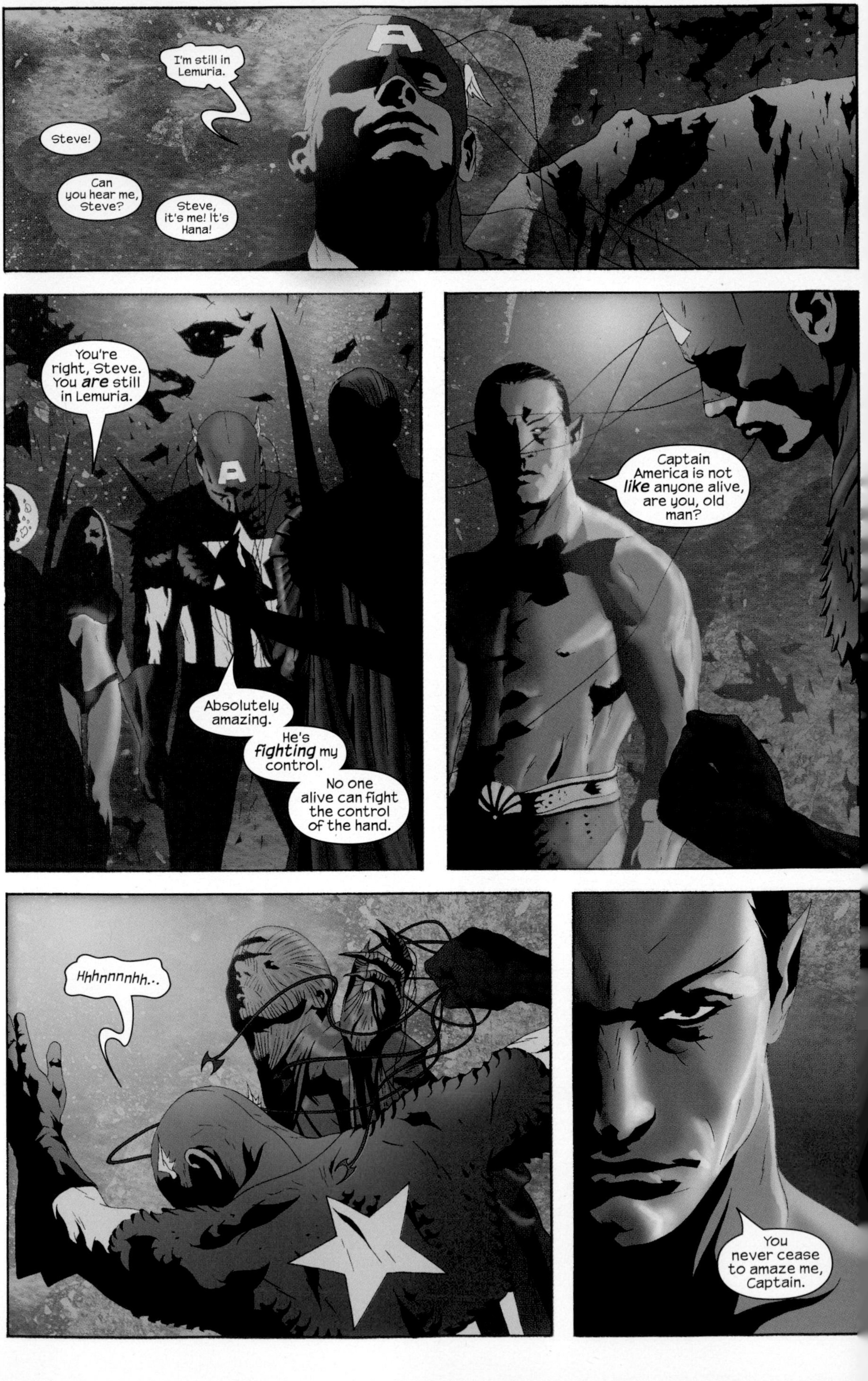
I'm still in Lemuria.
Steve!
Can you hear me, Steve?
Steve, it's me! It's Hana!
You're right, Steve. You *are* still in Lemuria.
Absolutely amazing.
He's *fighting* my control.
No one alive can fight the control of the hand.
Captain America is not *like* anyone alive, are you, old man?
Hhhnnnnhh...
You never cease to amaze me, Captain.

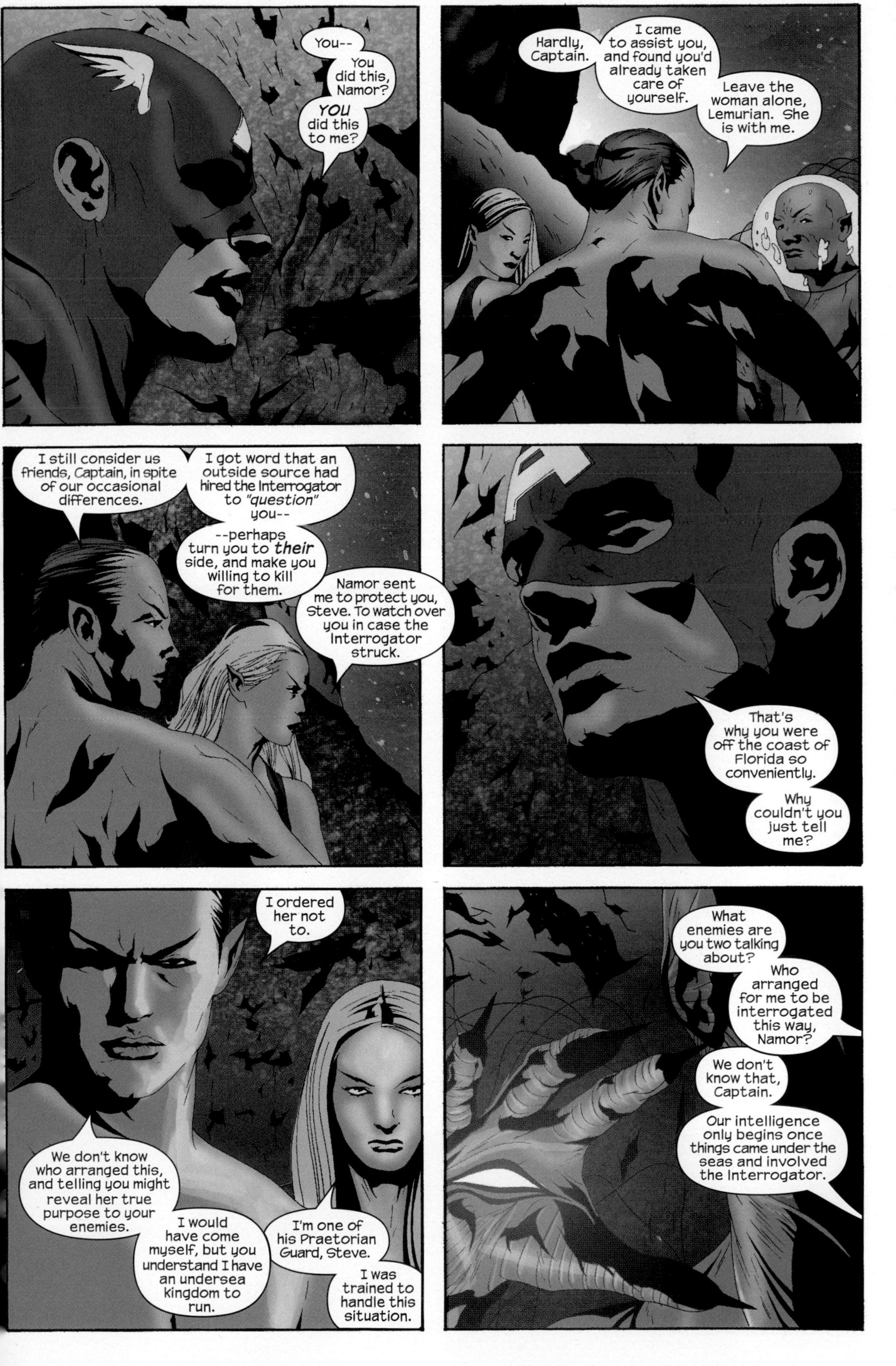
You--
You did this, Namor?
YOU did this to me?
Hardly, Captain.
I came to assist you, and found you'd already taken care of yourself.
Leave the woman alone, Lemurian. She is with me.
I still consider us friends, Captain, in spite of our occasional differences.
I got word that an outside source had hired the Interrogator to "question" you--
--perhaps turn you to their side, and make you willing to kill for them.
Namor sent me to protect you, Steve. To watch over you in case the Interrogator struck.
That's why you were off the coast of Florida so conveniently.
Why couldn't you just tell me?
I ordered her not to.
We don't know who arranged this, and telling you might reveal her true purpose to your enemies.
I would have come myself, but you understand I have an undersea kingdom to run.
I'm one of his Praetorian Guard, Steve.
I was trained to handle this situation.
What enemies are you two talking about?
Who arranged for me to be interrogated this way, Namor?
We don't know that, Captain.
Our intelligence only begins once things came under the seas and involved the Interrogator.

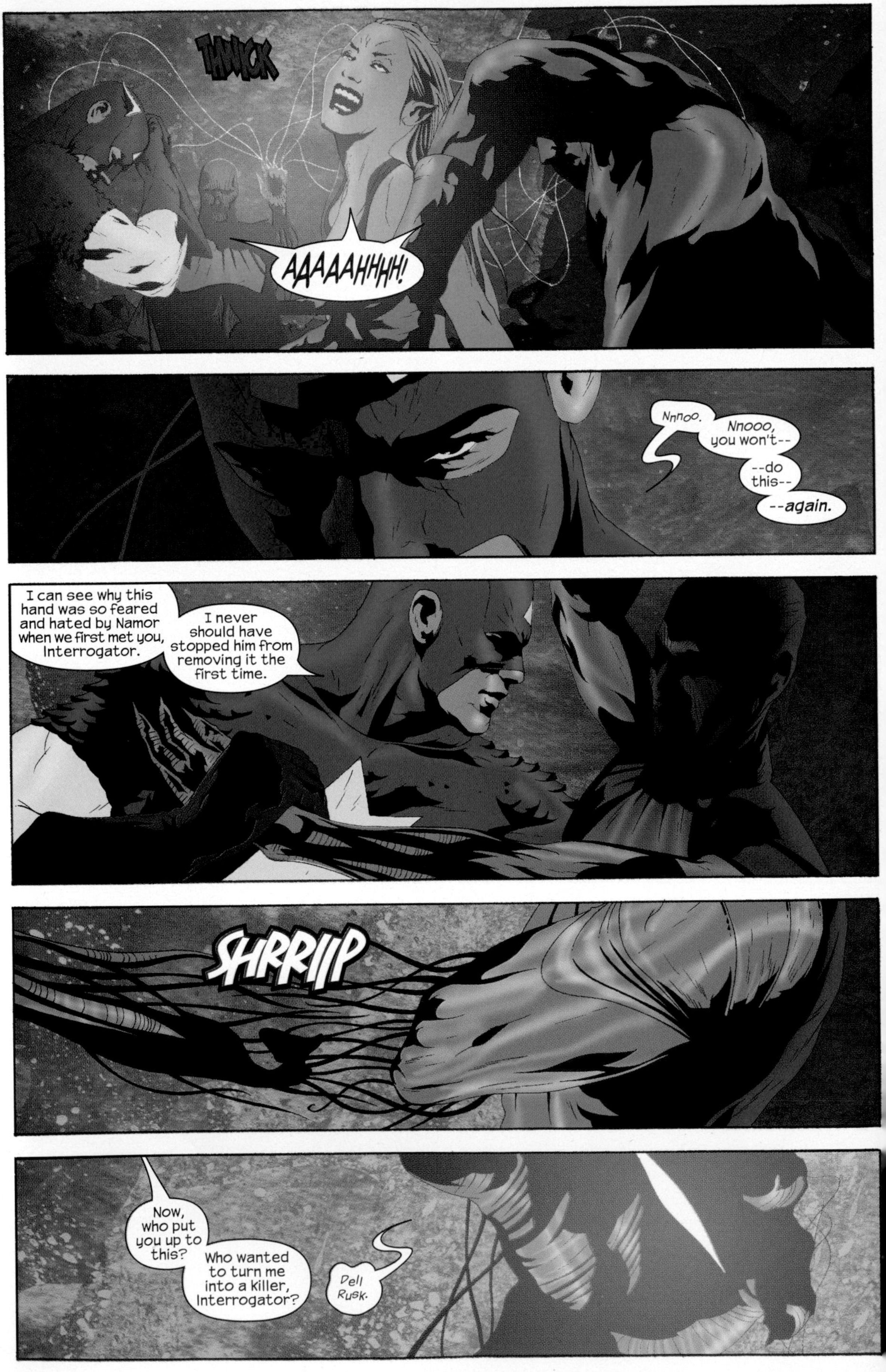
THWICK
AAAAAHHHH!
Nnnoo.
Nnooo, you won't--
--do this--
--again.
I can see why this hand was so feared and hated by Namor when we first met you, Interrogator.
I never should have stopped him from removing it the first time.
SHRRIIP
Now, who put you up to this?
Who wanted to turn me into a killer, Interrogator?
Dell Rusk.

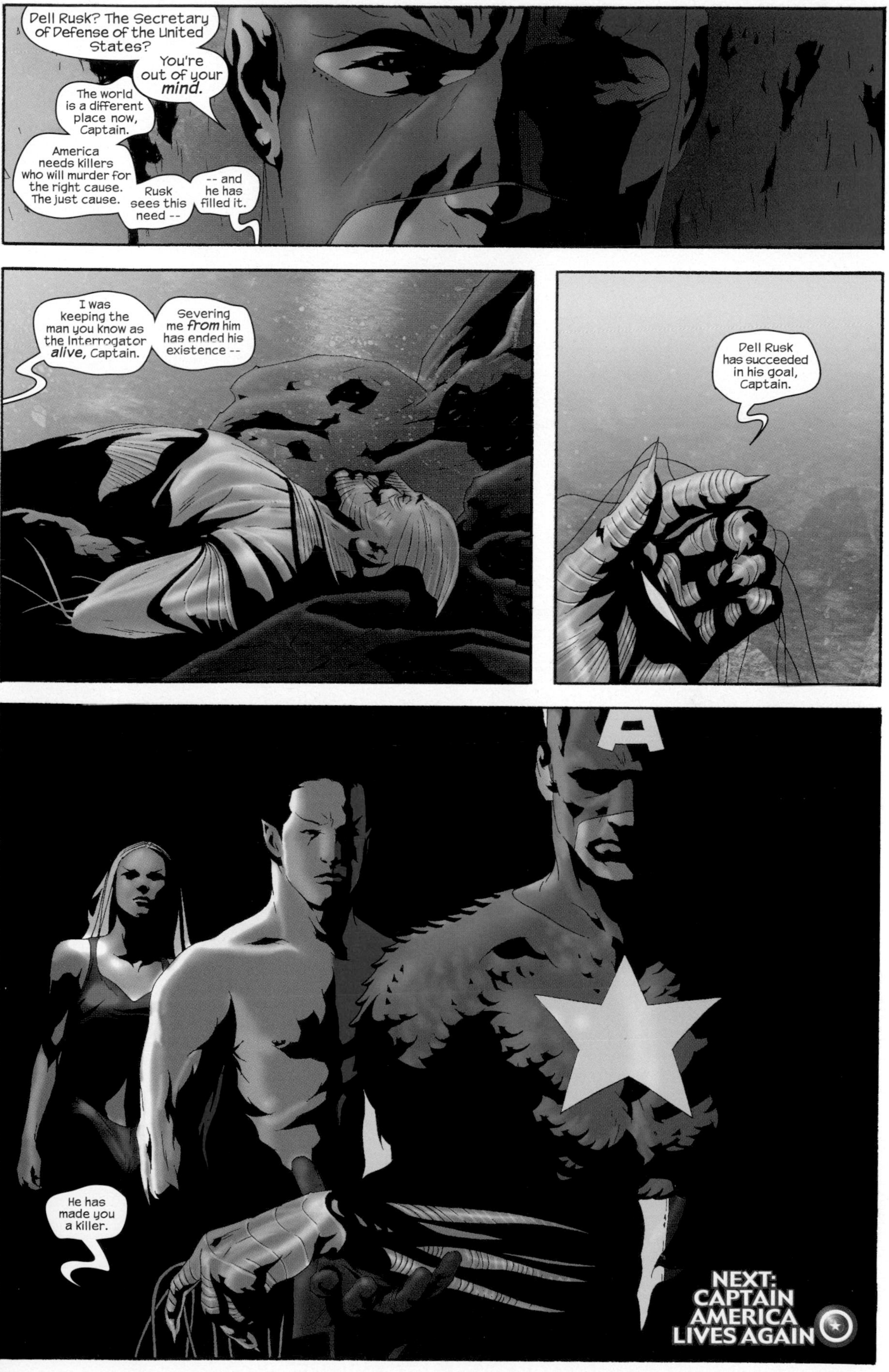
Dell Rusk? The Secretary of Defense of the United States?
You're out of your *mind.*
The world is a different place now, Captain.
America needs killers who will murder for the right cause. The just cause.
Rusk sees this need --
-- and he has filled it.
I was keeping the man you know as the Interrogator *alive,* Captain.
Severing me *from* him has ended his existence --
Dell Rusk has succeeded in his goal, Captain.
He has made you a killer.
NEXT: CAPTAIN AMERICA LIVES AGAIN

UNUSED COVER

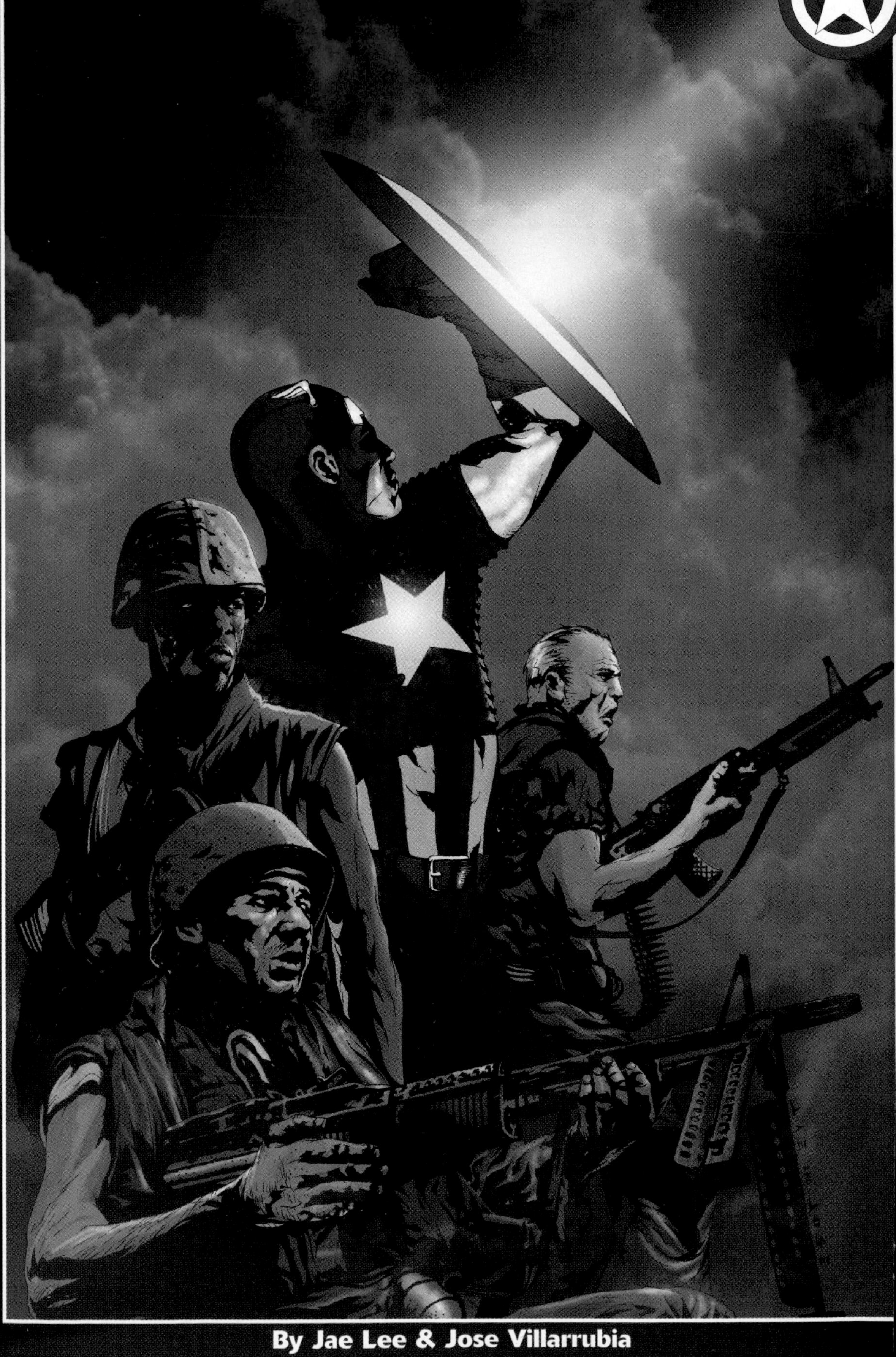

By Jae Lee & Jose Villarrubia